SPLIT THE PIE

ALSO BY BARRY NALEBUFF

Thinking Strategically: The Competitive Edge in Business, Politics, and Everyday Life (with Avinash K. Dixit)

The Art of Strategy: A Game Theorist's Guide to Success in Business and Life (with Avinash K. Dixit)

Co-opetition (with Adam Brandenburger)

Why Not?: How to Use Everyday Ingenuity to Solve Problems Big and Small (with Ian Ayres)

Lifecycle Investing: A New, Safe, and Audacious Way to Improve the Performance of Your Retirement Portfolio (with Ian Ayres)

Mission in a Bottle: The Honest Guide to Doing Business Differently—and Succeeding (with Seth Goldman)

SPLIT THE PIE

A Radical New Way to Negotiate

BARRY NALEBUFF

HARPER
BUSINESS
An Imprint of HarperCollinsPublishers

HarperCollins books may be purchased for educational, business, or sales promotional use. For information, please email the Special Markets Department at SPsales @harpercollins.com.

All illustrations by Dan Ashwood.

Image on page 42: ©2020 Honest Tea, Inc. "Honest" is a registered trademark of Honest Tea, Inc.

Image on page 250: Reprinted from the *Journal of Political Economy* with permission under fair use provision. Matthew Backus, Thomas Blake, and Steven Tadelis (2019) "On the Empirical Content of Cheap-Talk Signaling: An Application to Bargaining," *Journal of Political Economy*, 127(4), 1599–1628.

FIRST EDITION

Library of Congress Cataloging-in-Publication Data.

Names: Nalebuff, Barry, 1958- author.
Title: Split the pie : a radical new way to negotiate / Barry Nalebuff.
Identifiers: LCCN 2021044351 (print) | LCCN 2021044352 (ebook) |
    ISBN 9780063135482 (hardcover) | ISBN 9780063135499 (ebook)
Subjects: LCSH: Negotiation in business. | Negotiation. | Success in business.
Classification: LCC HD58.6 .N28 2022 (print) | LCC HD58.6 (ebook) |
    DDC 658.4/052—dc23/eng/20211104
LC record available at https://lccn.loc.gov/2021044351
LC ebook record available at https://lccn.loc.gov/2021044352

22 23 24 25 26 LSC 10 9 8 7 6 5 4 3 2 1

To Herb Cohen and David Stern (1942–2020),
two negotiation giants from whom I've had the privilege to learn.

CONTENTS

Part I | The Pie

Part II | Splitting the Cost

Part III | Complex Negotiations

Part IV | How to Grow the Pie

Part V | Negotiation Mechanics

SPLIT THE PIE

INTRODUCTION

Negotiation is stressful. That's even true for me. A great deal is at stake: money (sometimes life-changing money), opportunity, time, relationships, and reputations. Negotiation can bring out the worst in people as they try to take advantage of the other side or just naïvely imitate the tough negotiatiors they hear about.

Wouldn't it be better if there were a principled way to negotiate? Wouldn't it be even better if there were a way to treat people fairly and get treated fairly in a negotiation? *Split the Pie* does both via a radical new approach to negotiation, one I have been teaching to MBA students and executives at Yale School of Management for the last fifteen years and to over 350,000 online learners at Coursera. It's the approach I used in selling my company to Coca-Cola. It's a simple, practical approach based on ideas from game theory. Like all good new ideas, it is also old. The fundamental insight can be traced back to the two-thousand-year-old Babylonian Talmud. (We explore this connection in Chapter 9.)

I start by helping you identify what's really at stake in a negotiation—what I call "the pie." The pie is the *additional* value created through an agreement to work together. Once you see the pie, you will change how you think about fairness and power in negotiation. The notion of "dividing the pie" is commonplace in negotiations. But most people are splitting the wrong pie; they focus on the total amount, not the gain created by an agreement. As a result, they argue over the wrong numbers and issues, and take positions they perceive as reasonable but are, in fact, self-interested. The hard part of negotiation is to measure the pie correctly. When the stakes are correctly understood, it is far easier to reach an agreement.

In a nutshell, negotiation is about creating and capturing value. When it comes to creating value, Roger Fisher and William Ury's *Getting to Yes* taught the world how to succeed by focusing on interests, not positions. Left unresolved is the messy problem of how to divide the gains created, whether they be synergies in a merger or cost savings from sharing an Uber. The resulting tension is why many people so dislike negotiating.

To resolve the tension, some negotiators appeal to fairness: "I've given you a fair offer. You should take it." But what looks fair to one side may not look so fair to the other. One side could offer less than half and still call this fair if the other side cares more about the deal. In other circumstances, one side might argue it's fair to split everything down the middle, even if the starting points are different. I think such divisions don't reflect the true nature of fairness in a negotiation.

Other negotiators appeal to arguments based on power. One side will argue it is "entitled" to a larger share because it is bigger, because it brings more to the table, because it can walk away more easily, because it has more options, and so on. Such appeals to power often prevail. The typical result is to divide things up proportionately, where the proportionality may be in terms of size (units, revenue, profit, dollars invested), or some other supposed metric of power. I think such divisions are flawed and don't reflect the true nature of power in a negotiation.

This book introduces a new approach, one that reveals the true power of the players and is fair in representing their contributions. The radical part is the conclusion that the pie should be divided evenly. That doesn't mean both sides end up with the same amount.

What is evenly divided is not the total but only the additional value created by the agreement, namely the negotiation pie. Because this even split fundamentally changes how people look at power, there will be resistance—especially from people who benefit from the illusion of power under the status quo. However, that resistance can be overcome, and I'll explain how.

What you will get from *Split the Pie* is a practical and theory-based approach to negotiation. When I say the approach is practical, I mean it has been field-tested. You'll read how it helped reframe what was for me a high-stakes negotiation when Coca-Cola purchased Honest Tea, a company I cofounded with my former student Seth Goldman. (We are the "Seth & Barry" on the back label.) That negotiation in 2008 was when the theory first moved beyond the classroom. Until then, it had been an idea germinating in my Yale negotiation course. The pie approach was developed out of necessity to help overcome Coke's reasonable objection that they didn't want to pay for value they helped create. Early on, we agreed to split the pie, whatever it turned out to be, and that gave both sides an incentive to make the pie as big as possible, which is just what we did.

The pie framework isn't just for high-stakes corporate negotiations. You'll learn how the pie will help guide negotiations should you ever need to break a lease with a landlord or buy a domain name from a squatter. You'll learn a better way to split costs between partners when the benefits are unequal. You'll learn how smart real estate lawyers in New York City employ the pie to rebalance an unfavorable default split of tax savings and thereby gain several thousand dollars for their clients—and you'll learn how to do it, too.

The pie framework will change the way you approach negotiations in business and in your personal life. It will allow you to see the negotiation more clearly and more logically. It will lead you to an agreement where the principle applied doesn't depend on the specifics of your situation. It will help you make arguments that persuade others by identifying inconsistencies in their approach.

Splitting the pie works when there is an opportunity to cooperate with the other side to maximize the value you can create together.

As you'll soon see, it also works when going up against someone who doesn't care about fairness or the pie perspective. Because it is principled and because it leads to fair results, this approach offers the potential for negotiation without all the posturing. Achieving a fair division allows both sides to focus their energy on making the biggest possible pie. The pie framework goes a long way toward resolving the tension between creating and capturing value.

It will soon be apparent that this book has more numbers than your typical negotiation guide. The numbers serve a purpose. They help build your understanding of the pie logic across different applications. The details allow you to fully engage with the examples. You are given enough information so that you can push back rather than take the answers on faith. I hope you will get some of the exciting experience of being in an MBA case discussion. At the same time, I do my best to keep the numbers simple: no Excel is required.

You may wonder if this is asking you to be too logical and too analytical. What about emotions and empathy? Of course, emotions matter. Yes, empathy is critical. Indeed, it is fully rational to be empathetic. But logic in negotiation is fundamental and is far less understood. Having a logical argument—a principle to refer to—can help bring down the emotions. The pie logic is what allows you to find truly fair solutions. The logic is what allows you to make a principled stand.

Don't worry, this book is not *The Vulcan Guide to Negotiation*. While the first half of the book focuses on the logic, the second half focuses on empathy. The tools and cases there are designed to help you be less egocentric and more allocentric—more centered on others. Empathy, not sympathy or charity, will help you better understand the other party's objectives and thereby expand the pie. Logic will ensure you get your fair share. If you can combine logic and empathy, you'll have the best of Mr. Spock and Captain Kirk.

With that, we boldly go where no negotiation book has gone before.

PART I

————

THE PIE

Chapter 1

A PIZZA

I live and work in New Haven, Connecticut. Alongside Yale University, New Haven is famous for its pizza. Some are fiercely loyal to Sally's and others to Pepe's. Based on their long lines, you might think they are harder to get into than Yale. That's because their clam pizzas are in a league of their own. At the risk of choosing sides, I look at a negotiation over a pie from Pepe's.

Pepe's will give Alice and Bob one of their 12-slice clam pizzas if the two can agree on how to divide it up. If they can't agree, Pepe's will still give them some pizza, but only half a pie, and with some favoritism: 4 slices will go to Alice and 2 to Bob.

There's plenty of incentive to reach a deal. The challenge is there are many deals that work for both sides, some more favorable to Alice and others to Bob. But they need to pick one. Most people employ one of two perspectives for how Alice and Bob might negotiate an agreement.

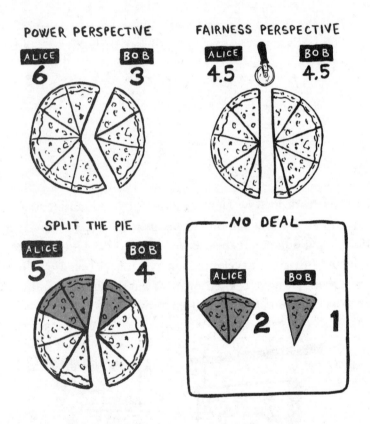

The first is the power perspective. Alice starts with more power—her fallback of 4 slices is twice as good as Bob's—so she should get twice as much: 8 slices for Alice and 4 for Bob.

The second is the fairness perspective. The two sides focus on what each ends up with. In this scenario, they divide the pizza in half: Alice gets 6 slices and Bob gets 6 slices.

There is a different—and more logical—way to divide the pizza. It's more logical because it focuses on what the negotiation is really about: the extra 6 slices created by an agreement. If Alice and Bob don't reach a deal, they will have a total of 4 + 2 = 6 slices. If they reach a deal, they will have a total of 12 slices. The value of reaching a deal is to go from 6 to 12 slices. That increase of 6 slices is what's at stake or what I call the negotiation pie. To get those 6 slices, Alice and Bob are equally needed. Because they have equal power, the 6 slices should be split equally. In addition, each side gets their fallback. This leads to an overall division of 4 + 3 = 7 slices to Alice and 2 + 3 = 5 slices to Bob.

While it seems odd to say this, most people end up being confused over what their negotiation is really about. They argue over the 12 slices, rather than the 6 slices. They focus on the whole pizza pie, not the relevant negotiation pie. The negotiation pie feels like an obvious idea hiding in plain sight. Once you frame the negotiation in terms of the relevant pie, the logical conclusion is that the relevant part of the pie should be divided evenly. That's what I need to convince you of. And then I'm going to give you the tools to convince others.

As a first step, I want to explain what's wrong with the status quo. In my view, the power perspective confuses power *outside* the negotiation with power *inside* the negotiation. Why should the total amount be divided up in proportion to the fallback options? The slices are not negotiating with each other—Alice and Bob are. While 8:4 seems like a reasonable outcome because it mimics the ratio of their respective fallbacks, there is no inherent reason why the outcome should be based on that ratio.

One way to see the weakness of the ratio argument is to consider a different scenario, one where Bob would get no slices, just a few crumbs, if there's no deal. Trying to mimic the ratio of fallbacks in that instance would lead to absurdly high ratios of slices (approaching infinity), suggesting nearly all 12 slices go to Alice.

Some might argue that Bob is in a weaker bargaining position since he will get just 2 slices if there's no deal, while Alice will get 4 slices. That argument misses the point of the negotiation. If they don't reach a deal, Alice will get nothing more than her 4 slices just as Bob will get nothing more than his 2. Effective negotiation is about beating your fallback. For Alice and Bob to beat their fallback, they are equally needed and hence equally powerful.

The second approach, an equal split of the total, is an oversimplified view of fairness. When it comes to dividing the 12 slices, Alice and Bob are not in equal positions. Alice has a better fallback. If 6:6 is really a viable view of fairness, it should work for any set of fallbacks. It doesn't. Look what happens if Alice's fallback option rises to 7 slices, while Bob's remains at 2 slices. If fairness means a 6:6 split, Alice would reject it. She'd rather keep her fallback of 7 slices than accept 6. While this flaw in an even split may not be apparent when the fallbacks are 4 and 2 slices, we see that as a rule for fairness, splitting the total in two is fundamentally flawed.

Splitting the total is a common mistake. Let's say we assign the fallbacks for Alice and Bob at random and then have them negotiate. What do you predict? Just such an experiment was done by Nejat Anbarci and Nick Feltovich.[1] Provided both fallbacks were less than half the total, the two sides split the total equally 42 percent of the time. It sounds fair and neither side does better by walking away. But as soon as one of the fallbacks exceeded half, equal division was chosen less than 8 percent of the time.

What is going on is the two parties were grasping for a solution that looks fair. The problem is they haven't learned to see the relevant pie as $12 - (4 + 2) = 6$ slices and so they end up splitting the wrong total. They split the 12 slices, not the 6 slices. It is fine to care about fairness, but fairness has to be applied to the relevant negotiation pie, not to the total. When it comes to the 6 slices of the negotiation pie, Alice and Bob are perfectly symmetric, equally positioned, and equally necessary. Dividing the negotiation pie equally is what's fair.

Under the pie perspective, the negotiation pie of 6 is split 3 and 3.

Each side gets their fallback plus half the pie. Alice ends up with 4 + 3 = 7 slices, and Bob gets 2 + 3 = 5 slices.

Splitting the negotiation pie is not just about fairness. Alice and Bob have equal power. If Alice doesn't agree to the split, the negotiation pie is lost. The same is equally true for Bob. Neither party can be said to contribute more than the other to creating the negotiation pie of 6. Inside the negotiation, where the object is to create incremental value beyond where the parties are starting, the two parties are entirely symmetric. The two do have differential power outside the negotiation as reflected in their unequal fallbacks. But that has no bearing on how to divide up the negotiation pie.

Now you've seen the secret sauce. It may look deceptively simple in the pizza case, at least in hindsight. When we apply this approach to more complicated real-world problems, the pizza example underlies everything we do.

Henceforth when I use the term "pie" I will always mean the relevant negotiation pie. That's the pie that matters. As I said up front, the hard part of negotiation is to measure the pie correctly. It isn't always as straightforward as in the pizza example. You may have to work with the other side to discover the pie. Recognizing the pie is the key to getting half. And once you resolve the problem of dividing the pie, you can focus your attention on working together to grow the pie.

Let's get started.

Chapter 2

NEGOTIATING
WITH
A TROLL

I know what some of you are thinking. This is all fine if Alice and Bob are reasonable and rational. But what if the other side doesn't care a whit about fairness and isn't interested in learning about the pie. What then? And how do you calculate the pie in a real setting?

I have this friend who thought he could save some money by filing a trademark without hiring a lawyer. That led to a rookie mistake. He didn't know that trademark filings are public information. When he went to register the associated domain name, he discovered that someone had recently bought the URL. That led to a negotiation via email.

The squatter—I'll call him Edward because that was his real name—offered to sell back the domain. He wrote:

Sorry that we did not know and expect that our domain is related to your trademark. Sorry if it made you feel bad. . . . So here we propose you that with USD 2500, we can transfer the domain to you. Kindly let me have you confirmation ASAP.

Edward was trying to anchor the negotiation with a high starting price, $2,500. This is a typical negotiation tactic. As for his apologies, my friend wasn't buying it. The purchase of the domain name was no coincidence: it was bought the same day the trademark filing was made public.

The friend had a very high value for the domain name, perhaps $5,000 or even $10,000. (Of course, Edward had no way of knowing that.) Edward's value was zero. That might suggest the stakes were quite high. But to figure out the size of the pie requires understanding what would happen if there were no agreement. That led my friend to do some research.

He discovered that there's a nonprofit organization called ICANN that manages domain names on the internet. Under ICANN rules, what Edward had done was registration in bad faith. ICANN has a dispute resolution process that costs $1,300 and was virtually guaranteed to assign the domain to the trademark owner. If my friend didn't reach an agreement with Edward, he could get the domain name back by paying a $1,300 fee to ICANN. No matter if the domain name's value to my friend was $5,000 or $10,000, the pie was only $1,300. The reason to negotiate was to save the ICANN $1,300 fee. He would save a bit of time as well, but that was a minor concern. And he was in no hurry since the business was still a few months from launch.

In his reply to Edward, the friend explained the ICANN dispute resolution process and pointed out that its $1,300 cost was a lot less than Edward's $2,500 asking price.

I appreciate your concern. While I feel bad that you have the domain, I would feel even worse paying $2,500. I would rather spend $1,300 and proceed with the ICANN dispute process. . . . Based on *your $2,500 asking price, if I proceed with the ICANN process, I will save money and you will end up with nothing. Thus I suggest that you accept $500. If you truly feel bad, this should more than cover your costs. And, if you don't feel bad, I am prepared to employ the dispute process.*

Edward was experienced in this type of holdup and knew he would lose. (A little digging at the World Intellectual Property Organization website showed Edward's track record was 0–3.) He came down to $1,100, a little below the $1,300 ICANN fee. This time he tried another tactic, adding a deadline.

Sorry that USD 500 is too low for me. Considering the dispute cost and time, I kindly suggest you that we meet up in USD 1100. I am leaving for my vacation from 9/1, so can you please confirm me ASAP?

Up until this point, it was fairly standard haggling. Now was the time for my friend to employ the pie framework. He emailed:

Here is how I see things. Avoiding the ICANN dispute process will save me $1,300. That is what is available to share between you and me. Under your proposal of $1,100, I would end up only $200 ahead and you would end up $1,100 ahead. That does not sound fair to me. It would be just as unfair as my offering you $200 so that I would end up saving $1,100 over the ICANN dispute process. I am willing to split the savings evenly with you, $650/$650, but that is as far as I will go. That is, I will pay you $650. That will leave you $650 ahead of where you would end up if I pursue the dispute process and I will end up $650 ahead.

The email presented the $1,300 pie. The strategy was first to explain what the negotiation was about, then to highlight the symmetry of the two sides, and finally to insist on an equal split.

In reply to Edward's proposed $200/$1,100 split, the friend had an equal and opposite counteroffer. There was no better justification for a $200/$1,100 split than for a $1,100/$200 split. It made sense to provide that counter as a hypothetical rather than an actual offer, since Edward would likely have been insulted by getting too strong a taste of his own unfair offer. The ability to flip any offer naturally led to the only fair result, an even split of the pie.

Edward made a quick counter.

Let's meet up in USD 900. This is my final price. I think that if you cannot accept this price, we have no choice. Kindly understand that my original price was USD 2500. And I am leaving very soon. Let's seal the deal.

The fact that Edward had made a big concession, having come down from $2,500 to $900, was irrelevant. His starting point was just for show. Most of the movement—the step from $2,500 down to $1,300—shouldn't count for anything. The friend had a $1,300 option on the table from ICANN. The negotiation only began once Edward was below $1,300.

As for meeting up at $900, Edward was suggesting they split the difference, not the pie. He had been at $1,100 and proposed moving halfway toward $650 (with a bit of rounding up). Meeting in the middle sounds procedurally fair, but the $1,100 asking price was arbitrary, while the $650 offer was fair. Halfway between arbitrary and fair is still arbitrary and no longer fair.

Edward tried all the tricks of anchoring, splitting the difference, ultimatums, and deadlines. These can work when the other side is unsophisticated. In this case, my friend saw through the tricks, and, more important, had a principled argument that defeated these tactics. He let the email go unanswered. Three days later, Edward accepted the $650 offer.

Edward was not interested in the pie, fairness, or negotiation theory; he just wanted to exploit the situation as best he could. So why did the pie argument work? It worked because it allowed my friend to stand his ground. Both sides understood the deal could be done at any price in the $0 to $1,300 range. Absent the pie, Edward's $900 "final" price might be just as credible as my friend's $650 proposal. But there was a key difference. Edward had no principle on which to base his number. In contrast, my friend made the case that he was proposing something fair based on an equal split of the pie.

Even if Edward didn't care about fairness, what mattered was convincing him that the other side did. That's why the pie proved powerful. My friend was insisting on doing something fair. If Edward wanted a deal, he would have to come to the $650 number or end up with nothing. And therein we see how the pie adds principled reasoning to a negotiation. The principle of splitting the pie allowed my friend to make a fair offer and stick with it.

The $650 deal was the friend's plan all along. He didn't start with $650 because he didn't think Edward would accept his first offer. He waited until they were getting close to each other and inside the $0 to $1,300 range before bringing out the pie argument.

It may seem peculiar to talk about pies and fairness when one is engaged in a hostage negotiation. Yet that's what this must have felt like. Edward had taken the domain name hostage and was negotiating a ransom payment. The potential ransom could be anything between $0 and $1,300. Unless my friend and Edward agreed on a price, my friend would call in the ICANN cavalry and rescue the hostage.

But that would cost $1,300. It was a bitter $1,300 pie. My friend couldn't save the ICANN fee without Edward's agreement, and Edward couldn't get any of those savings without my friend's agreement. Perhaps as a matter of principle my friend should have said no so as not to reward Edward's behavior. That was another reason why he was unwilling to give Edward more than half the pie. To save $650, he was willing to let Edward get $650, though not a penny more.

As you might have guessed, this "friend" was yours truly. There's one more takeaway: spend twelve dollars and buy the domain before filing the trademark.

Chapter 3

THE PIE

The starting point of any negotiation should be: What is at stake? While this might seem an obvious question, the answer turns out to be subtle.

The scope of a negotiation is what the two sides can jointly create *over and above* what they can do on their own—the pie. To create the pie takes both parties. By definition, what is jointly created is what neither side can create alone. When viewed from this perspective, neither side is more powerful. This is the simple but profound insight that leads to the claim that the pie should always be divided 50:50.

In the domain name case, the pie was relatively simple to calculate and to explain. In other circumstances, people have difficulty seeing the relevant pie and even when they do, they follow convention and propose a proportional division. There's a long history in favor of the conventional approach. According to Aristotle in his *Nicomachean Ethics*:

The just, then, is a species of the proportionate. . . . the unjust is what violates the proportion; for the proportional is intermediate, and the just is proportional.

While it is daunting to disagree with Aristotle, I believe proportional division violates a central tenet of justice: *If a rule for dividing the pie is to be considered fair, it must be considered fair for any possible set of starting points.* As we will see in the next example and throughout the book, a proportional division that sounds fair in one context breaks down in another. That's not just a problem with proportional division. An equal division of the total also breaks down. Splitting the pie is the only approach that constitutes a robust, principled commitment to fairness.

Just Interest

It was Diwali. Anju and her older brother Bharat were together back in their childhood home celebrating with their parents. After dinner, Bharat turned to his sister for some financial advice. She did have a Yale MBA after all. He couldn't decide how to best invest his money. The stock market was volatile, but bonds paid little interest. With the $20,000 he had to invest, he could get 2 percent on a one-year CD (certificate of deposit).*

Anju said she felt the same dilemma, but even more so. She had been planning to buy a one-year CD with the $5,000 she had to invest. Because she had a smaller amount to invest, the bank was only offering her a 1 percent interest rate. While $50 in interest was better than nothing, it wasn't that much better than nothing.

The two quickly agreed it made sense to pool their funds and invest together. With a bit of online searching, Anju found that they could get a better rate—3 percent—if they were to purchase a $25,000 CD.

---

* I've rounded up the interest rates to keep the calculations simple.

	AMOUNT INVESTED	INTEREST RATE	INTEREST
ANJU	$5,000	1%	$50
BHARAT	$20,000	2%	$400
ANJU & BHARAT	$25,000	3%	$750

So far, everything was smooth sailing. Now it came time to figure out how they would divide up the interest. Bharat presented what he thought was a fair solution and what pretty much everyone in this situation would propose: the two of them would each earn 3 percent on the money invested. That means Anju would get $150 in interest (3 percent on $5,000), while Bharat would get $600 (3 percent on $20,000). This was fair because everyone was getting the same interest rate. Bharat was dividing the $750—the whole pizza—in proportion to the money invested.

Anju had taken my course and saw things a bit differently. The money wasn't a big issue, as all dollars involved were pretty small. But she wanted to be treated fairly. The way she saw things—and the way I hope you now see things—was that investing together created $300 of value. The two of them were able to earn $50 + $400 = $450 before they decided to pool their funds. Teaming up increased that total to $750. She was equally responsible for the $300 increase. In our language, we'd say that $300 increase is the pie.

Anju wanted the $50 she could earn on her own plus half the pie or $50 + $150 = $200 in total. The gain over Bharat's proposed $600/$150 split wasn't worth getting into a big fight over, but she did have her pride at stake.

She made the pie argument to Bharat. She explained that she wasn't looking to split the $750 (which would leave Bharat with less than if he acted alone). She was only looking to split the $300 gains created by investing together. She emphasized that he needed her help to create those gains.

Bharat pointed out that without his help, she would be stuck at $50. She should be happy to end up with $150. Wasn't she getting a bit greedy?

Anju was ready for this. Without her help, Bharat was stuck at $400 of interest. He was asking for $200 of the $300 increase or two-thirds of the gains. He was the one being greedy.

At this point, it turned into a friendly argument. Each side wanted to be right. Ever the gentleman, Bharat offered to split the difference between his proposal of $150 and hers of $200. He proposed Anju accept $175 in interest.

Halfway between unfair and fair was still unfair, so Anju was not ready to give in. She told me with some pride how she managed to convince him. "Bharat," she said, "imagine for a moment that a $25,000 CD pays the same 2% interest rate as a $20,000 CD. It still makes sense for us to invest together as that leads to an extra $50 in interest."

	AMOUNT INVESTED	INTEREST RATE	INTEREST
ANJU	$5,000	1%	$50
BHARAT	$20,000	2%	$400
ANJU & BHARAT	$25,000	2%	$500

"Under the scheme you proposed, we'd each earn the same 2% on the money invested. That means you'd still get $400 (your 2% on $20,000) and I'd get $100 (my 2% on $5,000). I'd go up from $50 to $100. I'd be getting *all* the gain. That wouldn't be fair to you. In this case, we earn an extra $50 interest and I should split that $50 evenly with you."

Bharat agreed he should get $25 in the case where a $25,000 CD only pays 2 percent. It was game over. He had accepted the general idea of splitting the pie. Bharat realized the proportional division he had proposed wouldn't generally be fair to him. He couldn't ask Anju to adopt proportional division in one case if he wouldn't be willing to accept it in another where it didn't work in his favor. Although it was hard to lose an argument to his little sister, he was coming around to seeing that she wasn't that little anymore.

I really like Anju's approach. A great way to convince someone that their solution isn't right is to give them an example where they would end up being the disadvantaged party under their rule. It is one thing for Anju to say to Bharat, put yourself in my shoes. Even better is to give an example where he gets to stay in his shoes, but they no longer feel comfortable.

To convince someone to adopt the pie approach, you have to persuade them (of the truth) that splitting the pie is fair. If you can also help them see why proportional division is unfair—and potentially unfair to them—then you are home free. They expect you to say why proportional division is unfair to you. You elevate the discussion if you present an example where proportional division goes against their interest. Such an example shows the solution they are proposing isn't a robust commitment to fairness, one that works for any set of conditions.

What people are doing in proportional division is treating each dollar of investment the same way. While that might superficially sound fair, it's not, since each dollar doesn't come at the same cost or create the same gain. Before the two sides figure out how to split the total, each side should first be compensated for what they could earn on their own. What is left over is the excess return and that is what is divided equally. If Anju were to walk away, Bharat would not be able to get any of the additional $300 on his own. This $300 gain is equally reliant on the two parties. It is not proportionally reliant on the amounts contributed.

By coming together, Anju's $5,000 investment created $100 of extra interest on her money and $200 on Bharat's money. Each party should keep half of what is created on their money and get half of what they enabled to be created. Why not keep only what's created on your part? Recall Anju's hypothetical example; her $5,000 investment created $50 of extra interest on her money and nothing on Bharat's. It isn't fair for Bharat to get nothing extra. Anju needs him to earn that $50. He is entitled to half of Anju's extra $50 just as Anju is entitled to half of Bharat's extra $200 of interest in the actual negotiation (where she plays an essential role in making that extra interest possible).

Behind the idea of fairness is equal treatment. The question is:

What should get treated equally? It isn't the dollars that have power. It is the two parties needed to make the deal happen. When the pie is correctly measured, the parties are equally essential and therefore equally powerful. That is what leads me to treat people equally, not dollars.

Anju was Bharat's only potential investing partner and vice versa. Given the small stakes, neither of them was going to go out and look for another partner. In other circumstances, it is likely easier to replace someone with a $5,000 investment than someone with $20,000. If so, Bharat's fallback option would be to find another person to invest $5,000 and work out a deal with that investor. If Bharat can more easily find alternative investors than Anju can, Bharat can strike a better deal with Anju.

For example, if someone else, say Chiragh, will invest $5,000 with Bharat and take his initial 3 percent offer, then Bharat can earn 3 percent on his $20,000 or $600 in interest. That's an improvement for Bharat, but it still makes sense to do a deal with Anju, especially if Chiragh won't accept anything less than $150.

Anju has to undercut Chiragh, but she can hold out for more than

	AMOUNT INVESTED	INTEREST RATE	INTEREST
BHARAT & CHIRAGH	$25,000	3%	$750
PAYMENT TO CHIRAGH	$5,000	3%	– $150
MONEY TO BHARAT			$600

$51. The pie logic still applies. Absent a deal, Anju and Bharat will earn $50 + $600 = $650, which is $100 below the potential $750 interest they can make together. Anju and Bharat split the diminished $100 pie, which leads to Anju collecting $50 + $50 = $100 and Bharat collecting $600 + $50 = $650.

Sometimes when people are thinking about a two-person negotiation they have in mind that other people can be brought in. Doing so changes the pie and what each side ends up with. If there are only two people who can come together to make this deal possible, the pie is $300 and Anju, even with the worse fallback, is equally entitled to half. If there are more than two people, there is still a two-person negotiation between Anju and Bharat. It is a different negotiation with a smaller pie, but they still split the smaller pie. We come back to this issue in Chapter 14, where we discuss multi-party negotiations.

A Framework for Negotiation

Negotiations call out for a framework, one that integrates fairness and power into a single principle. Game theory provides such a framework. Two parties entering a negotiation have alternative choices outside the negotiation available to them (though they may not be attractive options). Game theory's concept of the pie takes these alternatives into account and thereby determines what is at stake.

The definition of the pie can be expressed in a simple formula:

Pie = Total value with deal − (Value of A's BATNA + Value of B's BATNA).

In this definition, "Total value with deal" is what the two parties, A and B, can do together. The BATNAs (Best Alternative To a Negotiated Agreement) are the actions A and B will pursue on their own if they don't reach a deal—in other words, each one's fallback option. The pie is how much more value is created by coming together compared to the largest value created when the parties pursue their best fallback options.

To keep things simple, I'll identify the BATNAs by their value (or cost). In the pizza example, Alice's BATNA was getting 4 slices and Bob's was getting 2 slices. In the domain-name negotiation, my BATNA was paying $1,300 to ICANN and Edward's was getting zero. In the interest rate negotiation, Anju's BATNA was earning $50 of interest on her own and Bharat's was earning $400.

The purpose of a negotiation is to beat one's BATNA. The pie is the extent to which the parties collectively beat their BATNAs. In the pizza example, the pie is $12 − (4 + 2) = 6$ slices. In the domain-name

negotiation, the total value with a deal was $0, which is $1,300 better than my paying $1,300 to ICANN and Edward getting nothing.*
With Anju and Bharat, working together brought $750 of interest, which beats their collective BATNAs of $50 and $400 by $300.

The definition of the pie doesn't care about your wealth, your gender, or which role you have, A or B. It doesn't even care about your individual BATNA. The pie is the same if the BATNAs are [4 slices to Alice, 2 to Bob] or [2 slices to Alice, 4 to Bob] or even [0 slices to Alice, 6 to Bob]. All that matters is how much gain is possible over the collective BATNAs. That's why the negotiation is taking place.

The pie perspective reveals that the two sides are always perfectly symmetric and equally powerful. By power, I mean one's essentiality in creating the pie. If either A or B drops out, there is no pie: A and B are equally essential and thus their power is always equal. Equal power should lead to an equal split. An equal split is also fair—the symmetry of the two sides means they are equally positioned under the pie perspective. This leads to the negotiation principle: *calculate the pie and split it equally.*

It is natural to conclude that people in symmetric positions should be treated equally. If A and B are the same in every way, of course they should get the same amount. The advantage of the pie approach is it reveals the hidden symmetry in situations where the symmetry is not immediately apparent. In the pizza example, Alice and Bob are not symmetric in terms of their fallback options. Thus, there is no claim that they each end up with the same number of slices. They are perfectly symmetric, however, when it comes to creating the six-slice pie. Their perfect symmetry in the pie lens leads to an even split of the pie. Anju and Bharat are not symmetric in terms of how much money they have to invest. But they are perfectly symmetric in terms of creating the extra $300 of interest. This is the importance of

---

* Paying $1,300 means my BATNA was a negative number. The pie is $1,300 = $0 - (- $1,300 + $0).

the pie framework. The essential symmetry only appears when one understands what the negotiation is about. Hence, you calculate the pie and split it equally.

I know it seems simple—perhaps too simple. Over the years I've taught the pie approach, I've heard plenty of "Yes, but . . ."

What if there is a third party?
What if the pie is hidden?
What if one side cares more?
What if the two sides don't agree on the pie?
Why should the side that traditionally does better adopt this approach?
Why can't one side have more power?

I have answers to all these questions and more. As we just saw with Anju and Bharat, adding a third party changes the pie, but it doesn't change the idea of splitting the pie. There is a tendency for people to jump in with all the complications that come into play with negotiations. I ask that you let me continue with some examples of relatively simple negotiations to help get our grounding. Simple negotiations end up being plenty complicated. I promise we'll address all these issues. Along the way, I'll also explain why someone who might normally get more than half should still adopt the pie approach.

_____

Chapter 4

TWO NEGOTIATION MYTHS

Peter Thiel is a famous Silicon Valley entrepreneur and investor. He cofounded PayPal and Palantir and was the first outside investor in Facebook. He is also famous for his unorthodox interview questions. Specifically, he likes to ask:

What important truth do very few people agree with you on?

It's almost a trick question. The statement has to be true. It has to be important. And, the hard part, almost nobody believes it. You can't say: global warming is the world's greatest threat. It's true and important, but too many people already agree with you. Cucumbers and green beans are fruits, not vegetables. That's true and not commonly understood, but it isn't important.

In the case of negotiation, there are two important truths that almost no one appreciates.

1. Having a poor BATNA does not put you in a weak position in the negotiation.
2. No matter the disparity in size or capabilities, both sides make equal contributions to the pie.

I'll try to convince you of each of these in turn.

A Bad BATNA

The standard argument made in the negotiation literature is that having a higher BATNA gives you more power. According to Roger Fisher and William Ury in *Getting to Yes*:

> *The better your BATNA, the greater your power. . . . [T]he relative negotiating power of two parties depends primarily upon how attractive to each is the option of not reaching agreement.*

As explained by Professors Robin Pinkley, Margaret Neale, and Rebecca Bennett, a low BATNA puts you in a weak position:

> *[I]f a negotiator has few or very unattractive options to the current negotiation, then he or she is unlikely to be willing to walk away from this negotiation. Thus, the negotiator should theoretically be in a less powerful position than that of an opponent with more attractive alternatives.*[2]

I disagree. A better BATNA doesn't lead to a person having more power in a negotiation. It simply means they are starting out with more, which means there is less to negotiate over. But they shouldn't get more than half the pie. And someone with a low BATNA should be no more or no less willing to walk away from a negotiation.

In the pizza negotiation, Alice's BATNA was twice that of Bob's,

4 slices versus 2 slices. And yet there was no sense in which Bob was in a weaker position to get any of the additional 6 slices than Alice. If Alice walks away, she loses the chance to improve upon her BATNA the same as if Bob walks away. When the two sides correctly understand what is up for negotiation—the pie—Alice and Bob are equally well positioned, equally strong, in the negotiation.

I had a worse BATNA in the domain name negotiation, but that didn't prevent me from getting half the pie. I offered $650 and Edward was holding out for $900. Edward's offer was only $400 better for me than walking away, while my offer was $650 better for him than walking away. That's why he didn't walk away when I didn't answer his email. The person offered less than half the pie is the one more willing to walk away.

I could give you examples of other negotiations where someone did equally well even though they had a poor BATNA, but you wouldn't know if that was just a lucky break or I was cherry-picking my examples. To really answer the question, we should run an experiment where we give one side a better BATNA and then see the result.

Just such an experiment was done by Professors Francesca Gino and Don Moore.[3] The negotiations involved the sale of a used car. Here's the setup. You're moving overseas to take a new job and thus you need to sell your trusty Toyota Prius. You've been to CarMax and they've given you a no-haggle offer. You have one other option, a person who will buy your car right now if you can agree on a price. You're leaving tomorrow, so this is your last chance to beat the CarMax offer. The potential buyer has seen a similar car to yours and will buy your Prius if you offer a better deal.

In the high-BATNA case, you have a good offer from CarMax and the buyer has a less-competitive fallback. In the low-BATNA case, you have a less-attractive offer from CarMax and the buyer has a better fallback.

Seller high-BATNA case: The offer from CarMax is $8,000. The buyer has seen a nearly identical car that can be bought for $10,000. What price do you think you can get?

Seller low-BATNA case: The offer from CarMax is $7,000. The buyer has seen a nearly identical car that can be bought for $9,000.

What price do you think you can get?

Do you have less power in the low-BATNA case? It may seem so. But in the experimental data, the average transaction price was $9,027 in the high-BATNA case and $8,061 in the low-BATNA case. While the price is just about $1,000 more in the high-BATNA case, looking under the hood we see that your power is really the same. In both cases, the buyer is willing to pay $2,000 more than the seller's BATNA. In both cases, the pie is $2,000. In both cases, the split is just about 50:50.

	HIGH-BATNA	LOW-BATNA
BUYER'S BATNA	$10,000	$9,000
SELLER'S BATNA	$8,000	$7,000
PIE	$2,000	$2,000
TRANSACTION PRICE	$9,027	$8,061
GAIN TO BUYER	$973	$939
GAIN TO SELLER	$1,027	$1,061
SPLIT OF PIE	49 : 51	47 : 53

Once the negotiation is framed in terms of the pie, there is no reason to think the same $2,000 will be divided differently in the two cases. Under our equal-division principle, the predicted prices are $9,000 in the first case and $8,000 in the second, and both parties will end up $1,000 ahead. And that's what the experiment found—although the numbers never come out exact. *The seller's power (and the buyer's power) are equal across the two cases.*

In the language of negotiation analysis, there is a ZOPA (a Zone of Possible Agreement) of size $2,000. The ZOPA in the "High-BATNA" case is $8,000 to $10,000, while in the "Low-BATNA" case it is $7,000 to $9,000. The negotiation is over where in the

ZOPA the two parties will land. The pie is the size of the ZOPA, and splitting the pie is the same as meeting in the middle of the ZOPA.

As I hope you now recognize, the seller has no less power in the second case. Of course, as a seller, you will do worse in the second case than in the first. Indeed, you should do $1,000 worse. But that doesn't imply you have less power.

You do worse only because you have a less valuable product to sell. In the high-BATNA case, you might have a 2011 Prius for sale, while in the low-BATNA case you have a 2010 Prius. The negotiation, however, is not over the valuation. The negotiation is over how to split the *differential* valuation between the buyer and seller. In both cases, that differential is $2,000.

I don't deny the advantage of coming into a negotiation with a better BATNA. Having a higher BATNA leads to getting more. If your BATNA is $8,000 rather than $7,000, I expect you will end up with more for your car. But I don't expect you will end up with a greater share of the pie. The extra money doesn't come from the negotiation. It comes from factors outside and prior to the negotiation, such as having a better car to sell.

This might seem like a semantic point. It isn't. The reason it isn't is that people double-count the gain of having a better BATNA. Even in the extreme case where one side's BATNA is worth zero and the other's is positive, both sides are equally necessary to beat their BATNAs. The side with few or very unattractive options should be no more or no less willing to walk away. So long as the negotiation is framed in terms of the pie, both sides have exactly the same potential gains from the negotiation and thus the same incentive to keep negotiating. A party with a weak BATNA is giving up too much if they don't hold out for half the pie.

Returning to our pizza example, if Alice can increase her BATNA from 4 to 5 slices, the pie shrinks from 6 to 5 slices since $12 - (5 + 2) = 5$. The key point here is that the pie, now 5 slices, still gets divided evenly between Alice and Bob. The reason for the negotiation is to get the extra 5 slices. Just because Alice has a better BATNA doesn't mean she will get any more of the 5 slices than Bob will.

The fact that Alice has a better BATNA means she has less of a reason to engage in the negotiation. And so does Bob. Coming together only creates a mutual gain of 5 rather than 6 slices. It is also true that Alice now ends up with more. The reason is that Alice starts out with 5 rather than 4 slices. The gain from the higher BATNA is a gain that took place prior to the negotiation. Alice ends up with 5 + 2.5 = 7.5 slices, while Bob ends up with 2 + 2.5 = 4.5 slices.

I don't want you to take away the wrong conclusion. Increasing the value of your BATNA is the surest way to end up with more money. You get 100 percent of your BATNA and only 50 percent of the pie. If you find a way to improve your BATNA, you will do better. Indeed, you will do 50¢ better for every extra dollar of BATNA. Your starting point is $1 better and the pie is $1 smaller, so the net gain to you is 50¢.

Similarly, if you can find a way to lower the BATNA of the other side you will also get an extra 50¢ for every dollar of reduction. The other side's starting point is now $1 lower and the pie is $1 bigger, so the net loss to the other side is 50¢, which goes into your pocket.

What Player A ends up with is

$$A\text{'s Total} = A\text{'s BATNA} + 50\% \text{ Pie}$$
$$= A\text{'s BATNA} + \tfrac{1}{2}\left[\text{Total Value} - (A\text{'s BATNA} + B\text{'s BATNA})\right]$$
$$= \tfrac{1}{2}\left[\text{Total Value} + A\text{'s BATNA} - B\text{'s BATNA}\right]$$

Similarly

$$B\text{'s Total} = \tfrac{1}{2}\left[\text{Total Value} + B\text{'s BATNA} - A\text{'s BATNA}\right]$$

There are three levers that are all equally effective in helping you get more: (1) make the deal a better deal by increasing the Total Value; (2) improve the value of your BATNA; (3) reduce the other side's BATNA.

If you are negotiating with someone who has read this book, these are the *only* levers to employ. The two of you will be splitting the pie. Since you can't get a bigger share of the pie, your only move is to change the total value created or the BATNAs.*

If BATNAs are so important, why then do I say that they don't give you power? My reason is simple. People with poor BATNAs not only start at a low point, they also feel pressured to accept less than half the pie. There is no sense in which they have any more or less reason to walk away from the negotiation. I can't count the number of times I've heard people say: You need this deal more than I do. Implicit or explicit in this argument is that the person with the worse BATNA should take less than half the pie. No! Both sides need the deal the same amount. They each need the deal equally to improve upon their BATNAs. And they each contribute equally to creating the pie. That's why the pie should be split evenly no matter the BATNAs.

Equal Contributions

People have a hard time seeing the equality of contributions made by parties bringing what looks like very different items to the table. That's why the bigger player generally gets more in a negotiation. Most people wrongly believe that contributions are related to size and thus are unequal.

I want to convince you that in all two-party negotiations, no matter how different the parties, their contributions to the pie must always be equal. That has to be true at the macro level: if the deal doesn't happen, the pie disappears. But when we get into the details, it may be harder to appreciate the equal contributions.

---

* Negotiations are based on perceived BATNAs. Changing perceptions therefore changes the negotiation result. People often imagine that their BATNA is better than it really is. You may want to help the other party understand that their true BATNA is less attractive than what they might wish.

Two Newspapers

The *Gazette* and the *Planet* are considering a partnership if they can agree on the terms. The *Gazette* is twice the size and can bring 10,000 new subscribers to the *Planet*, while the *Planet* can bring 5,000 new readers to the *Gazette*. The increased profits from these new readers would be $150,000. The *Gazette* says it's entitled to a 2:1 profit split as it's bringing twice as many readers and hence is bringing twice as much to the table.

Are they really bringing twice as much? No, the contributions are equal. The mistaken impression comes from comparing the number of new readers rather than looking at each set of new readers in isolation. Consider the 10,000 new readers the *Gazette* can bring to the *Planet*. What is the *Planet* contributing in return? The answer is its content. Without the *Planet*'s content, there is nothing for the *Gazette* readers to read. The two companies are equally needed to create the value of the 10,000 new readers.

Similarly, when the *Planet* provides 5,000 new readers to the *Gazette*, the *Gazette* is contributing its content. The contributions are not 10,000 new readers versus 5,000 new readers. Each of the two contributions requires both parties. The increased profits should be split $75,000 to each.

Sisyphus

Sometimes one side must do a lot more work to make the pie happen. In those cases, it doesn't seem fair to split the pie. The reason it's unfair is that the pie isn't being measured correctly. I'll explain the confusion using my spin on the myth of Sisyphus.

Zeus is prepared to pay Sisyphus 100 silver drachmas to roll a heavy boulder to the top of a mountain. There is a tricky pass near the top where Sisyphus keeps slipping and the rock then rolls back down to the bottom. Fortunately, Athena is there to assist. With just a bit of a push at the right time, she can help Sisyphus navigate the pass and reach the top. Is Athena really entitled to 50 drachmas for her moment of help?

Giving Athena half generally elicits a visceral reaction of unfairness. She hasn't worked anywhere near as hard as Sisyphus. She doesn't deserve as much! There is some truth to that sentiment.

Yes, she and Sisyphus are equally essential and so each should get half the pie. But, no, the pie isn't 100 drachmas. The pie is the value the two create above their BATNAs. The value created has to take into account the cost—in this case all the hard work—associated with the task.

Let's say it requires 4 hours of strenuous work and that Sisyphus can earn 15 drachmas/hour for such work. The pie isn't 100 drachmas; it is only 40 drachmas after taking into account Sisyphus's foregone 60 drachma wages. If Zeus had only offered 50 drachmas for the job, Sisyphus would have turned him down (at least in my version). There would be no pie: the 4-hour effort required wouldn't have been worth the compensation. We can say Sisyphus's BATNA is 60 drachmas if he could have earned that elsewhere for the same amount of hard work. Equivalently, we can say the job comes alongside 60 drachmas' worth of costly effort, leaving an effective pie of 40.

Athena and Sisyphus really only have 40 drachmas to split. She gets 20 and Sisyphus 80, 60 of which compensate him for all the heavy lifting and 20 from the pie.

It may still seem that Athena is doing quite well for her moment of help. But Sisyphus is missing an essential ingredient without which he can't earn more than his regular 15 drachmas/hour. If there are other goddesses he can tap, Athena is no longer essential, and Sisyphus will get more of the 40. If Athena is the only one available, I'd advise her to hold out for half of the 40 (or see if Atlas might roll the rock up for less).

The Coke Side of Savings

We saw in the pizza example that dividing the pie in proportion to BATNAs made no sense when one party's BATNA went to zero. Proportional divisions are more typically connected to size, not BATNAs, where size is measured in units or dollars. Even here, it leads to absurd results.

The problem with proportional division becomes obvious when the ratios become extreme. What looks like a glitch when the ratio is 2:1 becomes untenable when the ratio is 1,000:1. I was the small guy facing just this issue in what was my most important negotiation.

As I mentioned in the introduction, along with being a professor, I started a ready-to-drink organic iced tea company with my former student Seth Goldman. It's called Honest Tea. The company ended up having several negotiations with Coca-Cola, and I was the point person.

I'll share two stories from the negotiations. The first is a little bit embellished, and the second one is completely true. In the next chapter, you will read about the negotiation between Honest Tea and Coca-Cola over the sale of the company. Here I want to share one of the preliminaries to the main event.

Before the two companies began talking about an acquisition, there was the potential for Coca-Cola to help Honest Tea with purchasing. Coca-Cola has tremendous purchasing power. They get super low prices on all their ingredients and packaging. In the discussion of potential synergies between Coke and Honest Tea, it came out that Coca-Cola could help Honest Tea dramatically cut the cost of its bottles—from 19¢ a bottle to 11¢ a bottle. That's a savings of 8¢ a bottle, and at the time, the company was selling 40 million bottles a year. The business was growing at nearly 100 percent, so over a three-year agreement, the predicted number of bottles sold would be 250 million. The cost savings was worth $20 million! That was an almost impossible number to imagine at the time. With that cost structure, the business would be profitable. The question was how to divide the $20 million between Coca-Cola and Honest Tea.

One option, certainly favorable to Coca-Cola, would be to divide the $20 million savings in proportion to unit sales volume. That way, each company would save the same amount per bottle sold. While units and dollars are not perfectly aligned, sales revenues provide a good estimate of the likely result. Coke's sales volume was $40 billion a year. Honest Tea sales volume was $20 million. That's a ratio of 2,000 to 1. If the companies shared the $20 million in pro-

portion to revenues, Coca-Cola would get $19,990,000 and Honest
Tea $10,000. Ouch.

As you might imagine, that didn't sound fair to me. And it didn't
even sound fair to Coca-Cola. Proportional division clearly doesn't
work when taken to an extreme. And that means it isn't fair anywhere else, either. Proportional division isn't a robust rule. That
suggests you should be suspicious of proportional division when
the ratio is 2:1 rather than 2,000:1. It is still unprincipled, but the
unfairness is just less apparent.

Recognizing the unfairness of dividing the savings in proportion
to sales, the Coke team presented a more reasonable offer: We'll take
$19 million. You can have $1 million. It's our purchasing power.
You're not bringing the same value to the table.

But is Coke bringing more to the table? Without Coke's purchasing power, there would be no savings. That is true. What is Honest
Tea bringing to the table?

In my head I was thinking: Your purchasing power is great, but
you need our inefficiencies. Okay, this might not be the best time to
be cute. Instead, I went with: You need our tea to fill your bottles.
Your purchasing power is great, but to get the savings on an extra
250 million bottles you need access to our customers. It's only by
putting your purchasing power together with the people who like
this not-too-sweet organic tea that we create the ability to save $20
million. That's why we should split the savings evenly: $10 million,
$10 million.

Coke had already harvested all the potential savings on its own
bottles. To create another $20 million in savings, it needed to find
someone who both was paying too much for bottles and used a lot of
bottles. That was us.

Trying to determine which side contributes more to the pie is like
asking which is more important to the Reese's peanut butter cup, the
chocolate or the peanut butter? There's no answer to that question.
You need both.

Even if you agree we are both equally needed, some of you will be
thinking I'm asking for too much. I'm negotiating with the Galactic

Empire—or at least it felt that way. Coke is a Fortune 100 company with one of the best-known brands in the world. I'm the small guy and I care a lot more about the deal. You might expect Coca-Cola to come back with something like: We're Coca-Cola. For us, $19 million isn't even a rounding error on a rounding error. For you, $1 million matters a huge amount. It's more money than you've ever made. You should be happy with $1 million. We'll take $19 million.

That was all true. One million dollars would have been a very big deal. And yet . . . every argument about splitting the pie can be flipped around. In this case, here's how that would work: Okay, Coca-Cola, you just told me you don't care about money. Nineteen million dollars is a rounding error on a rounding error. It doesn't matter to you if you don't get it. But we really do care. We'll take the $19 million, and you can have the $1 million. Nobody on your end will even notice.

One reason large firms often end up getting more is they argue they care less and therefore need more to get the same gain. But that doesn't really make sense. If you argue you should get more because you don't care, that argument can be turned around. The response is: Well, in that case, if you don't care, it's easy for you to make a sacrifice and give up more. We return to this topic in Chapter 11.

At the end of the day, the conversation about joint purchasing was soon superseded by a conversation about buying the company. We never had to reach an agreement about the price of the bottles. Instead, we had to reach a much more important agreement about the price of the company. I'll take a step back and provide some more background before diving in.

Chapter 5

AN HONEST PIE

Negotiation guru Herb Cohen offers some very practical advice: You should care, really care, but . . . not that much. It is hard to be objective when the negotiation is personal and the stakes are extremely high. That is why people hire lawyers and bankers to represent them in a negotiation.

Back in 2008, I didn't have the luxury to follow Herb's excellent advice. I was involved in a high-stakes negotiation with Coca-Cola—at least high-stakes for us. Coke was interested in buying Honest Tea, the company I cofounded with Seth Goldman. Coke had said early on: NO investment bankers. They didn't want to be in an auction situation. I didn't much like the ground rules, but I didn't want to take the risk Coca-Cola would walk away.[4]

For the previous ten years, Seth and I had been working to build Honest Tea. Truth is, the business should have been a recipe for disaster. Neither Seth nor I had any prior experience in running a company. We were going against Coke, Pepsi, Nestlé, Arizona, SoBe, and a dozen more players in what is often considered the world's most competitive market.

And yet, we survived, even flourished. Honest Tea succeeded by taking a different approach. No syrup, no concentrate, no flavorings, no high-fructose corn syrup, no low-fructose corn syrup. The recipe was premium organic tea leaves, hot water, and just a bit of honey, maple syrup, agave, or organic cane sugar. While others were selling iced tea that tasted like liquid candy, Honest Tea was tea that tasted like tea.

Ten years in, the company still felt like a start-up. At the time, Honest Tea's annual sales were around $20 million. It was the number one tea brand at Whole Foods in every region of the country. It was also the fastest-growing tea brand in the natural foods channel. But there was little mainstream distribution.

The future was far from assured. The company had survived deformed bottles, car accidents, even a national recall. To cover the cash needed for inventories, the company had taken out a $5 million loan—but the bank required us to provide personal guarantees. If things went south, we would lose everything.

It is most every entrepreneur's dream to get a call from Coca-Cola saying they are interested in buying your business. While Seth and I were excited to be talking with Coca-Cola, we weren't ready to sell. We were having fun and it felt like we were just hitting our stride.

On the other hand, not selling was scary. Our BATNA wasn't the status quo. It was going to be much worse than that. Back in 1991, Coke and Nestlé had formed a partnership to market Nestea.* That partnership wasn't working out. What that meant was for the first time in a long time, Coke and Nestlé were free to pursue other tea ventures on their own, outside of their Nestea partnership.

---

* Honest Tea had a history with Nestea. When the company was first launched, the name was Honestea. Nestlé's lawyers blocked the trademark filing on the grounds that the name was using their trademark, as in HoNESTEA. We resolved the issue by adding a space and an extra T. The result, Honest Tea, was a much better name.

Over the summer, Nestlé USA had tried to purchase our company. The two sides had made some progress in terms of price, but when the Swiss headquarters saw the number, the CEO got sticker shock and nixed the deal. The head of Nestlé USA came back to Honest Tea with a much-reduced number. I said no. The head of Nestlé USA then wrote to Seth implying I had ruined the hopes and dreams for Seth, his family, and all their future generations. This was getting personal.

The interest from Nestlé and Coke meant one thing. Both companies were determined to buy a tea business. If they didn't buy Honest Tea, they would be buying one of Honest Tea's rivals. Honest Tea wouldn't be competing with other start-ups like Long Life, Inko, Sweet Leaf, and Tradewinds—we would be competing against these businesses backed by the big guns. And if Honest Tea sold to Coke or Nestlé down the road, we would be an add-on and not the main event.

Seth and I weren't just imagining this. The folks at Coca-Cola let us know this in the kindest possible way. They didn't say: "If you don't sell to us, we will crush you like these tea leaves." (That's what the CEO of Tetley conveyed when Honest Tea wasn't interested in his offer.) What they said was: "We have been given a mandate by the board to bring a tea company into our portfolio. We have looked at 150 different options. You are our first choice. We are excited by what you've done and can do. But please understand we have a mandate."

Competing against former rivals backed by the big guys was daunting. But Seth and I weren't just focused on the downside. The opportunity to be part of Coca-Cola created tremendous upside to the mission. As Muhtar Kent, then CEO of Coca-Cola, said to us, "We don't want Coca-Cola to change you; we want Honest Tea to change Coca-Cola." Honest Tea would be Coke's first organic tea. With their help, Honest Tea could bring down the cost of its plastic bottles. It could improve production quality. It could help democratize and mainstream organics. It could demonstrate that you can create a successful company without having to sacrifice your ideals.

Thus the paradox. Seth and I wanted Coca-Cola's help but didn't want to sell. Could we get the best of both worlds? What we all agreed to early on was that Coca-Cola would buy a minority interest in the company today and then have the option to buy the rest in three years. And after some more back-and-forth, we also got what is called a put, the right to ensure that Coca-Cola bought the company in three years if the Honest shareholders wanted them to.

That solved one problem but created another. What price would Coke pay at the end of the three years? Coke had promised to help with purchasing, production, and distribution over the next three years. They quite rightly didn't want to have to pay more due to all the help they were giving.

This is where I first put the pie approach into use. Up until then, it had been an idea germinating in my negotiation course at Yale. Could it resolve the paradox?

What is the pie created by this deal? Working with Coke would allow Honest Tea to reach a level of sales well beyond what it could achieve on its own. Coke didn't want to pay more for the company because of the sales it made possible.

My counter was that the two parties were equally needed to make those additional sales possible. Yes, Honest Tea couldn't get the sales without Coke's trucks, but Coke couldn't make those extra sales without Honest Tea to put on their trucks. Only by coming together could we create a pie.

And hence the solution. Coca-Cola would pay Honest Tea a price based on a multiple of sales. The multiple would represent the full value for sales up to a level of $X (which I need to keep confidential) where $X was projected sales based on current trends. For sales above that level, Coca-Cola would pay 50 percent of the multiple. In other words, the two companies would split the pie, where the pie is the value of the extra sales made possible by this deal.

There was a good deal of back-and-forth over what was full value (what is known as the market multiple) and what was the right value of $X. Think of that as hashing out the details. Those were data-driven questions.

Early on everyone agreed to the concept of splitting the pie. Thanks to the pie framework, the hard part ended up being the easy part. With the agreement in place, everyone could work together to create a giant pie. Writing now, a dozen years after the deal closed, the teas are sold worldwide, and the business is more than ten times its size in 2008.

Along with being a good deal for both sides, there's one last point I'd like you to notice about the Honest Tea deal. The two sides didn't have to know what the pie was in order to split it. They agreed to do an ex post split of the pie—whatever it turned out to be. That is really helpful when you are negotiating in an environment of uncertainty. The two sides know there is a pie to be created but neither side knows how big the pie will be or each side has its own view and they don't agree. They don't have to agree. So long as the pie can be measured after the fact, the two sides can agree to split it. That's a key insight we'll use in many of the upcoming examples.

Chapter 6

A LEGAL PIE

Contracts get broken. When that happens, people get upset. They argue about being made whole. They sue each other. The pie approach can help resolve the conflict. It can help determine how much someone should pay in damages, and can also help provide better incentives to make the resulting losses as small as possible.

A way to think about this issue is as follows. One side took a unilateral action. Instead of negotiating its way out of the contract, it walked away. But what would we expect to have been the result if the two sides renegotiated the terms? The agreement the two sides would have come up with is my starting point for how to resolve the dispute. Of course, that solution is splitting the pie.

Breaking a Lease

Shayne had just taken a new job 2.5 hours away from where he was living. That was good news for Shayne but not so much for his landlord. Shayne would be moving in a month's time. The problem was there were five months left on his lease, so that's four months early. When he told the landlord he'd be breaking the lease, she was none too happy. She talked about how she was on the hook for any lost rent. She talked about how she has kids to take care of.

She insisted Shayne pay $2,400 for two of the four remaining months of rent. On top of that she said breaking the lease forfeited the $1,200 security deposit and, to add insult to injury, the extra $500 pet security deposit. Shayne was out $4,100. Yikes.

Shayne reluctantly agreed. It was marginally better than paying the full four months of rent. Four days after he moved to his new home, Shayne came back to his old place to pick up some tools left in the yard. To his surprise, new tenants had already moved in. The landlord had lined them up during the month's notice Shayne had provided.

I learned about Shayne's case when I was driving home listening to my Slate Plus podcasts and up popped *How To!* with Charles Duhigg. In each episode, Duhigg brings in an expert to help a listener solve a problem. That day Duhigg was helping Shayne from Virginia learn how to do a better job negotiating. The visiting expert was Chris Voss, former FBI hostage negotiator and author of *Never Split the Difference*.

Chris Voss helped walk Shayne through what he might've done differently. For starters, Voss wanted Shayne to demonstrate that he understood the landlord's position. He asked Shayne to start his landlord conversation with "You feel." Shayne offered:

> *You feel like we're leaving you in a bad spot because it's not a good rental season and nobody's really moving. And you're afraid the apartment's going to be vacant for a month or two before you can get a renter.*

Voss thought that was great and I agree. As I discuss in Chapter 18, you want to make the other side's case. That's the best way to demonstrate you understand their position.

Next Voss had Shayne practice asking "How" questions. Shayne proposes: How do we come to a solution that we can both be happy with? Voss approves but wants to flip the phrasing: How do we come to a solution where we both don't end up hating each other after this is all over? As Voss explains:

> *When you say that we can both be happy, my reaction is you're only interested in your happiness. You could care less if you're happy about me.*

I love the allocentrism and the verbal jujitsu. To my mind, there's just one thing missing: the pie framework.

I contacted Shayne and together we figured out the pie. Let's start with his BATNA. Shayne could have paid the remaining four months of rent and kept the apartment empty and thereby not broken the lease. In that case, he would be entitled to get his security deposit back. The apartment would be vacant for four months. That's a loss of $4,800.

But that wasn't his best alternative to no deal. According to Virginia law (Va. Code Ann. § 55.1–1251 (2020)), the landlord must make reasonable efforts to re-rent the unit, even if the tenant breaks the lease. This isn't true in all states. In Florida, the landlord has no such requirement. Fortunately, Shayne was in Virginia. He was only on the hook for the lost rent until the landlord found a new tenant.

Since Virginia had a tight housing market, the unit wouldn't end up vacant for four months or even two. Most likely, it would take the landlord fewer than six weeks to find a new tenant. While I'd want to do some more research to get better data before an actual negotiation, for now we'll assume that with the landlord doing the minimal effort legally required, the unit would be empty for a month. Sometimes it would be more, sometimes less, but it would take a month on average. That's the economic harm caused by Shayne's breaking the lease.

DO YOUR RESEARCH

To determine your BATNA (and hence the pie) often requires research. In the domain case, it required understanding ICANN's dispute process. Here it meant finding out the landlord's legal responsibilities. We return to this topic in Chapter 20, where we focus on how to prepare for a negotiation.

For the landlord, her BATNA was doing the minimal reasonable effort. She collects rent from Shayne until a new tenant appears.

The potential pie is finding a replacement tenant sooner so that the unit doesn't sit empty. If the landlord puts in real effort, she might find a new tenant in a week or less.

The landlord was asking for $4,100, more than three times the expected loss. That's unreasonable. As a starting offer, Shayne could offer to pay $1,200 to cover the expected loss of a month's rent. That gives the landlord a month's notice plus an extra month of rent covered to find a new tenant.

I wouldn't be surprised if the landlord asked for more. Under the status quo, Shayne is on the hook for lost rent and the landlord has no risk. Now she'd be forced to work extra hard and take on risk she didn't sign up for. Perhaps she'd insist on getting $1,800 to cover the risk and her extra effort.

While paying $1,800 is a lot better than paying $4,100, that's giving too much of the pie to the landlord. If she can find a tenant ready to move in when Shayne leaves (as she did), she comes out $1,800 ahead. She gets the full rent from the new tenant plus $1,800 from Shayne.

A better option for Shayne is to split the pie. Shayne agrees to pay $1,800 for six weeks of rent—well more than the average time required when the landlord is hustling. Anything the landlord recovers during that time, 50 percent goes back to Shayne. In theory, the law says that Shayne should get 100 percent of anything the landlord recovers, but then the landlord doesn't have any incentive to hustle and find a new tenant quickly. Shayne wants her to hustle.

If she hustles and gets a replacement right away, Shayne would be out $1,800 but get back $900 for a net loss of $900. The landlord would be $900 ahead. If it takes two weeks before someone moves in, Shayne would get back half of the last four weeks' rent, or $600 for a net loss of $1,200. The landlord would be $600 ahead. This seems a more reasonable approach as Shayne should take on some of the risk and the landlord should share in the gain from re-renting the apartment.

Now that we understand the pie and how to deal with risk and incentives, we have to sell it to the landlord. This is where empathy and examples come into play. Here is what I would propose saying. Let's start with the "You feel."

You feel like we're leaving you in a bad spot. You need the rent.

Let her talk about the need to take care of her kids. Then continue with:

Here's the good news. We can work together so that you end up with more money, not less. With my four weeks' notice, I figure you can find a new renter before I move out. Virginia is a tight rental market. Just to be safe, I'll guarantee six weeks of rent. At the same time, I want to recognize and reward the effort you make to find a replacement. Once you find someone, we'll split whatever rent you get for what's left of those six weeks.

I like providing examples. I do this in every contract I write. An example helps eliminate any potential ambiguity of what was intended. Thus, I'd continue with:

For example, if you find someone right away, we'll split the $1,800 rent guarantee and you'll be $900 ahead. If it takes you two weeks after I move out, you'll still end up $600 ahead.

If she complains about all the extra work, this seems like pretty good compensation for a few hours of time. If she replies that it is unreasonable to expect to find a new tenant with no downtime, you might reply that it is equally unreasonable for it to take six weeks. If she balks about splitting the rent she gets, that might be the time to bring up her responsibility to mitigate damages and effectively rebate all the rent recovered. Under the law, she doesn't get to keep any of the extra rent. By striking a deal, your leaving early provides an opportunity for her to collect 50 percent more rent.

Damages

In some cases—like Shayne's—there's a potential to reduce the damages from a broken contract. In other circumstances, there's nothing to be done other than figure out how much the person who breaks the contract should pay. We have to be extra careful as the rule we pick will determine when people will choose to break their contracts. We don't want people to stick with an existing contract when breaking it would create a much bigger pie. (Remember, that bigger pie has to take into account any losses from the person on the other side.) And we don't want people to break an existing contract when doing so destroys pie.

The case of Alice's broken car deal shows how to walk this path. Alice had agreed to buy a 2013 Prius for $9,000 from a graduating senior who seemed to be in a hurry to sell the car. She knew it was a steal. The car had low mileage and was in great condition. She figured it was worth $11,500. She signed an agreement with the seller and left him with $500 in cash as she went off to the bank to get a cashier's check for the remainder.

When she came back, the car was gone! The seller, whom we'll call Bob, explained that someone had come by while she was at the bank and had offered him $13,000. The buyer had paid via PayPal and drove off with the car. Bob apologized and returned Alice's $500.

I called up my friend Richard Brooks, a professor at NYU School of Law who teaches contract law. I asked what Alice could do.

In the field of law, there is a view that sometimes it makes sense to intentionally break (or in legalese, breach) a contract. This is called an "efficient breach." This was the case with Shayne in that it did not make sense for him to remain in his apartment and commute five hours a day rather than move to his new job location.

The question arises as to how much someone should get compensated when their contract gets broken. We don't want to encourage this behavior, especially when it is not efficient to do so.

As Richard explained, the law suggests three possible options for how much Alice should get paid.

1. Restitution or Reliance
2. Expectation
3. Disgorgement

Let me go over what each of these terms means and why none of them offer a good solution.

Under "restitution," Alice gets her money back and nothing more, while Bob gets to keep the full $13,000 received from Mr. PayPal. That doesn't seem fair. Alice valued that car at more than she paid for it, so just giving her back the purchase price is a bad deal. Indeed, if restitution is all that is required, Bob could sell the Prius to someone else for just $10,000 and pay Alice nothing. Bob has an incentive to break the contract if he can get anything above $9,000. This could easily lead to what is called an inefficient breach. The person who takes the car away from Alice might value the car less than she does. The end result is like forcing Alice to sell back to Bob a car she values at $11,500 for just $9,000. She loses all the gains she made on the deal.

Under "expectation," Alice gets compensated an amount based on her full value of the car. She thought she had bought a car worth $11,500.[5] Thus if Bob gives her back the deposit plus $2,500 for breaking the contract, that would be as if she had resold the car to Bob at its full value to her. This would ensure that the seller would not break the contract unless there was someone willing to pay more than Alice's value of the car. Expectation is certainly better for Alice than restitution. And it prevents inefficient breach.

Under "disgorgement," Bob has to turn over all the extra money to Alice. Disgorgement seemingly works out the best for Alice, so much so that she is happy to have her contract broken. Now she ends up with a gain of $4,000, which is $1,500 better than keeping the car. It is as if she had the car in her possession and resold the car back to Bob at the price he received from Mr. PayPal. The problem with disgorgement is that the seller doesn't end up with any reward. Bob nets the same $9,000 whether he sells the car to Alice or to the PayPal buyer. That's a problem because it means Bob won't ever break the contract and sell the car at $13,000, and thus there won't be any money to disgorge.

We summarize the payments to Alice and Bob in the table below. Note that the total always adds up to $13,000, the money Bob collects from Mr. PayPal.

	RESTITUTION	EXPECTATION	DISGORGEMENT
MONEY TO ALICE	$0	$11,500 – $9,000 = **$2,500**	$13,000 – $9,000 = **$4,000**
MONEY TO BOB	$13,000 – $0 = **$13,000**	$13,000 – $2,500 = **$10,500**	13,000 – $4,000 = **$9,000**

The gain in terms of the pie when the PayPal person buys the car compared to Alice is $13,000 – $11,500 = $1,500. The pie is $1,500 because that is the extra value created by selling the car to Mr. PayPal rather than to Alice. (In calculating the pie, I leave out the gain to Mr. PayPal as he is not part of the negotiation between the seller and Alice over the broken contract.)

Restitution gives more than 100 percent of the pie to the seller or more generally to the person who breaks the contract. (Bob gains $4,000 by breaking the contract.) As such, it creates terrible incentives and goes beyond unfair into the realm of theft.

Disgorgement gives all the pie to the buyer or more generally the party that didn't break the contract. Expectation gives all the pie to the seller or more generally the party that did break the contract. While both options are far better than restitution, that isn't saying much. Why should either party get all the pie?

The obvious solution—though not to the courts—is to split the pie. Bob returns Alice's deposit, and then pays her an extra $2,500 to compensate her for the gain she would have had were the contract carried out. That leaves $1,500 to split. Alice ends up with $2,500 + $750 = $3,250 in cash and her deposit returned. This is $750 better than getting the car. Bob ends up with $13,000 − $3,250 = $9,750, which is also $750 better than his original $9,000 deal with Alice.

	SPLIT THE PIE	GAIN FROM BREAKING CONTRACT
MONEY TO ALICE	$11,500 − $9,000 + 50% x ($13,000 − $11,500) = $2,500 + $750 = $3,250	$750
MONEY TO BOB	$13,000 − $3,250 = $9,750	$9,750 − $9,000 = $750

What we are doing is forcing Bob to split the profit that Alice would have made had Alice sold the car to Mr. PayPal. Think of the following negotiation. Alice has the registration in her possession so that Bob can't sell the car to Mr. PayPal. But Bob has Mr. PayPal's contact info in his possession. Alice doesn't know the identity of the mystery buyer willing to pay $13,000. Only by coming together can Alice and Bob create this $1,500 pie. Although Alice and Bob were denied the opportunity to negotiate over the $1,500, the courts could impose a split-the-pie outcome on them.

This solution isn't perfect in terms of incentives to the seller in that he only gets 50¢ on every dollar of pie he creates. Thus he might not work hard enough to find buyers who are willing to pay the high prices that lead to an efficient breach. But 50¢ is still a lot better than the $0 incentive that comes with disgorgement.

Incentives

The incentive issue is a common problem, and the underlying reason is that we haven't taken into account the cost of effort when calculating the pie. Just as Sisyphus had to be compensated for his effort in rolling the rock uphill, the landlord has to be compensated for her effort in finding a new tenant and Bob has to be compensated for any effort required to find a better car buyer.

When we introduced the idea of the pie, the size was given: six slices in the pizza example or $300 of interest with Anju and Bharat. It took no special effort to create the pie. In other circumstances, one or both parties have to exert effort either to create the pie in the first place or to make it bigger. Here I focus on the case of expanding the pie.

When the pie is correctly measured, any costs associated with expanding the pie are reimbursed. If one party spends $10 to create an extra $18 of value, they should be reimbursed for the $10. The expanded pie is only $8 and that is what should be split evenly. Incentive problems arise when the time and effort involved to expand the pie are hard to observe or measure and thus hard to compensate. That may lead people to incorrectly see the extra pie as $18, not $8, and thereby split the wrong total. If there's no reimbursement and the two sides split the pie and any mismeasured increase in the total, neither side will find it worthwhile to spend $10 and only get back half of the $18 or $9.

This issue arises to a lesser extent in our proposed solution to the negotiation between Shayne and his landlord. Shayne pays $1,800 to cover six weeks of rent, and anything the landlord recovers during that time, 50 percent goes back to Shayne. The landlord is the one putting in the effort to find the new tenant but only collects 50¢ on every dollar of recovered rent. That recovered rent isn't really the pie as it leaves out the cost of the landlord's effort. She will put in some effort—but not the ideal amount—since she bears the full cost and only gets half the benefit. (Splitting the recovered rent creates far better incentives than Virginia law, which has all the recovered rent go to Shayne.)

If there's no reimbursement for effort, we can still create the proper incentives if all the extra revenue goes to the party doing the work. In our earlier example, if the party gets all $18 while paying $10, the effort is worthwhile.

This leads to a paradox. How do we give all the extra revenue to one side and still split the pie? The answer is to split the expected or anticipated pie. One side keeps all the extra revenue but gives the other side a fixed payment equal to half the anticipated pie. If the landlord were to keep all the extra revenue, she would hustle even more and likely find a replacement tenant by the time Shayne moves out. That saves six weeks of the apartment being empty (using the landlord's more conservative estimate) or $1,800. The six weeks saved is not the pie as we have to first reimburse the landlord for her extra effort. Say that effort comes at a cost of $300.

EXPECTED REVENUE GAIN	Six weeks of rent = $1,800
EXPECTED PIE	$1,800 – $300 = $1,500
PAYMENT TO LANDLORD	50% of $1,500 + $300 = $1,050

In this case, Shayne would pay the landlord half the $1,500 pie plus her $300 cost for a total of $1,050 no matter what happens. Another way to see this is Shayne pays the landlord the $1,800 for the lost six weeks and the landlord gives Shayne back half the expected pie, or $750 (for the same net payment of $1,050). The landlord makes this $750 payment in return for the right to keep 100 percent of the recovered rent.

The anticipated pie is split and landlord is now fully compensated for her work since she gets to keep all the recovered rent. The solution isn't perfect—while the incentives are right and the end result splits the anticipated pie, all the risk is now on the landlord. The pie calculation should reflect that as well, which means Shayne should pay a bit more to the landlord. Upon reflection, the earlier proposed fixed $1,200 payment to the landlord looks like a fair deal for all parties and one that gets incentives right.

In our examples of broken contracts, only one side had the capability to expand the pie. In other situations, both parties might have opportunities to expand the pie and it may not be possible to properly reimburse them for their effort. If one side is getting all or most of the extra pie, that party is well motivated to make the pie bigger, but the other side has little or no incentive to do so. One party will work and the other won't. When the two sides agree to split the increased revenue, not the pie, each side is half motivated to make the pie bigger. They may pass on some small opportunities to create pie, but they will still take on the big ones, even if they aren't reimbursed. Two people each with a half incentive typically works better than giving one side a full incentive and the other side nothing.

_____

Chapter 7

DO YOU
HAVE TO
SPLIT THE PIE?

Most people haven't heard about the pie approach. I've been empha-
sizing situations where you are the little guy and would get less than
half unless you employ the pie. What if you are poised to get more
than half the pie? The other side, unaware of the pie, is also unaware
they are getting less than half. They'd be more than happy for you to
highlight the pie and then split it with them. Or you can keep silent.
What do you do?

CEMA

I have a colleague who for reasons that will soon be apparent would
prefer to remain anonymous. We'll call him Arturo. He had signed a
contract to purchase a brownstone in Brooklyn and was in the process
of getting a mortgage. Much to his surprise, he learned that in New

York City, a person taking out a mortgage pays a 1.8 percent recording tax on mortgages below $500,000 and 1.925 percent on mortgages at or above $500,000. That was a big number. He had been planning on taking out a $1 million mortgage, so the recording tax would be $19,250.

After overcoming his shock and doing some googling, Arturo learned that the tax code makes it possible to reduce the bill by doing a CEMA—which stands for a Consolidation, Extension, and Modification Agreement. Under a CEMA, the buyer takes responsibility for the seller's mortgage and deducts the mortgage amount from the sale price. Of course, this is only operative if the seller has a preexisting mortgage.

The good news was that the seller did indeed have a preexisting mortgage. The mortgage was for $600,000. What that meant was Arturo could take over the seller's mortgage and consolidate it into his. The recording tax would then only apply to the new part of the mortgage, the additional $400,000, not the existing $600,000. The tax would fall to $7,200, a savings of just over $12,000!

There was more good news. Because he was taking responsibility for the seller's mortgage, the sale price would be offset by that amount. That meant the seller would also pay lower taxes. In New York State, the seller pays a 0.4 percent transfer tax on the sale price. The seller would save 0.4 percent on $600,000, or $2,400.

	NO CEMA	WITH CEMA
PURCHASE PRICE	$1,300,000	$1,300,000
BUYER'S MORTGAGE	$1,000,000	$400,000
SELLER'S MORTGAGE	$600,000	$600,000 taken over
TRANSACTION PRICE	$1,300,000	$700,000
MORTGAGE RECORDING TAX	$19,250	$7,200
SELLER TAX	$5,200	$2,800
TAX SAVING		$24,450 – $10,000 = **$14,450**

The CEMA route would save a combined $14,450 in taxes. There would be some small increase in legal fees. Arturo estimated the net total savings at around $14,000. In our terminology, that was the pie.

This led to a moment of truth. To complete a CEMA, Arturo had to get his lender to agree and the seller had to give permission as well. Both parties needed to sign off. What would Arturo tell the seller?

There were two options.

1. Ask the seller for his cooperation in facilitating the CEMA. Explain in general terms that this would lead to his saving some money.
2. Explain the situation in more detail and propose that the two sides split the $14,000 savings equally.

At this point, you can guess what Arturo did. He kept his mouth shut and went with option 1. The seller was happy to help out. He wasn't familiar with how a CEMA worked. He just signed the forms he needed to. Based on the tax defaults, the seller would get $2,400 of savings and Arturo would get almost five times as much, $11,600.

You shouldn't beat up Arturo too much. Most people are happy to accept the default split that comes based on buyer and seller taxes. They don't see the world in terms of the pie, and they don't recognize their equal power. Indeed, thousands of buyers who arrange a CEMA end up getting over 80 percent of the savings. According to New York City star real estate lawyer Sandor Krauss, "When I represent the buyer, we ask for all the CEMA credits and usually get it, and when I am on the seller side, we always get half."

On the morning of the closing Arturo's real estate lawyer called him to report some more good news. The lawyer had explained to the seller that he was about to get a $2,400 tax savings. The seller was delighted, so much so that he offered to split that savings with Arturo! The lawyer called to say what a great job he had done. The buyer would be getting all the $11,600 plus half the $2,400.

Even for Arturo this was too much. He told the lawyer to direct all $2,400 of the transfer tax savings back to the seller. But before the lawyer could reach back to the seller, he got another call. The seller's curiosity had been piqued. After a bit of research, the seller had figured out that Arturo was about to save $11,600. He was livid. He wanted half.

There really wasn't any principled counterargument. Had the seller understood the situation from the beginning, he would have been willing to do the CEMA if and only if the two sides agreed to split the combined savings equally. While the seller was unlikely to walk away from the deal over $5,000, he might have delayed the closing or proved difficult in some other way.[6]

Okay, there was one semi-principled counterargument. The seller had implicitly agreed to the 5:1 split by not bringing this up at the time he agreed to the CEMA. But holding him to that division wasn't worth doing. Arturo didn't want to move into a new house and have the seller bad-mouth him to all the new neighbors. He mumbled something or other and threw in a few extra thousand. They shook hands and closed the deal. Even so, the experience left a bad taste in the seller's mouth. And Arturo didn't feel great about it, either.

I have two morals.

Sometimes you can get away with getting more than half the pie. But it is a dangerous strategy. And you might have some trouble looking at yourself in the mirror.

The second moral comes from taking the perspective of the seller's side on this transaction. When someone says this will be good for you, make sure to find out how much they will be gaining. Be allocentric. Don't just look at your gain. Figure out the pie. Get half.

This message is part of our larger theme: be on the lookout for default splits of the pie that come from tradition, regulations, proportionality, or misguided equality (splitting the 12 slices, not the 6). There is nothing stopping you from undoing the default and proposing an even division of the pie. Arturo's seller would have gotten half the pie if he had only asked for it.

Chapter 8

WILL THE OTHER SIDE BUY IN?

I recognize this view of negotiations is novel. I fully appreciate that most people do not negotiate the way we've discussed. This is not surprising. Unless they had independently discovered the pie framework, they would not see the force of equal division nor have the tools to convince others. While there are exceptions, most often the norm is a simple heuristic that varies with the situation and who is making the proposal.[7] In some cases, we see proportional division; in other cases, one side proposes an equal split of revenues or costs that only looks at part of the picture or proposes an equal split of profits but ignores the different BATNAs. The result are offers that appear fair to the side making the proposal, but not to the other. My aim is to use the pie to provide one consistent framework, a framework that is fair to both sides and that reflects their equal power.

Yet there is a wrinkle. It may seem the pie framework is one-sided in favoring the smaller or perceived weaker party. The approach certainly has the potential to lead to better outcomes for the smaller parties, but it requires the larger party to go along. They may do so because they want to be seen as fair. They may do so to get the deal done. They may do so because if the two sides can amicably resolve the division problem, this allows them to focus on creating value. But in other cases, they will resist.

The job of this book is to first change the way you see negotiation and then to give you the tools to change the way the other side sees the negotiation. The illusion of power will be hard for the other side to give up. You may need to educate them.

Education begins with setting up some ground rules for the negotiation. You can introduce the concept of the pie and explain why power is equal in that framework. You might sum up the ground rules with "Our shared goal is to reach a fair outcome based on equal power. Let's try to create as much value as possible in the negotiation and share equally in this value creation." If the other side agrees to these terms, you can move to framing the negotiation in terms of the pie and then look for opportunities to make it bigger.

There's a danger if you don't start with ground rules. If, instead, you start the negotiation with an offer that leads to an even split of the pie, you may well end up with less than half. Starting this way puts you at risk if the other side is stuck negotiating the old-fashioned way and sees your opening as your aspiration, not your principled solution. In my view, the first thing to settle is how the two sides will negotiate.

It is not enough just to propose these terms of engagement. You want to get agreement on these terms. Then you want to ensure that the other side is living up to this agreement—and that you are, too. If you can get agreement on the ground rules, you have a shared interest in creating the largest possible pie. It turns a negotiation into a joint optimization problem.

If you don't start with the ground rules, leave yourself some room to move up to half the pie once you introduce the pie framework.

That's why in my negotiation with Edward over the domain name I started with a number that offered him less than half the pie. I guessed that he expected there would be some give-and-take, and so I played along. Edward was asking for more than the pie. Early on, I steered him toward the pie by framing things in terms of my BATNA (which was paying the $1,300 ICANN dispute resolution costs). That framing quickly brought his asking price to something below $1,300. At that point, we had done a little dance and I felt it was time to explain the pie.

I used the pie to explain why his proposed division was unfair. Then I made an ultimatum—take a fair deal or no deal—though I was more polite. "I am willing to split the savings evenly with you, $650:$650, but that is as far as I will go." He tried to present his counteroffer as an ultimatum, but it was an arbitrary number and thus didn't stick. After I didn't respond to his counter, he thought things over and took the fair deal.

In this case, the pie came up pretty quickly and there wasn't a cost of delay since there was no expectation we'd build trust or find a way to expand the pie. Indeed, even after we agreed to split the pie there was no trust; we used escrow.com to handle the transfer of the domain name and the cash.

Of course, not everyone will agree to these ground rules whether presented up front or later on. The other side might be a bully or act like a bully and make demands, threats, and ultimatums. If the other side rejects this approach, at least you know who you are negotiating with. This might be a good time to look for another negotiating partner. Or, if that is not an option, you might want to explain again why the pie represents what is at stake, why power is equal, and why without a fair split there may be no deal.

That last explanation is why both parties should agree to negotiate in this fashion. Once the negotiation is framed in terms of the pie, power is equal, an even split is fair, and absent a fair split there may be no deal. Agreeing to an equal split doesn't hurt the larger party: an even split is better than no split.

Of course, if you are the smaller or traditionally weaker party, you will want to present this approach. To do so convincingly, you first need to convince yourself. That may be enough. You can insist on an equal split and explain why that is being reasonable. There is no equally compelling counter the other side can insist on. Since any unfair division is arbitrary, there is no stickiness to any counter. The other side will come around as they realize you have taken a principled stand. If they want a deal, they have to accept a fair deal.

If you are the traditionally advantaged party and the other side presents our principled approach, I proudly admit I have no rebuttal. There is no principled position you can offer as a counter. You might not care about fairness or the pie, but the other side does and is right to insist on getting half. Be reasonable and accept that your perceived greater power was illusory. Refusing to accept principled arguments about equal power will paint you as intransigent and may cost you the deal. And even if you do get a deal, the other side may not trust you and may be less willing to explore how to create the largest pie. If you don't agree to split the pie, it is hard to imagine the other side will trust you and work with you to explore how to create the largest pie.

If you are the advantaged party and the other side is unaware of the pie approach, what do you do? This is more challenging. You may have made sincere arguments in favor of your having more power. You weren't trying to trick the other side—you believed you had more power and thus were justified in demanding more than half. Now you know. Should you try to preserve the illusion of power?

Some will choose to share our approach. People who dislike negotiating because they don't want to be taken advantage of generally don't want to take advantage of others even if they can. It violates their ethics. Following the Golden Rule, they treat others the way they wish to be treated. They want a fair solution. Now they have it and will want to share it.

Others will choose to share our approach for tactical reasons. If you don't employ the pie, you end up focusing on measures, such as size or market share, that are extraneous. The other side may feel that its contribution is not being appropriately respected, even if it doesn't have the pie vocabulary to articulate its concern. It may block any deal it perceives as unfair. Better to share the principled approach to negotiation and reach an agreement.

It might well be a better agreement since the other side is more willing to work with you to maximize the pie when they feel they are being treated as the equal partner they are. Split-the-pie deals are done quickly and efficiently. Over the long run, parties that are principled negotiators will enhance their reputation for fairness and be attractive deal counterparties. That means more pie creation, even if it also means more equal sharing.

Chris Voss (author of *Never Split the Difference*) suggests opening a negotiation with a promise to offer a fair deal. He asks the other side to let him know if they feel he is being unfair. This is not just advice to the weaker party who is hoping to get treated fairly. It is advice directed to the stronger party. His reasoning is that if people feel they are being treated unfairly, they shut down. They won't work with you to expand the pie. They may not even be willing to do a deal. Acting fair and being clear that you want to behave in this fashion will help you close more deals.

I fully agree with Chris Voss on this point, and I take it a step further. Unless the two sides have a common view of what fairness means, each side can and often will pick a perspective on fairness that works to its advantage. A promise to offer a fair deal has more bite when it comes with a common understanding of what fairness entails. Splitting the pie provides the much-needed neutral perspective on fairness that both sides can adopt.

The reasons for the advantaged party to split the pie are ethical (Golden Rule), practical, and tactical. Most often they should carry the day. And yet there will be times when you might want to keep your mouth shut. In a flea market, you don't have to offer $100 for the teacup that completes your set. And if the other side volunteers a proportional division that favors you, you can choose to go along. You don't have to take the lead. But don't fight logical arguments when the other side makes them.

What about Using Objective Criteria?

Fisher and Ury advise employing objective criteria to split the pie. They provide examples such as market value, costs, precedent, efficiency, tradition, what a court would decide, and equal treatment. I get concerned when there are multiple criteria as people can then pick the one that works best in their situation. I certainly agree with equal treatment, but one has to be careful about what is being treated equally—dollars or people? Equal treatment of investment dollars leads to proportional division, while equal treatment of people can lead to dividing the pizza 6:6 or 7:5 depending on whether we focus on the total or the pie.

Objective criteria such as market value and costs help determine the pie, but they don't provide guidance for how to split it. Take my negotiation with Edward over the price of a domain name. The relevant number was not the market value of the domain name (if there were one) but the cost of the ICANN process. Even that objective number didn't provide an answer. All it did was provide the range of possible answers, $0 to $1,300. We knew what a court would decide: I'd win. Our negotiation was to avoid my $1,300 cost of going to ICANN's court. What objective criteria would help us divide the $1,300 pie?

There's one universally relevant objective criterion: when the pie is correctly measured, the two parties are equally essential in creating value. That's why I argue for a specific type of equal treatment: split the pie. I agree with Fisher and Ury when they write "objective criteria need to be independent of each side's will." I believe objective criteria also need to be independent of the specific negotiation, and it's best if there's just one so they are never in conflict. We want one objective criterion that's independent of each side's will and can be applied to all negotiations. Framing the negotiation in terms of the pie, recognizing the equal contributions, and then splitting the pie equally fits the bill perfectly.

The upcoming Part II provides examples of how to divide the pie in the context of cost sharing. In Part III, we answer the remaining "Yes, but" questions. It may seem that we are deferring the topic of how to grow the pie.

I started with and continue to emphasize how to divide the pie for a simple reason: if you have to watch your back the whole time, it is hard to work together to create the largest pie. Compare your comfort levels in the two following scenarios:

1. Let's find a way to cooperate. I'm sure we can find a fair way to divide what we create.
2. Let's agree to split evenly what we can create together. I'm sure we can find a way to make a bigger pie.

Route 1 is basically saying "Trust me." Just like I get my guard up when someone says "truthfully," I get worried when I have to trust the other side.* Under route 2, the contentious part has been resolved and in a way that is principled and fair. That provides the framework for cooperation.

There's an old saying that it is easier to share a shirt that you don't yet have. If we can't agree how to share something we haven't yet created, I'd be worried about the fight to come when the shirt is there between us. That's why I've been so focused on how to divide the pie. Ultimately, I think solving the division problem is what unlocks the potential to create the biggest pie. The tools for doing so are the topic of Part IV. In Part V, we cover how to prepare and what to reveal. There are even some tools for creating (or at least not destroying) and capturing pie for when you're stuck in more traditional negotiations.

---

* When someone says "Truthfully, . . ." or "To tell you the truth, . . ." it makes me wonder if everything else they said is equally true.

In the meantime, let's not lose sight of a key step in creating pie: you have to reach an agreement. A "No deal" outcome destroys pie. If we need to work together to create value or save costs, there's no pie if we can't agree on how to split it. The arbitrary approaches people have traditionally taken are unfair and thereby make it harder to reach an agreement.

PART II

SPLITTING
THE COST

So far, we have focused on dividing up a positive pie. For example, Anju and Bharat earn more interest by joining forces; the *Planet* and the *Gazette* create value by sharing subscriber lists. The very same approach also applies to dividing up a negative pie. By a negative pie, I mean there are costs that have to be paid. The negotiation is over who should pay how much.

The issues here range from the minor matters such as how to allocate an expense report across company divisions or split the cost of a car ride to fundamental challenges such as how the world's countries should split the cost of reducing carbon emissions. Everyone sees the benefit of working together, but no one wants to pay more than their fair share.

Negotiating who pays what cost is less fun, more emotional, and more problematic than the task of sharing gains. That's why I put it off until we first covered the more enjoyable problem of splitting a positive pie. When things are tough, there is even greater value in a fair, logical structure. Hence our split-the-negative-pie approach.

In some cases, the parties are involved in an actual negotiation. Other times, the parties are looking for a cost-allocation rule that is fair to all the parties. You can think of a fair cost-allocation rule as what a fair negotiation process would lead to without having to do the negotiation. As you can predict, I think a fair cost-allocation rule is one that splits the pie.

We begin this section with a lesson from the Talmud on how to split the cost. As far as I know, this is the earliest example of applying the pie approach. I appreciate that this is a bit of a detour, so it's fine if you'd rather skip ahead to Chapter 10 and go right to the modern examples of cost sharing. Those interested in the historical connection, read on.

Chapter 9

A TALMUDIC SOLUTION

The fundamental idea of splitting the pie can be traced back two thousand years to the Babylonian Talmud. The Talmud forms the basis for Jewish civil, criminal, and religious law. It consists largely of case studies, where the reader is left to discern general lessons from them. A particularly fascinating case concerns the proposed resolution of a financial dispute.

The Talmud offers the following prescription:

Two persons appear before a court holding a garment. One says it's all mine and the other says half of it is mine. The first will receive three-quarters and the latter one will receive one-quarter.

This may seem strange. One person has claimed the whole garment and the other has claimed half. Proportional division would propose a 2:1 split, two-thirds to the first person and one-third to the second. But the Talmud says the division should be 3:1, three-quarters to the one asking for everything, and only one-quarter to the one asking for half.

There's a simple logic underlying the solution. It's known as "the Principle of the Divided Cloth," and it turns out to be the same as splitting the pie.[8]

Imagine the two parties in the dispute—we'll called them Cain and Abel—are holding on a cloth starting from different ends. Abel makes a claim starting from the left; he claims the entire pie or cloth for himself, conceding nothing to his brother Cain. Cain makes a claim to half the cloth starting from the right end, thereby conceding the other half to Abel.

If we look at both claims together, we see the dispute is really only over half the cloth. Cain has conceded half to Abel, so that is not in dispute. The Talmud solution is to give each party what has been conceded to him by the other and then split the amount in dispute. Abel gets what Cain has conceded him, half the cloth, plus half of the disputed half, which adds up to three-quarters. Abel conceded nothing to Cain, so Cain only gets half the disputed amount, which is half of half or a quarter.

At this point you might be wondering: Why is Cain asking for only half the cloth? If Cain asked for more, he'd get more. Yes, this is true under both proportional division and the Principle of the Divided Cloth. We expect each party will try to make the largest claim he or she can justify. Abel's larger claim may be justified by external factors such as Abel is owed twice as much money.

It helps to think of a negotiation as having two stages. One is making claims and the other is dividing things up once the claims are made. The Talmud focuses on the dividing-up question. In some negotiations, the claims are not malleable. Take the case where an estate owes money to two different creditors, $100 to Abel and $50 to Cain. Unfortunately, the estate has only $100 in assets. In this case, the size of the debts is not in dispute. The relevant question is how the creditors should divide up the $100, given that the two debts more than exhaust the assets.

Absent the Talmud's approach, you probably had one option in mind: proportional division. A $100 creditor will get twice as much as a $50 creditor, making the split 66:33. The Principle of the Divided Cloth gives you a second fair option. The $100 creditor (Abel) gets the conceded $50 plus half of the $50 in dispute for a total of $75, leaving Cain with $25. Proportional division treats each dollar of claim equally. The Principle of the Divided Cloth treats each creditor equally with regard to the disputed amount.

The Principle of the Divided Cloth can be reinterpreted as splitting the pie, though this is far from obvious. Our next examples illustrate the connection.

Let's return to our original negotiation over a 12-slice pizza. When I first presented the story, Alice would get 4 slices absent an agreement and Bob would get 2 so that the real negotiation was over the additional 6 slices they'd receive from Pepe's if they could come to an agreement. Under the Talmud interpretation, Alice and Bob have incompatible claims on a 12-slice pizza. Alice has been promised 10 slices and Bob has been promised 8, but there are only 12 slices to go around. The fact that Alice "only" claims 10 slices means she is conceding 2 slices to Bob. As a backup plan, Bob can give Alice her full claim of 10 slices and keep 2. Similarly, Bob's claim of 8 slices concedes 4 slices to Alice. Thus, Alice and Bob go into the negotiation knowing they can get at least 4 and 2 slices, respectively. The point of the negotiation is to go from those combined 6 slices to 12. The conflict is over the 6 slices that both sides want. According to the Principle of the Divided Cloth, the disputed 6 slices are split evenly, leaving Alice with a total of 7 and Bob with 5.

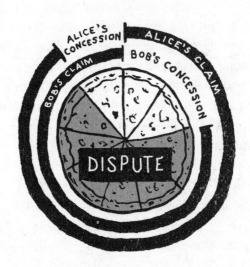

The Principle of the Divided Cloth has a natural application to cost sharing. We'll stick with Cain and Abel but modernize the story a bit, or more than a bit. Cain and Abel are shepherds, and they are tired of shearing their sheep with scissors. They are looking into buying an electric sheep clipper on Amazon. Since sheep only need to be shorn once a year, the two brothers can easily share the same clipper.[9]

Before they hit the Buy Now button, they have to agree on how to split the cost. The answer would be easy if Cain and Abel had the same number of sheep: they would split the cost evenly. The situation is challenging, as Abel has twice as many sheep as Cain and therefore stands to benefit twice as much.

Acting self-interestedly, Cain and Abel would each like the other to cover as much of the cost as possible. At the same time, each is looking to be fair. But what is fair here? No surprise, Cain makes a stand for proportional division: Abel should cover two-thirds of the cost as he will use it twice as much and get twice the benefit. Abel wonders if this is Cain's jealousy arising over Abel having more sheep. He counters that fairness implies equal treatment: the two should each pay half the cost. They are stuck with incompatible positions and no way forward.

According to the Talmud, the way the cost is split depends on the total cost relative to the potential benefits to each party. We'll put some numbers on the example to illustrate. Let's say the value of the electric clippers is $200 to Abel and $100 to Cain.

The Principle of the Divided Cloth provides an answer for any possible clipper price.

If the clippers cost $50, Abel gets his way and the costs are divided equally.
If the clippers cost $150, Cain gets his way and the costs are divided proportionately.
If the clippers cost $250, Abel pays $175 while Cain pays $75.

This is represented in the table below:

COST OF CLIPPERS	ABEL ($200 BENEFIT)	CAIN ($100 BENEFIT)
	Abel pays	Cain pays
$50	$25	$25
$150	$100	$50
$250	$175	$75

At first glance, the Talmud's solution looks arbitrary and mysterious. The principle becomes clear when we look at the negotiation in terms of the pie.

Look first at the case where the clippers cost $50.

If Cain and Abel reach an agreement, they share an electric clipper. They have a combined benefit of $300 and the clippers cost $50, so their combined net gain is $250. But the pie is the gain compared with no agreement. Thus, we also have to figure out what Cain and

Abel will do if they don't reach an agreement. Abel will buy his own set of clippers. With a benefit of $200 and a cost of $50, his net gain is $150. Similarly, Cain will also buy his own set. With a benefit of $100 and a cost of $50, his net gain is $50. Absent a deal, the two of them will still come out $150 + $50 = $200 ahead.

CLIPPERS COST $50	ABEL BENEFIT $200	CAIN BENEFIT $100	TOTAL
Combined Gain if Deal			$300 − $50 = $250
Gains if No Deal	$150	$50	$200
Pie			$50

The pie is the $250 gain when they share a clipper minus the $200 gain when they each buy one. Thus, the pie is $50. This makes intuitive sense. Cain and Abel avoid buying a second clipper and save $50. Cain and Abel are equally responsible for this savings. If Abel walks away from the deal, the $50 is lost. If Cain walks away from the deal, the $50 is lost. There is no sense in which one side is more responsible than the other for creating the $50 savings.

The Talmud proposes the two split the savings right down the middle. Each saves $25. That means Abel pays $25 (rather than $50) and Cain pays $25 (rather than $50).

We can also explain this result in terms of the divided cloth. The cloth is $250—the amount the two of them have to divide up after paying for the clippers. Abel can claim $200 as that is his maximum possible benefit. Abel is therefore conceding $50 to Cain. Cain can only claim his maximum benefit of $100. Cain is conceding $150 to Abel. The concessions add up to $200, leaving $50 in dispute. They split the disputed amount, $25/$25. Cain ends up with the $50 conceded to him plus $25 for a total of $75. Abel ends up with the

$150 conceded to him plus $25, for a total of $175. When each pays $25, the net gains are $75 and $175 to Cain and Abel, respectively. While I think it's easier to explain the answer in terms of the pie, the two approaches lead to identical answers.

What if the cost is $150?

If they share a clipper, they have a combined benefit of $300 and a cost of $150, so their combined net gain is $150. Once again, we have to ask what Cain and Abel will do if there is no deal. Abel will still buy the clippers on his own. With a benefit of $200 and a cost of $150, his net gain is now $50. As for Cain, if he bought clippers on his own, he would end up losing $50. He is better off sticking with the status quo and getting $0. Thus, absent a deal, the two of them will come out $50 + $0 = $50 ahead.

The pie is now $150 − $50 = $100. This also makes intuitive sense. Cain was getting nothing without a deal. Now it is possible for Cain to get his full $100 of value by sharing Abel's clippers at no additional cost. If the pie is evenly split, both sides should come out $50 ahead. You can think of this as Cain paying Abel $50 to borrow the clippers. Cain is paying $50 for something he values at $100, so he ends up $50 ahead. And Abel is $50 ahead from the money that comes from Cain.

CLIPPERS COST $150	ABEL BENEFIT $200	CAIN BENEFIT $100	TOTAL
Combined Gains if Deal			$300 − $150 = $150
Gains if No Deal	$50	$0	$50
Pie			$100

In terms of the divided cloth, here the cloth is $150. Abel has a claim of $200 so he is not conceding anything to Cain. But Cain is only able to claim $100, and thus concedes $50 to Abel. Thus $50 of the $150 cloth is allocated via concessions and the remaining $100 is in dispute. Each side gets an additional $50 (half the disputed amount), leaving Abel with a gain of $50 + $50 = $100 and Cain with $0 + $50 = $50 gain. The last step is to turn the gains back into costs paid. When Abel pays $100, he comes out $100 ahead; when Cain pays $50, he comes out $50 ahead. Those are the proposed gains in the divided cloth solution.

A key feature of the Principle of the Divided Cloth is that once you ask for the entire pie, you don't get extra credit for asking for anything more. If there is $150 to divide and Abel has a $200 claim, he doesn't get anything more than if he asked for only $150. The most you can legitimately ask for is everything.

Cain and Abel aren't splitting the costs equally in one case and proportionately in the other. In both cases, they are splitting the pie equally. You can predict the answer for the case where the clippers cost $250. Cain and Abel will split the pie evenly. Let's check.

If they combine forces, they come out $300 − $250 = $50 ahead. If they can't reach an agreement, the $250 cost of the clippers is so high that neither one will find it worthwhile to buy the electric clippers on his own. Absent an agreement, both end up with $0. Consequently, the pie is $50 − ($0 + $0) = $50. Splitting the pie implies each side ends up $25 ahead. If Abel chips in $175 for something worth $200 to him, he ends up $25 ahead. And if Cain contributes $75 for something worth $100 to him, he, too, ends up $25 ahead.[10]

The clipper example may seem a bit far-fetched, but it is representative of a large set of business negotiations. Instead of clippers, there could be a software package that lowers the administrative costs by $1/employee. Abel has 200 employees, while Cain has 100. Thus, Abel has twice the potential benefit. Or there could be a joint marketing campaign such as "Got Milk?" Abel's dairies have twice the market share of Cain's so Abel will get twice the benefit from increased demand. As we saw, just because one side stands to benefit twice as much does not mean they should pick up two-thirds of the cost. Whenever there are unequal benefits—which is pretty much all the time—the Talmud offers a fair solution to the negotiation problem.

The fact that the idea of splitting the pie can be traced back to the Talmud is remarkable. This one idea unifies what would otherwise look like three idiosyncratic solutions. It solves the problem of treating people in unequal positions equally. The result is fair in that each side ends up with an equal benefit—when the benefit is measured in terms of what is at stake in the negotiation.

The Principle of the Divided Cloth illustrates the profound idea that the negotiation is about the disputed amount or what we call the pie. When you first look at the problem, you might think that Cain and Abel are negotiating over how to split the $200 and $100 benefits. Or you might think they are negotiating over how to split the cost, whether it be $50, $150, or $250. Neither perspective is correct. The point of the negotiation is to create the pie. That is what is at stake. If you don't understand what the negotiation is really about, there's little hope you will come up with a principled solution.

___

Chapter 10

WHO PAYS?

We've all been in situations where we've had to pay more than our fair share. At least it's felt that way. When we do projects with others, whether work or play, we need to figure out who pays what. Splitting the cost equally is often unfair. When two couples share a vacation home, what if one gets the master bedroom? Or what if one of the couples has kids and uses two of the three bedrooms?

The same issues arise on a much bigger scale when companies come together. Carmakers are building a network of high-speed electric charging stations in Europe. How should the companies divide the multi-billion-euro cost? Not equally. You can think of their very different market shares as akin to using a different number of bedrooms.

Beyond business, cost-sharing challenges arise on a global scale. How should the industrialized countries split the cost of supporting economic development and humanitarian aid? An equal split would be fair if all the industrialized countries had the same size, same population, and same level of economic activity (GDP). But when they are all different, as they are, what should each country contribute?

The typical solution is to divide costs in some proportional fashion, whether it be related to bedrooms, market share, or GDP. The underlying motivation is that this is a proxy for the benefits attained in the first two cases, but then it's more like an equal burden borne when it comes to humanitarian aid. As we will see, the proportional solutions fail logic and fairness.

The basic problem is: How do you treat parties in unequal positions equally? In some contexts, this is the search for a fair cost-allocation rule. There's not always a negotiation involved. With friends and family, the parties may not want to negotiate because they are concerned about the effect on the relationship. They are just looking to do something fair.

Inside a company, costs have to be shared across projects and divisions. Managers don't want to spend their time negotiating with each other. Like a family, they just want a fair rule. In other settings, there is an actual negotiation involved—if the parties can't agree on how to divide the costs they won't be able to proceed with the project. In all these settings, you want to frame the problem in terms of the pie. Splitting the pie implies a specific cost division, and that's the one that's logical and fair.

I'll show how the pie works in the cost context starting with some small-stakes examples, such as splitting an expense report or sharing an Uber. While the stakes are small, I think they are interesting in their own right. They show how hard it can be to see the pie even when it is there in plain sight. Moreover, these examples illustrate the logic we apply when we turn to sharing the multi-million-dollar cost of a water pipeline or the multi-billion-dollar cost of a charging station network for electric cars.

An Expense Report Dilemma

I had a speaking opportunity in Houston and one in San Francisco. Without any coordination between the two parties I would have had to make two round trips. Fortunately, the two groups had some flexibility in terms of the dates. By coordinating the two schedules, I was able to make a triangle route. The total airfare ended up being $2,818.*

The negotiation question: How should that $2,818 be split up between the party in Houston and the one in San Francisco?

The two parties weren't actually negotiating with each other. I was trying to represent both parties and do the negotiation in my head. To come up with a fair solution, I want you to follow along and imagine how an actual negotiation would play out. That's because in my mind a fair cost-allocation rule is what each of the two parties would pay had they gone through a negotiation.

In our example, you can think of the two parties as two divisions of a company trying to figure out how to split up the cost of an employee's travel. Each side is willing to pay its fair share. At the same time, each wants to pay as little as possible.

By now you know to ask about the BATNAs. If the two sides don't reach a deal, then I'd have to make two round trips. Houston would end up paying $1,332, which is just twice the $666 one-way fare to Houston. Similarly, San Francisco would pay $2,486, twice the one-way fare back home.

---

* I know that's a high number, but I was flying business class.

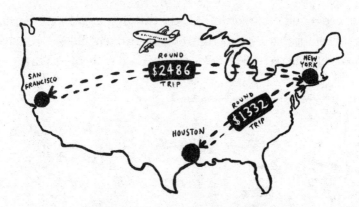

It is obvious that the two sides can't split the total airfare in half. That would mean that Houston ends up paying half of $2,818 = $1,414, which is more than the New York to Houston round-trip cost. Echoing the line from *Apollo 13*: Houston, we have a problem.

Houston and San Francisco quickly reach a partial agreement. They reckon that I had to fly out to Houston in any case, so Houston should be on the hook for the $666 one-way fare from New York to Houston. Similarly, San Francisco should cover the $1,243 cost of the San Francisco–New York trip home. The question remaining is how to cover the $909 Houston to San Francisco leg.

San Francisco proposes they split the cost of leg equally. Each side pays $454.50.

Houston counters with the proposal that they split the cost of the leg in proportion to the one-way fares. Houston would pay $317 and San Francisco would pay $592. This proposal is the same as splitting the entire $2,818 in proportion to the ratio of the round-trip fares, $2,486: $1,332.

Which seems more reasonable to you?

Hopefully, you haven't fallen for either approach. The right way to approach the problem is to look at the situation in terms of the pie. Why are the two sides coordinating their dates? The goal is to save money. The amount of money saved is

Cost of Round Trips − Cost of Triangle Route

= ($2,486 + $1,332) − $2,818 = $1,000

See, there is a round number hiding in there. While we have framed things in terms of sharing costs, the actual pie ends up being the cost savings, which is a positive number.

If the two sides coordinate, they can save $1,000. If they don't, the $1,000 is lost. Each party is equally responsible for the $1,000 savings and so each should get half. Each side pays the full price of the round trip minus the $500 savings:

> Houston pays $1,332 – $500 = **$832**
>
> San Francisco pays $2,486 – $500 = **$1,986**

I picked this example because it shows how the pie can be hiding in plain sight. Negotiators typically look for some fairness justification behind their proposal. Split the total in half, split the cost of the leg in half, split it proportionately. These are all ways of treating airfare equally or travel legs equally (or proportionately). But fairness should not be focused on airfares or travel legs. Fairness is about treating people equally, for it is the people who are negotiating with each other, not the airline legs.

Some readers will be wondering if I should be getting some of this pie, too. Perhaps. In the way I framed the negotiation, I was an employee of the company and so the negotiation was between the two divisions. I have also left out of the calculation the time savings for me along with reduced wear and tear, and the reduced greenhouse emissions.

Sharing a Runway

I picked the next example because it is a case where you can explain the pie solution without using the pie vocabulary. And it makes crystal clear the problem with proportional cost sharing.

Two airlines are looking to share a runway. The runway hasn't yet been built. Airline A runs small turbo-prop planes and only needs a 1km runway. Airline B flies Boeing 737s and needs a runway that's 2km long.

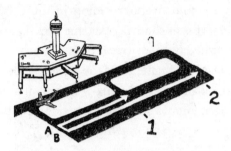

Runways are expensive to build. A one-kilometer runway costs around $5 million and a two-kilometer one is around $10 million. If the two airlines can't agree, they will each go ahead and build separate runways. (Of course, that's very unlikely to happen since they have such a large incentive to agree.)

How much should each airline pay? There are two common answers.

1. Airline A pays $3.33m and B pays $6.67m
2. Airline A pays $2.5m and B pays $7.5m

The argument for option 1 is that Airline B is using twice as much runway so it should pay twice as much. This is the proportional solution where the costs are divided in proportion to runway length used.

The argument for option 2 is that Airline A isn't using any of the second half of the runway. Thus the entire cost of that second half should be paid by B. The two airlines are really only sharing the first half, so that's the cost they should split equally. Thus Airline A pays half of $5m, while Airline B pays the other half plus the full $5m cost for the second half.

The second argument is the one that makes sense to me. Imagine that Airline B were flying A380s and needed a 3km runway. The total cost would rise to $15m. If the cost were divided up in proportion to usage, Airline A would pay 1/4 of the total or $3.75m (and Airline B would pay the remaining 3/4 of the cost). This makes no sense to me. What Airline A pays should not depend on the needs of Airline B that are irrelevant to A.

In this example, we can resolve the negotiation without having to call up the pie. But it will come as no surprise that the pie solution coincides with option 2. If the two sides don't agree, the total cost will be $5m + $10m = $15m. If they do reach an agreement, the total costs will be just $10m. Working together will save the two of them $5m.

Who is more responsible for the savings? They are equally responsible. Neither airline can save the $5m without an agreement. Thus, they should split the $5m in savings. That means Airline A pays $5m − $2.5m = $2.5m and Airline B pays $10m − $2.5m = $7.5m.

It is comforting to see that the pie solution aligns with our intuition. Sometimes you will be able to intuit your way to the pie answer. That said, I always advise starting with the pie answer. You may not choose to use the pie in your explanation to the other party, but it's a good way to check that your intuition is right.

Let's compare the runway solution to the triangle route. I think this is useful because it shows just how misguided the non-pie approach can be.

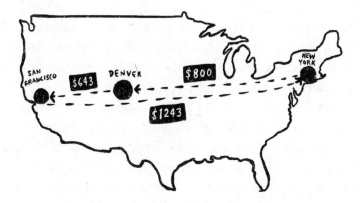

Say the first speaking engagement was in Denver, which was right on the way to San Francisco. The runway and the pie approach would have the two cities split the cost of the New York–Denver round-trip. If we think of the plane as more like a long-distance Uber, the two cities can share the ride out to and back from Denver.

In contrast, if we apply the original expense report logic, Denver should pay for the New York to Denver leg since I had to get to

Denver in any case, while San Francisco should pay for San Francisco to New York since I had to get home from San Francisco in any case. The question would be how to split the cost of the Denver to San Francisco leg.

The reason that logic is mistaken is that getting to Denver brings me closer to San Francisco. That's why San Francisco should split the cost of getting me to Denver and getting me back from Denver. You can think of the New York to Denver leg as akin to the first part of the runway where both parties share the cost. The second leg is all on San Francisco. But this is the hard way to come up with the answer. It's easier to calculate the pie.

With the numbers in this revised example, the total savings are $1,600. Denver would pay $800 rather than the $1,600 New York-Denver round trip. And San Francisco would pay $2,486 − $800 = $1,686.

Our intuition works well when the runways or flight paths overlap. Things go awry when detours are involved. That will be the focus of our ride-sharing examples in the next section.

While the example of the runway may seem a bit artificial, and it is, this turns out to be a quite common problem. In Chapter 14, we'll look at a case where several housing developers had to split the cost of a water feeder to their adjacent properties. The properties were laid out west to east, just like a runway. The property farthest to the east needed the longest feeder line and the one to the west needed the shortest one. (The reason we didn't use the pipeline example here is that there were five different companies involved. We'll come back to the example when we discuss multi-party negotiations.)

For urban dwellers, an example that hits close to home is the question of how owners in a multi-story condominium should share in the cost of an elevator. In the United States, it is common to share the costs equally among all the condo members in spite of the fact that the value is not at all equal. You might think that's just the way it is done.

In France, the law dictates owners pay "in proportion to the advantages" gained. The folks on the ground floor don't use the elevator at all.[11] Those on the first floor only use a small fraction of the elevator's lift. Those on the second floor need twice the elevator runway, while those on the top floor need the full elevator run. Those on the higher floors pay proportionally more as the formula attempts to split the pie. If an elevator needs to be built or substantially upgraded, the pie framework leads to a much more reasonable result. This ended up mattering after many French apartment buildings were privatized and the upper-floor residents proposed expensive upgrades to outmoded elevators. Those on low floors didn't block the renovations because they only paid a small fraction of the cost. Using the pie framework helps us live together better at work and at home.

Sharing a Ride

Both Uber and Lyft are large enough so that when you call a ride, the driver shows up in a few minutes. Often it will be the same driver. Where Lyft has a harder time competing is in pooled rides, what Uber calls UberPool and Lyft calls Lyft Shared. This is where Uber's larger size provides a competitive advantage.

For the last few years, the relative market shares between the two rivals have held at roughly 70:30 in favor of Uber. If there are 70 people taking rides on Uber, there are about 2,500 ways to put people together in a pool. (The exact number is $70 \times 71 / 2 = 2,485$.) For the 30 people on Lyft, there are only 465 options. While Uber has a little more than twice the market share, they can make 5.4 times as many pooled-ride combinations.

The following thought experiment might help. Airline 1 has just one flight going back and forth between New York and Los Angeles each day, while Airline 2 has 10 in each direction. In terms of schedules, Airline 1 only has one round-trip option, while Airline 2 has 100 possible schedule options, 10 on the outbound and 10 on the return. Ten times the number of flights means 100 times the number of flight options for a round trip.

The same relationship is true for Uber and Lyft. The ratio of their market sizes is $7/3 = 2.33$, which implies the ratio of the number of ways to pool their riders is $(7/3)^2 = 5.44$.

Ride sharing isn't just a way to save money, reduce congestion, and lower greenhouse gases. It is also a way for Uber to press its advantage over Lyft. But for ride sharing to work, the company has to figure out how much each passenger should pay. The good news is that the two strangers don't have to do a negotiation with each other. What's a fair way to split the fare?

We'll take the case where Alice and Bob are both heading to LAX. Alice starts at the Getty Museum and Bob is picked up at Tsujita Noodles. As you can see from the map, Bob is right on the way.

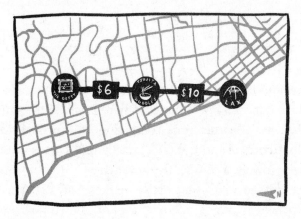

If Alice had gone by herself, the fare would have been $16, while the cost to Bob on his own would be $10. Since Bob is right on the way, the combined cost is $16. This is identical to the runway example. Alice should pay the full fare between the Getty and Tsujita and then the two of them split the remaining amount. Alice pays $6 + 50% × $10 = $11, while Bob pays 50% × $10 = $5.

It is easy to explain this without using the pie. Why should what Bob pays depend on where Alice starts? He shouldn't pay more if she began her trip at the Hammer Museum rather than the Getty. All that matters is the part where they ride together.

This is exactly the result we get from splitting the pie. The savings from coming together are $10. If each went alone, the combined fare would be $16 + $10 = $26, but together the cost is $16. If they split the pie, each party saves $5. Alice pays $16 − $5 = $11 and Bob pays $10 − $5 = $5.

Now I want to make the ride sharing example a bit more challenging. As we see in the next figure, Alice and Bob share a ride to LAX. Just as before, Alice gets in first and then picks up Bob. The total fare is $10. How much should Alice and Bob each pay?

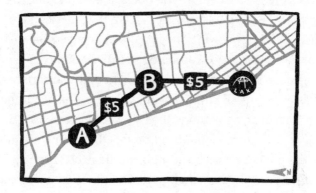

The tempting—but wrong—answer is Alice pays the full $5 for the leg in which she is solo and then Alice and Bob split the next leg 50:50. Thus Alice pays $7.50 and Bob pays $2.50.

The main reason this is wrong and why this is not the same as the runway problem is that Bob is a bit out of the way. Were Alice to head straight to the airport, the total fare would only be $9, not $10. I admit that fact was left out of the original picture. But out in the world, people don't just hand you the pie. You have to do some exploration to get the information you need to calculate the pie.

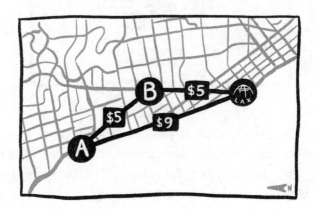

In this case, the research is easy. Uber and Lyft offer fixed fares. Alice could know in advance how much it would cost to go on her own straight to airport. That is where the $9 comes from.

Another reason the pie calculation would be off is that Alice is losing a bit of time via the detour. The ride is longer and perhaps even a bit less pleasant having to share the car. On the other hand, she takes some pleasure from knowing she is reducing congestion and carbon emissions. We'll call these combined negative and positive effects a wash. And since Bob is getting to go straight to the airport, he doesn't lose any time. He doesn't mind having a bit of company for the ride.

Hence, absent an agreement, the two would spend $9 + $5 = $14, not $15. The savings from them riding together is only $4, not $5.

Since the pie is $4, Alice and Bob should each save $2 from the pooled ride. That means Alice pays $2 less than going alone or $9 – $2 = $7, while Bob pays $5 – $2 = $3.

Alice is not fully convinced this is correct. She points out that Bob is out of the way. If only he lived at location B', there wouldn't be the need for a detour. The detour costs an extra $1. She wants Bob to cover the detour costs and pay an extra dollar.

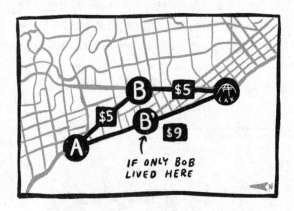

If you were Bob, how would you respond? There are two ways to answer this. One is the high-level answer. If the two of them don't come together, there is no ability to save $4. If Alice wants to save $4, she has to accept the detour as part of the deal.

But there's another answer. When you are in what I call pie-land, any argument the other side makes can be turned around. If Alice says Bob is out of the way, Bob can equally well say Alice is out of the way. If only Alice lived over to the left at A', Bob would be directly on the way and there would be no detour.

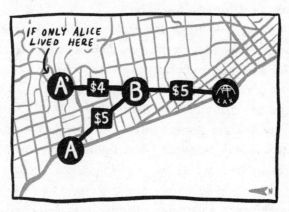

There is no sense in which Bob or Alice is more out of the way. They are each *equally* out of the way if the two of them want to share a ride. In fact, the first answer in which Alice paid the first $5 leg and then split the second leg is a case where Alice paid the full cost of the detour. If they split the cost of the detour, then Alice would pay 50¢ less than $7.50, which is $7, the same answer as when the two split the pie.

I want to work though one last ride-sharing example. I pick this one because it looks super scary. But if you use the pie, it's a cakewalk.

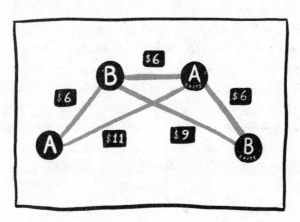

In this example, Alice gets in at point A, Bob gets in at B. Next, Alice gets dropped off, and then Bob gets dropped off. Each of the three legs has a cost of $6. Just as in the previous example, picking up Bob does cause some level of a detour. If Alice were to go straight to her destination, the cost would be $11. If Bob were to go straight to his destination, the cost would be $9.

When the two share a ride, the total cost is $6 + $6 + $6 = $18. If they each went separately, the cost would be $20. Hence the savings or the pie is $2. Thus, each side saves $1 compared to going alone. That means Alice pays $11 − $1 = $10 and Bob pays $9 − $1 = $8. I hope you'll agree that wasn't too hard.

I can't say that going through all this work is necessary over a dollar or two for one ride. But Uber needs to come up with a plan for how to split the cost between the two (or more) people sharing a ride. One goal should be to treat their customers fairly. Another is to give all potential riders the same incentive to share. Otherwise, those getting too little incentive won't share as often and so there will be fewer shared rides. Splitting the pie is fair and provides equal incentives to both parties. The more Uber can incentivize people to pool, the bigger its advantage over Lyft.

Ionity

For electric cars to take off, there needs to be a much more robust network of high-speed charging stations. In the United States, the multi-billion-dollar cost of building these charging stations is being subsidized by Volkswagen's diesel emissions settlement (although more needs to be done). In Europe, the carmakers are on their own.

As a result, BMW, Daimler, Ford, Hyundai, Kia, and Volkswagen are working together in a joint venture called Ionity to build ultrafast electric charging stations across Europe. The advantages from cooperating are enormous. Even if some carmakers were willing to go it alone, there would be a massive duplication of effort and a much less efficient network as there would be no coordination of locations.

This leads to a negotiation problem. How should the alliance members split the price tag? It wouldn't work to split the costs equally. The partners have significantly different market shares, and those with a small share would walk away.

When hearing this question, most propose that costs should be divided up in proportion to market share. But this doesn't settle the matter. There are several ways to measure market share. The automakers have different price points and different profit margins. It is unclear if costs should get divided up in proportion to unit sales, dollar sales, or profits. Costs could also be divided up in proportion to miles driven. Each party has its favorite answer. And even if the parties agree that costs will be divided in proportion to unit sales, there is still the question of whether unit sales numbers should be current sales of cars with internal combustion engines or future sales of electric cars.

As I wrote at the start, the pie approach is not meant to describe how parties negotiate. In cases like this one where equal cost sharing won't work, some type of proportional division is the norm. But that doesn't make it reasonable or principled. I think proportional division misses the point of the negotiation. The purpose of the agreement is to prevent duplication of effort and to share in the cost savings.

Consider how the negotiation might go between a two-partner version of Ionity. Rather than make up names, I'll call them BMW and Daimler. The first step is to figure out each side's BATNA. Given the critical importance of charging stations to each party and given their substantial market position, I assume both parties would proceed on their own absent any agreement. For purposes of this example, I also assume there are no other possible partners available to defray the cost.

Say that each party would have spent €1 billion acting alone, and together they can build an equally effective network that covers both automakers for €1.5 billion. The savings from reduced duplication and improved coordination are €500 million:

(€1 billion + €1 billion) − €1.5 billion = €500 million

This is the pie.

This €500 million pie should be split evenly between the two companies. This is true even if their unit sales are unequal, or their revenues or profits are unequal. We don't have to look at miles driven or sales of internal combustion engine cars or battery-powered cars. The reason for the negotiation is to create a partnership that saves €500 million in costs.

I picked this example because it shows the challenge of seeing the world in terms of the pie. The world does not present itself and say: here are the BATNAs and this is the pie. The challenge in negotiation is to frame the problem correctly.

The natural inclination is to dive in and pick something that sounds fair. Proportional division of costs according to unit sales treats each car equally. Proportional division of costs according to revenue treats each dollar of revenue equally. Proportional division of costs according to miles treats each mile driven equally. The reason I think these answers are misguided is that the cars or dollars or miles are not negotiating with each other. It is BMW and Daimler that are at the table. BMW and Daimler have equal power in terms of creating the savings. Equal power leads to treating the two parties the same, not treating what they produce the same.

The example with BMW and Daimler was perhaps too simple. Once the pie perspective was adopted, the calculations were straightforward. Calculating the pie is not always that easy. Consider a scenario where the two potential partners are BMW and Kia. As before, BMW would still build out a network on its own at a cost of €1 billion. But Kia's market position is too small to justify this expense. Its value is only €700 million. Thus, on its own, Kia would not build a network. That's Kia's BATNA, and we'll assign it a value of €0.

If the two come together, the cost goes up, let's say to €1.4 billion, since they would need to build a larger joint network that works equally well for BMW when it has to share. This charging network allows Kia to enter the European electric car market, which we assumed is worth €700 million to Kia.

	BMW	KIA	TOTAL
WORK TOGETHER*	BMW Network value – (€1.4b – Kia payment)	€700m – Kia payment	BMW Network value – €700m
NO DEAL	BMW Network value – €1b	€0	BMW Network value – €1b
THE PIE			€300m

---

* When they work together, the total amount paid must add up to €1.4 billion. BMW pays the difference between Kia's payment and €1.4 billion.

When the two companies work together, they can create an extra €700 million of value at a cost of €400 million. The pie is €300 million. Splitting the pie means that Kia would pay €550m, essentially the full extra €400 million cost of the bigger network plus €150m to BMW for the original network. In this way, BMW comes out €150 million ahead from the payment by Kia, and Kia comes out €150 million ahead as it ends up with something worth €700 million at a cost of €550 million.

One can see that reaching this solution is more complicated in that it is based on what Kia thinks the network is worth. Kia might not know this exactly and BMW is even less likely to know what Kia thinks the network is worth. (Cost savings seem easier to verify than valuations.) Businesses might use a rule of thumb that the network value is proportional to the number of cars sold. Even so, this doesn't justify proportional division of costs. BMW's market share in Europe is almost exactly twice Kia's. But Kia pays more than half of what BMW contributes—in our example, BMW pays €850 million, while Kia pays

€550 million. The reason why proportional division isn't reasonable is that it effectively ignores BMW's positive BATNA. BMW can make do without Kia. There is no reason for BMW to share that profit. As in our prior example of splitting interest on a CD, proportional division ignores the BATNAs in deciding what each party should pay or get.

The actual Ionity negotiation wasn't just between a pair of automakers. The six carmakers involved agreed that costs would be divided in proportion to unit sales. They picked current sales in contrast to future sales in order to calculate the split at the time of agreement. No surprise, perhaps, since proportional division is simple to understand. But that doesn't make it reasonable and doesn't explain why unit sales makes more sense than revenue or other metrics. Proportional division misses the purpose of the agreement, which is to prevent duplication of effort and to get more parties to join in sharing the cost. It misses the pie.

Cost Sharing on a Global Scale

Just as car companies have to figure out how to split the cost of building charging stations, countries have to figure out how to share the cost of development aid and humanitarian assistance. Here the numbers are much bigger, roughly $260 billion in annual development aid and $30 billion in humanitarian assistance.[12] While some of the aid money is gladly donated and in other cases is used to build foreign support, there is still tension over how much each country should be contributing.

Starting in the late 1950s, the World Council of Churches proposed that industrialized countries contribute 1 percent of their gross domestic product (GDP) as foreign aid to support developing countries. A 0.7 percent contribution was proposed by the United Nations in 1970 and reaffirmed in the 1992 Rio Earth Summit. As with Ionity, contributions are supposed to be done in a proportional fashion, where here the proportion is based on GDP.

While that is a simple formula, it doesn't seem reasonable. Two countries can have the same GDP, but one has twice the population of the other and thus is half as rich. Should they really make the same contribution? For example, Switzerland and Turkey have similar levels of GDP, but Turkey has ten times the population and thus one tenth the per capita GDP.[13]

It isn't fair that foreign aid contributions should be the same percent of GDP when the donor countries are in such different economic positions. At the same time, I appreciate that many people might accept an unfair rule because it is simple to understand and apply. After first vaccinating health care workers against COVID-19, my state of Connecticut gave up on different priority rules for risk classes and moved to a simple age-based rule. This made it harder for the well-connected to game the system and thus led to a fairer application of an unfair rule. (If I were forced to stick with some type of proportional contributions for foreign aid, I'd suggest donations be assigned more like the way income tax is done—a percent of what might be called disposable GDP, which is GDP that exceeds $10,000 per person.)

Not seeing the pie also gets in the way of finding solutions to reducing carbon emissions. The 1992 Framework Convention on Climate Change had the so-called Annex 1 countries—pretty much the 44 wealthiest countries—target year 2000 emissions to their 1990 levels. There were no targets set for the other 110 countries of the world that signed the accord. Again, that wasn't fair. Some Nordic countries had already done a good deal of work prior to 1990, so their targeted 1990 emissions level was much harder to reach. Some countries were experiencing population growth and others decline. There was no sense in which the 1990 numbers were an equitable distribution of emissions.

Should emission goals be a total level, a per capita level, or a carbon-intensity level? In the 2015 Paris Agreement, China pledged to reduce its carbon intensity by 60–65 percent by 2030. But given the rapid growth of its economy, total carbon emissions will continue to rise.

There is confusion when people frame the negotiation in terms of what each country will pay or promise to achieve. Instead, we should frame the negotiation in terms of what is the benefit created—what is the pie—and then think about how to split the pie evenly. The division problem is highly contentious. One reason is that the pie is enormous. It is the future health of the planet. In economic terms, the pie is the savings created by avoiding the worst outcomes associated with global warming (flooding, droughts, famines, mass migration) net of the cost of reducing emissions. The rich countries can't realize this pie all on their own. (Greenhouse gasses all go into the same atmosphere, no matter where they arise from.) And yet, the rich countries aren't willing to share the pie equally. To do so would require a massive transfer of wealth to developing countries. Rich countries would need to pay enormous financial incentives to preserve rain forests and help developing countries transition more rapidly from coal to sustainable energy.

A second bedeviling problem is that those who will be most impacted—today's youth and future generations not yet born— aren't even at the bargaining table, and thus are denied their chance to get an equal share of the pie. The unfair fight over how the planet's future will be shared gets in the way of ensuring there will be any pie at all.

I realize this is a supremely important topic, and one I can't do justice to in a few paragraphs. I bring it up here for one reason: to see the potential impact of the pie approach on our thinking outside business settings. The simple defaults of proportional contributions or targets can get in the way of finding solutions to the world's greatest challenges, ranging from economic development to climate change. I want people to frame problems and solutions in terms of the pie.

We return now to focus on more mundane negotiations in business and everyday life. While I want to change the way people approach negotiations when the scale is global, I first have to convince them to think in terms of the pie for simple problems. To do so, there are some questions I need to answer. And that is what's next.

PART III

COMPLEX
NEGOTIATIONS

At this point, I hope you understand the pie approach and can see its merit. Now it is time to address the yes, but . . .

I've said that the result should be a symmetric split of the pie, but what if the two sides aren't symmetric? There are several ways in which asymmetries arise. We've dealt with the possibility that one side is bigger than the other. No matter the size difference, their contributions are always the same in a two-party negotiation.

Okay, but perhaps one side cares more than the other. Or the two sides can have different perceptions regarding the size of the pie. Negotiation protocols can advantage one party over the other. Negotiations with three or more parties also create asymmetries. These are the topics covered in Part III.

The biggest objection people have to the pie approach arises when one side obviously cares more about the outcome than the other. To take an extreme case, Bob is in the desert, nearly dying of thirst. Can he really hold out for half the pie? As we will soon see in Chapter 11, the answer is yes, but that doesn't mean he gets half the water.

Chapter 12 considers what it means to split the pie when the pie is uncertain. In these circumstances, the two sides can be equally uncertain or one side might have a better understanding of the pie than the other. The side with better information can exploit that advantage to get more than half the pie. A solution that levels the playing field is to agree to a contingent split of the pie—the split is based on what the pie turns out to be rather than its unknown size today.

We've been looking at negotiations without any rules or structure. If there are some rules to the negotiation, those rules can convey power. For example, if one side can make an ultimatum, it can get more than half the pie. This is covered in Chapter 13. Of course, negotiation protocols are themselves part of a larger negotiation, and so they may not provide as much power as one first imagines. When one negotiation result influences what happens in later negotiations, parties will care about their reputation. Chapter 13 also considers the role of reputation and explains why these concerns tend to reinforce an even split.

In Chapter 14, I show how things work when there are three or more active participants in the negotiation. Once there are more than two parties, it is no longer the case that each party is equally responsible for creating the pie. Even so, the pie framework applies, and the result is a generalization of our basic approach.

Negotiations with more than two people allow for the possibility that the contributions people bring to the deal are unequal. In the most extreme example, someone might bring nothing to the table. In Chapter 15, we discover how such an individual might still manage to get paid.

The material in these five chapters is more challenging. It's okay with me if you want to skip to Part IV where I turn to growing the pie. Here in Part III, my focus is on answering critics and dealing with the complications that arise in practice. I don't want to leave readers with the view that the pie approach only works with two players or when the parties care the same amount or the pie is known to all. Because these are complications, the material is more challenging. If you've already bought in to the pie approach, feel free to jump ahead to Part IV. (I won't notice.) The material on growing the pie is more fun.

Chapter 11

WHAT IF YOU CARE MORE?

It is not uncommon for a negotiation to feel like a contest between David and Goliath. Unlike the biblical outcome, the Davids tend not to fare as well. Why is it that the smaller party feels they are at a disadvantage?

One reason is that they care a lot more.* For David, the result could be life altering. For Goliath, it might just be a blip, nothing worth getting too excited about. While the smaller party is typically the one that cares more, that's not always the case. This brings us to the general question of whether caring more leads to getting less.

My view is that an asymmetry of caring shouldn't put one side at a disadvantage. Yes, the side that cares more is more eager for a deal.

---

* Another reason is that the smaller party may have fewer options. Their BATNA is worse. As we discussed in Chapter 4, that doesn't mean they should get less in the negotiation. That just means the pie is bigger.

But the side that cares less will find it easier to make a concession. In these circumstances, each side should still get the same share of the pie, but now it is a share of the pie as they each calculate it.

To illustrate, we'll jump right in with an extreme example, one that audiences regularly challenge me with. Bob is in the desert, nearly dying of thirst. Alice is properly hydrated. There are three 1-liter water bottles. How will the two divide them up?

The common view is Bob is so desperate he'll be happy to accept any division. This perspective leads to Alice getting the majority of the water. A competing view is Bob cares about the water so much more than Alice—he cares about every drop—that he's the one who will end up with most of the water.

Let's put some numbers on the situation and apply the pie perspective. We can say that Bob's value of the first bottle is $1,000,000/liter, and thereafter $5/liter. That first liter is hugely valuable to him. For Alice, her value is constant at $1/liter for all three bottles. What ultimately matters isn't how Alice and Bob divide the water; it's how they divide the pie.

This is the first time we've had to think about negotiating when the two parties have different preferences. To maximize the pie, the parties should allocate the items based on who values them the most. Thus Bob should get all the water. The resulting pie would be $1,000,010. To split the pie, Bob pays Alice $500,005. Bob gets what he values most highly (water) while Alice gets what she values most highly (money). Both sides come out $500,005 ahead. So far it seems the person who cares the most gets most (or even all) of what they most care about. The Davids do just fine.

There is a sense in which this solution doesn't capture the predicament real-life Davids find themselves in. Someone in David's shoes has fewer resources. A David doesn't have $500,005 lying around to pay Goliath. So what happens with Bob and Alice if Bob only has 50¢ to his name? Bob might say he values the first bottle at $1 million, but he has no real way of demonstrating it or compensating Alice. What Bob really means is that if he had $1 million, that's how much he'd value the first water bottle. Since he doesn't, they have to negotiate without the ability to use money to even things out and divide the pie.

In this case, the size of the pie—using Bob's somewhat hypothetical valuations—depends on how it is divided. If all the water goes to Bob, the pie is $1,000,010, while the pie is only $3 if all the water goes to Alice. Bob values the water much, much more than Alice. If we give all the water to Bob, that creates more value than if we give all the water to Alice.

As a result there is now a tension between maximizing the pie and how it is divided. It would appear we have to choose between a really big pie that's very unevenly split or a really small pie that's evenly divided.

The underlying issue is how we calculate the pie when the two parties can't transfer money. Adding up the values in terms of dollars makes sense when the two parties can pay each other and thus have a common currency. When there's no common currency, it is hard, perhaps impossible, to compare one party's valuation with the other's. Bob's $1 million valuation of the first bottle is no longer comparable to Alice's $1 valuation. Bob can say he values the first bottle a million times more than Alice does, but if he doesn't have to pay anything to Alice to back up those words, or can't, it is hard to really know what this means.

To resolve the issue of incomparable scales and potentially exaggerated claims, we can compare what each side gets relative to its ideal. In effect, that is like putting each party on a common scale where getting nothing is worth 0 and getting everything is worth 100.

Equal power still holds, but the implication of equal power has to be broadened to cover the case of noncomparable valuations. The broader implication is that *each side gets the same share of its ideal pie.* For Alice, that's what fraction of the $3 in value she could potentially achieve, while for Bob that's what fraction of the $1,000,010 in value he could potentially achieve.

Because the two sides value the water bottles differently, we can come up with a split that allows both parties to get more than half the pie as they value it. In the example of the water bottle, it is possible for each side to get roughly 75 percent of their ideal. Bob gets 750 ml from the first bottle, while Alice gets the other 250 ml and the two remaining bottles. Alice is at 75 percent of her ideal since she has 2,250 ml out of a potential 3,000. Bob is at (roughly) 75 percent of his ideal since 75 percent of the first bottle is worth $750,000 out of a potential $1,000,010.

If Bob got more of the water, he would be getting more than 75 percent of his ideal while Alice would be getting something below 75 percent. Conversely, if Alice got more of the water, she would be getting more than 75 percent of her ideal while Bob would be getting something below 75 percent. We've picked the one allocation where each side gets the same share of its ideal.*

We are not splitting the pie 50:50. We are splitting the pie 75:75! Our view of equal power and fairness still holds. Both power and fairness imply that each side should get the same share of the total pie as they value it. In cases where both parties value getting more of the item in a linear fashion, the best that can be accomplished is for both sides to get 50 percent of their ideal. But in other situations— for example, where Bob values the first water bottle more than additional ones—it is possible for both sides to end up with more than half of their ideal pie.

While Bob is more desperate, he still ends up with the same fraction of his ideal as Alice. It is true that he ends up with less than half the water, but since water doesn't have a linear value, the percentage of the water he gets isn't a reliable metric of how well he does. What really matters to Bob is how much he gets of the first bottle. There-

---

* Were I Alice in this situation, I'd give Bob an entire bottle. That's because I care about other people's happiness. I would get more indirect pleasure from seeing Bob greatly enjoy the last 250 ml than the 25¢ in value from drinking the extra 250 ml myself. The point of the example, however, is to explain how to split the pie in situations where one side appears much more desperate than the other. When people care about the happiness of the others in the negotiation, that should factor into the calculation of the pie.

fore, when we think about how well Bob does in the negotiation, we should focus on how much of the first bottle he gets or, more generally, how close he comes to his ideal, where the ideal is measured in value, not water.

OTHER SCENARIOS

What if Alice's value were $2/bottle? The answer would be unchanged. When Alice gets 2.25 bottles, she is still at 75 percent of her ideal, as is Bob.

What if Alice's value were $1,000,000/bottle, but for all three bottles? The answer would again be unchanged. When Alice gets 2.25 bottles, she is at 75 percent of her ideal, as is Bob. It is easy for Bob to give up the last two bottles. All he really cares about is the first bottle. In the negotiation, Bob gets credit for giving up something Alice values even if he doesn't.

It may seem inefficient that Bob doesn't get all of the first bottle, as he clearly values it more. The problem is that he doesn't have anything to offer in return for getting more water.

In the water-bottle negotiation, Bob was cash constrained. There are many other negotiations where it doesn't work to even things out with money. Think of negotiations inside a family. If a couple shares a common bank account, there's no real meaning to one side paying the other. The larger reason why it may not work to translate everything into money is that money itself ends up being like the lifesaving water: one side values it much more highly than the other.

When a start-up is negotiating with a larger established firm, the money involved will be life-changing if not lifesaving for the start-up while not material to the big player. The money is like the first water bottle for Bob: it matters a lot more to the start-up.

The larger player uses this asymmetry to argue that it needs to get more than half the dollars at stake as otherwise it won't get the same "value" from the deal. Such thinking underlies the common view that the larger party has more power in a negotiation. The larger player says, "You need this deal much more than I do," and the smaller side goes along.

While this is common practice, the arguments are not convincing. If the larger party cares so little, then why is it fighting so hard? If each extra dollar hardly registers, it is easier for the larger player to be more generous.

We'll put on some numbers to illustrate the point. As before, Honest Tea and Coke are negotiating over $20m in cost savings. We'll assume Honest Tea cares nineteen times as much about each dollar. In that case, Coke needs $19m of the $20m to achieve the same effective gain as the $1m going to Honest Tea.

It seems peculiar, even paradoxical, that the side that cares less gets more money. And yet, experimental work by Rudy Nydegger and Guillermo Owen suggests that people are taken in by the argument that both sides should get the same effective gain—so the side that cares less gets more of the money.[14] In their experiment, subjects negotiated a split of 60 tokens where each token was worth 1¢ to one side and 2¢ to the other. There was no settling up after the experiment. All eight subject pairs ended up dividing the tokens in a 2:1 ratio. The side that valued tokens at 1¢ got 40 tokens, while the side that valued tokens at 2¢ received 20 tokens. The intent of the negotiators was clear: they settled on the outcome where each side walked away with 40¢, equal gains measured in pennies.

To see if this really makes sense, consider the result as the asymmetry gets bigger. If the 60 tokens were worth 59¢ each to one side and 1¢ to the other, the Nydegger and Owen result implies the 59¢ person would get 1 token and the 1¢ side 59 tokens. If I were the person who values the tokens at 59¢ each, I'd be pretty unhappy with this outcome. I'd be making a huge sacrifice (59 tokens worth almost $35 to me) in order to give the other side a few pennies. I'd be giving up a great opportunity just to bring myself down to the level of someone who is very hard to please.

While people's first instinct is to focus on what each side is getting,

I think it is equally reasonable to focus on what each side is giving up. How far is each side from achieving its ideal? Let's go back to the negotiation between Honest Tea and Coke. At the split that leads to an equal gain—$1m to Honest Tea and $19m to Coke—Honest Tea is $19m away from its ideal, which feels like a $361m sacrifice, while Coke is only $1m away. The concessions made are highly lopsided.

If Coke makes the argument that it should get more because it cares less, Honest Tea can turn this argument around: "If you care so little, give us $19m of the $20m. Money matters a lot more to us and you would hardly miss it. When we get $19m, we are $1m away from our ideal and you are $19m away from your ideal. That's an equivalent sacrifice given how much more we care."

Any argument the larger party can make about getting more can be flipped into an argument for getting less. If Coke says it needs more because it doesn't care, that is equally an argument for getting less since it doesn't care about making the sacrifice.

At the equal-gain split—$1m to Honest Tea and $19m to Coke— the incentives to push for more are lopsided. If Honest Tea holds out for $1m more, that would double its take; making a $1m concession would only cost Coke about 5 percent. I'd push for the extra million. And I'd keep pushing. The next million would increase our position by 50 percent, but only cost Coke 5.5 percent. I'd stop when I got to $10m. At that point, an extra million is only worth 10 percent more, and costs Coke 10 percent to give it up. I'd stop when I was getting half the pie as I see it.

Our pie solution to these situations employs the same principle as with the water bottles. Each side has equal power and therefore each gets the same share of their ideal. Here that means they split the savings, $10m and $10m. Each side values that $10m differently, but they can agree each is getting half the potential pie.* Each is halfway

---

* The reason they can't each get more than half the pie is we've assumed money has a constant, albeit different, value to each side. If the first million were worth more to Honest Tea than later millions (just like the first water bottle was worth more to Bob), both sides could get more than half the pie.

between getting its worst outcome (no savings) and its best outcome (all the savings). At $10m to each, Honest Tea sees itself getting half of a large $20m pie, while Coke sees itself getting half of a small $20m pie. Even though they evaluate the $20m differently, they can agree that both sides are needed equally to create the pie. And they can agree that the pie is $20m, whatever that is worth. Consequently, each side gets the same share, here half, of the pie *as it values it*. Even though the start-up cares more, it doesn't end up with less.

When one side cares more, extra vigilance is required. It is easy to get confused about power and fairness in these situations. People are taken in by the argument that the side that cares less gets more so as to end up with equal gains. When one side cares twice as much as the other, equal gains don't lead to a preposterous outcome, especially when the stakes are measured in pennies. But once one side cares a lot more than the other and the stakes are real, the flaw with equal gains becomes apparent. The pie perspective is particularly valuable in these circumstances.

———

Chapter 12

WHAT IF THE PIE IS UNCERTAIN?

In the first negotiations we considered, the size of the pie was known or knowable. Edward and I both knew the cost and result of the ICANN dispute process; Anju and Bharat knew the synergies with CD interest rates; the two divisions knew the cost savings from flying a triangle route. In the CEMA example, the buyer knew more than the seller about potential tax savings, but a little research would have put the two parties on a level playing field.

In other cases, the negotiations are over a pie that hasn't yet been baked. That was the situation when Honest Tea was negotiating with Coke. We had to divide the pie before knowing its size. The uncertainty creates a problem on two counts. The other side might have a better idea of the pie's size and can use its information to take advantage of you. Even when both sides are equally unsure, if you agree on a price today, one side will likely end up with more than half.

In these situations, you can agree to split the pie ex post facto. Whatever the pie ends up being, the parties agree today to divide the pie as it materializes. For example, in the case of Coca-Cola buying bottles for Honest Tea, the expected savings were $20m based on 8¢/bottle on 250m bottles over three years. Of course, the 250m bottles was an estimate and could be far off. Even if Coke were willing to split the pie, it didn't want to pay out $10m only to discover down the road that sales came to 150m bottles. In that situation, Coke would have paid out $10m of a $12m pie.

The solution is to split the pie on a bottle-by-bottle basis. Recall that Coke's costs were 11¢ and Honest Tea was paying 19¢/bottle. The total savings are 8¢/bottle. Instead of splitting an uncertain $20m pie, Honest Tea buys bottles from Coke at 15¢ each. That way, Coke makes 4¢/bottle and Honest Tea saves 4¢/bottle. The pie is split evenly on each bottle and thus split evenly no matter how many bottles are sold.

An even ex post split is just what Honest Tea and Coke agreed to in terms of the buyout price three years down the road. As discussed in Chapter 5, the purchase price was the market multiple up to sales of X and then half the market multiple on the incremental sales above X. Coke and Honest Tea working together created the potential for sales to exceed X. The value created by those sales was split evenly when Coke got to pay half price on the multiple of those incremental sales, whatever they turned out to be.

Agreeing to split the pie ex post avoids the risk of an uneven split when the pie turns out to be different than expected. This strategy is even more important when one side has superior information. The side that knows more might offer you something that looks like a fair split, but only they know if this is true or not. You'd like to wait and see what the pie is before agreeing to how many slices you'll accept. To protect yourself, you can agree today on a formula for how to split the pie based on what materializes.

A Nice Painting

Anaïs was selling a large oil painting she inherited from her grandfather. She had no real idea what the painting was worth. It was unsigned and not in great condition. But her grandfather must have thought it was special since he hung the painting so that it was the first thing you saw when you entered the living room.

The local dealer offered $1,000. She thought about countering with $2,500. That risked losing the deal. Perhaps even worse, if the dealer said yes it would be a sign that the painting might really be valuable. Anaïs was concerned that the art dealer knew the true value and might be taking advantage of her.

To level the playing field, Anaïs could go and get the painting appraised. That would take time and cost at least $1,200. She could end up spending more on the appraisal than what the painting was worth.

Much better is to make a contingent counteroffer. Anaïs says to the dealer: I understand you are expecting to spend some money on restoration. You might even be planning to spend money on authentication if this is by a famous artist. Here is what I propose. I'll sell you the painting for your offer of $1,000, and you share with me 50 percent of the proceeds for anything you get above $10,000.

Anaïs is now protected even without knowing the value. The offer is fair to the dealer as well. If the painting is worth something in the $1,000 to $10,000 range, the dealer only pays the original offer of $1,000. If the painting ends up being worth $15,000, the dealer pays another $2,500, but that's good news because the dealer is also making more money.* If the painting ends up being worth $25,000 or $100,000, Anaïs will be very glad to be sharing in the upside. If the dealer absolutely refuses to accept these terms, that might be a hint it is worth spending some money to get an appraisal.

---

* For this scheme to work, Anaïs must be able to verify that the painting has been sold and verify the sale price. With an auction sale, records are public. Private sales are harder to verify. If Anaïs doesn't trust the dealer today, it isn't clear she should trust the dealer to report honestly in the future. Contingent deals work best when the contingencies are easily observed.

The case with the painting may seem out of the ordinary, but we are often in a situation where we are selling to someone and we don't really know what they will do with it or how much they value it. For example, the person buying your house may be able to get the property rezoned so that they can replace the house with four condos and thereby greatly increase its value. After the buyer makes an offer, you should ask: What do you intend to do with the property? The buyer who intends to go the condo route might well answer: That's my business. How is this of your concern?

The answer is simple. You want to split the pie. If the two sides are going to split the pie and only one side truly knows what the pie is, the other side either has to reveal its plans or agree to make a contingent split. You can say you're prepared to sell the property at price $X if the use will be residential or $Y if commercial. How the property gets used is your concern because you want to get half the pie. The contingent agreement allows you to split the ex post pie, whatever it turns out to be.

This is precisely the solution Deepak Malhotra and Max Bazerman propose to resolve the Hamilton property case in their book, *Negotiation Genius*. Your company has a parcel of undeveloped land and your job is to negotiate the sale. There's an offer of $38m on the table, but you think you can do better. In particular, you are talking to a second potential buyer. Based on your research, you estimate the buyer's valuation ranges from $40m to $60m depending on how they will use the property. A commercial development creates 50 percent more value than a residential development.

That wide range places you at a large informational disadvantage. They know their actual value and you don't. If you ask for the high end while the buyer is at the low end, the asking price will look unreasonable. If you ask for something closer to the low end and the buyer is at the high end, you'll leave millions on the table. That is why you don't want to go first in giving a number.

You may not have a choice as tradition says that sellers have a listing price. What do you do? A solution is to use your much tighter estimate of the *conditional* valuation. You level the information playing field by making the asking price contingent on the eventual use. Your asking price is $40m if the use is residential and $60m if commercial. If the buyer rejects this approach, it's a good indication that they have a commercial use in mind.

I want to contrast the conditional price with what might be called the big bluff as a way to learn the other side's value. A friend was selling his boutique software company. There was no revenue and the cost of making updates and managing engineers was driving him crazy. Indeed, he was on the verge of shutting the business down.

Before giving up, he had the chance to make one last pitch to a well-established firm. To his surprise, the CEO offered him and his partners a cool $1m for the business. He just about peed in his pants. But instead of saying "Where do I sign?" he came back with "You know that's too low." And sure enough, the price came up to $1.25m.

You might conclude that his negotiation helped reveal the seller's true valuation. Okay, the slick move helped reveal that the value was somewhere north of $1.25m. But, as far as we know, it could have been $1.5m or $15m or $150m.

Let's go back to Anaïs and the painting. If she rejected the $1,000 and demanded $2,500, she'd learn that the dealer valued the painting at something above $2,500 if he said yes. She still has no idea how much *more* the painting is worth. Moreover, insisting on $2,500 may cost her the deal and the $1,000. The contract where she shares 50 percent of what the dealer gets above $10,000 protects her when the painting has a high value and doesn't squash the deal when the painting is only worth a few thousand. You don't have to bluff your way to learn more about the other side's value.

I used this type of a contingent contract when I sold my second company, Kombrewcha, to AB InBev. There's a long backstory that I'll just briefly mention. At Honest Tea, we introduced our own version of a kombucha. For the uninitiated, kombucha is a fermented tea loaded with probiotics. Slightly tangy, it can be an acquired taste. I was hooked. Perhaps that was because the product was accidentally alcoholic.

At the bottom of each bottle is a live "SCOBY," a Symbiotic Culture Of Bacteria and Yeast. The yeast just does its thing and turns sugar into alcohol. Although Honest Tea's kombucha was legal when it was bottled, after a few weeks on the shelf the alcohol level rose to 0.7 percent, just above the 0.5 percent legal limit to be a nonalcoholic beverage.

As a result, we had to do a national recall. There were class-action lawsuits. It was a million-dollar disaster. Ultimately, we stopped making kombucha when we couldn't figure out how to keep the alcohol level below 0.5 percent.

You know the old saying: When life gives you lemons, make lemonade. While I didn't know how to make nonalcoholic kombucha, I did know how to make slightly alcoholic kombucha. Coke gave its blessing to this venture as they don't participate in the alcohol space. My new partner, Ariel Glazer, and I got the right alcohol licenses and launched Kombrewcha. The motto was "Get Tickled, not Pickled."

We were still early in the game, sales below $1m, when we were approached by ZX Ventures, the incubator arm for AB InBev (the folks who make Budweiser). If you take a broad view of their business, you'll see they aren't just about beer. They sell fermented food, and they were attracted by the idea of a healthy buzz.

The synergies were obvious. They were willing to commit to upgrading a brewery to help scale up production. I wanted us to build a big pie together. The only problem was how to measure the value of something at such an early stage.

Our solution was a long earn-out, a small share of revenue over a dozen years. The share goes up when revenue hits a predetermined target. We both knew it would take time to build the market. If the alcoholic kombucha business becomes a $100m business, we'll both be very happy. Certainly my investors will be. Meanwhile, we are still in the early years. Stay tuned. Or, better yet, give Kombrewcha a try.

A Merger of Equals

Many deals end up with a contingent split of the pie, even though it isn't advertised that way. For example, when it comes to the standard merger agreement, the two sides tend to split the synergistic gains in proportion to their pre-merger sizes. This is the outcome when companies do what is called a "merger of equals." While it is called a merger of equals, the pie is not split in a way that recognizes the equal contributions of the two sides. The pie is split in the same way as the equity shares, not 50:50.

Here is an example based on a real-world merger. Two companies, we'll call them Adelaide and Brisbane, can achieve large cost savings by consolidating their overlapping operations. Under the status quo, Adelaide has a market capitalization of $240b, and Brisbane's capitalization is $160b. If they merge in a stock-for-stock deal, their combined market capitalization will be $430b, the extra $30b representing the joint cost savings.

Under a merger of equals, each side retains its proportionate share in the combined enterprise. Since the size ratio of the pre-merger companies is 60:40, Adelaide would end up with 60 percent of the combined entity and thus 60 percent of the $30b gain, or $18b. Brisbane would get the other 40 percent, or $12b. Adelaide gets 50 percent more of the gains because it is 50 percent larger.

Most professionals think this is a perfectly reasonable outcome. As you know by now, I respectfully disagree. Both companies are equally responsible for the $30b cost savings. It is true that if Adelaide walks away, there is no deal and the full $30b is lost. It is equally true that if Brisbane walks away, there is no deal and the full $30b is lost. There is no sense in which Adelaide contributes 50 percent more to the cost savings. Since contributions are equal, the split of the pie should be equal, too: Adelaide and Brisbane should each get half the $30b pie, or $15b.

The $30b of cost savings is an estimate, not a sure thing. Adelaide doesn't want to pay out $15b and take on all the risk of the synergies panning out. Under the merger of equals, the result is a contingent deal, which solves the risk associated with uncertainty. The problem is that the contingent split ends up being 60:40. Since the Adelaide shareholders own 60 percent of the new combined entity, they will collect 60 percent of whatever gains arise. It's correct that Adelaide should end up with 60 percent of the base amount since they bring 60 percent of the assets prior to any synergies. The trick is to come up with a way to divide the synergies differently from the way we divide the base.

A MULTI-LAYERED SPLIT

Anju and Bharat divided the base differently than the gains in their CD negotiation. They bought a $25,000 CD that paid out $25,750. Bharat first got back his $20,000 while Anju got back her $5,000, a 4:1 split that reflected the different investments. Next Bharat got $400 interest while Anju got $50, an 8:1 ratio that reflected the different interest payments on what they could do alone. Finally, the additional $300 gains from the joint CD were split 50:50, reflecting their equal contribution to the pie.

One solution is for Adelaide to pay $3b up front to the Brisbane shareholders. That way, Brisbane shareholders get 40 percent of whatever gains arise from their merger share plus the $3b up front. Brisbane's 40 percent of the expected $30b gains should be worth $12b, plus the $3b up front adds up to an expected $15b, the same as what Adelaide expects from its 60 percent gain after the $3b payment. Both sides expect to come out $15b ahead. There's still a risk the gains won't come out exactly as predicted, but the risk is limited to 10 percent of the total. That isn't zero risk, but it is much more manageable.

To come up with the right true-up payment requires the two sides have a similar view of the potential pie. The two parties could agree in principle that contributions are equal but disagree as to the size. Correctly calculating the pie means knowing what the two sides can accomplish together, which may be confidential, and also requires each side knows both BATNAs.

If some of the relevant numbers are hidden or hard to confirm, this creates the potential for bluffing and misrepresentation. The experimental results discussed earlier showed that buyers and sellers of used cars were able to split the pie on average even when the BATNAs and valuations were private. In other situations, especially in mergers, the parties avoid this challenge by revealing the relevant numbers.

All the facts were on the table in the Adelaide-Brisbane example, which is based on the proposed merger between mining giants BHP and Rio Tinto. Far from trying to keep the $30b in synergies hidden, BHP publicized its estimate of the pie—it wanted to provide its shareholders, regulators, and the public with its rationale for the merger. The pie was relatively easy to estimate since there were no other options to create synergies. The value of the BATNAs were just the two company valuations prior to the merger proposal. The potential pie was thus the $30b in synergies. Ultimately, however, there was no pie since the European Commission blocked the deal.

Misperceptions

I recognize it won't always be possible to do a contingent deal. In these circumstances, one side might think it is getting half the pie, but the result could well be far away from an even split. This is particularly true when one side's valuation is idiosyncratic and there's no way to verify it.

The classic example takes place in a flea market. The seller has a teacup worth $5 to him. Along comes a buyer whose valuation is $300. As it so happens, this teacup will complete her set. The pie here is huge at $295.

The pie is large because the buyer has an unusually high valuation. Moreover, she knows that her valuation is exceptional. She understands that most potential buyers would value this teacup somewhere in the $10 to $20 range and that the seller would have the same expectation about her value. While she might not know the seller's exact BATNA, she is confident it's somewhere in the $5 to $10 range.

The buyer knows the pie is huge, and the seller does not. By keeping her valuation hidden, she can take advantage of the seller's misperception of the pie. She might ask about the price of a few different teacups and suggest that any one of them would do. Even if the seller asks for a price of $20, she might initially push back so as not to convey that the teacup is something she values much more highly.

The negotiation is taking place over a misperceived pie and that misperception is much to the buyer's advantage. She can capture well more than half the actual pie because the seller has little idea just how large the pie is.

Uneven splits can also arise when one side learns the two parties' preferences are aligned on an issue while the other side thinks they are opposed. For example, Bob might compensate Alice for getting his way on some issue, thinking this is splitting the pie. But if Alice also wants the same result, Alice gets her preferred outcome as well as compensation from Bob.

Being better informed doesn't mean you always get more than half the pie. If you know that the pie is *smaller* than the other side thinks it is, but you can't convince them, you might have to settle for less than half. This could arise if your BATNA is better than the other side appreciates, and there is no way of proving it. The other side is asking for too much, half of an exaggerated pie, and your choice is to take less or end up with no deal. The other side thinks it is being fair in demanding half the pie, but only you know that they are asking for too much. If you can do a contingent deal, that would solve the problem. Otherwise, you may have to settle for less than half. Just as you can get more than half if they don't appreciate how big the pie is, you may have to accept less than half if they don't appreciate how small the pie really is.

Uncertainty and Bias

I believe the pie framework helps those who have been historically disadvantaged in negotiations; it does so by revealing their equal power and providing a path to capture half the pie. But it is not a panacea. Pie logic will need to overcome ingrained biases. This is harder to accomplish when the pie is uncertain and the other side has superior information. Leveling the information playing field can help reduce the bias.

Job negotiations, especially those above entry level, are an arena where the pie is uncertain. This creates the potential for misperceptions, where the misperceptions are more likely to fall on the side of the candidate. The firm has more experience hiring employees than a job candidate has in negotiating with the firm, and consequently the firm typically has a better understanding of the BATNAs and the potential pie than does the job candidate.

Just as in the flea market, when one side has better information, this creates the potential for an uneven division of the pie. Unlike the flea market, the uneven divisions are of concern to society, especially when the unevenness of the division varies systematically across groups. An example is the salary gap between men and women. Nina Roussille, an economics professor at MIT, has shown how differential information contributes to gender differences in salaries.[15] Her data comes from a half million job offers at Hired.com, an online recruitment platform for high-paid engineering jobs. (The average salary is $120,000!) On this platform, job candidates post their desired salary along with qualifications and experience. After adjusting for qualifications, experience, and location, women asked for 3.3 percent less and ended up being offered 2.4 percent less.

The desired salary number on the website isn't a traditional negotiation, but you can think of it as an opening number. While employers can and sometimes do pay more than the ask, a lower asking number generally leads to a lower offer. The 3.3 percent gap in the asking number entirely explained the difference in salary offers.

That answered one question but left many more unresolved. Why were women asking for less? Was it due to different information, different preferences, or was it responding to biases in the market? What would happen if women asked for more? Quite remarkably, Professor Roussille got a chance to answer those questions.

When Hired.com learned of the gender disparity in asking salaries, they decided to change their policy. Previously, job candidates provided their desired base salary by filling in an empty text box. In mid-2018, Hired.com changed its practice to prefill the salary box using the median market wage based on the person's job title, desired location, skills, and experience. The enhanced information and guidance eliminated the gap in the asked wage and rendered the salary gap insignificant.

You might be concerned that asking for more would lead to fewer job interviews. It turned out just the reverse was true—at least within a reasonable range. On average, candidates who asked for 3 percent more (given similar qualifications) were *more* likely to be interviewed, perhaps because the firm interpreted this as a sign of unobservable quality.

It wasn't the case that everyone used the prefilled number. Those who thought they were above average asked for more, while others asked for less. The prefilled median provided a better baseline around which to adjust. The effect of a better baseline was most pronounced at the more senior end of the job distribution, where there is more variability in salaries. Hired.com leveled the information playing field and in so doing, leveled the negotiation.

What do we take away from this research? A naïve conclusion is that women would benefit from more networking and research to find out the market wage. I find this problematic as it puts the onus of eliminating bias on women. A better conclusion is this is an opportunity for systemic change.

One systemic solution is for companies to be more transparent about salaries. Let's get rid of "salary commensurate with experience" and put in a number. This also means going beyond salary ranges to provide information about median salaries inside the band and how they vary with experience and qualifications.

We almost had the chance to get broader transparency. President Barack Obama signed an executive order that required companies with 100 or more employees to disclose pay data broken down by gender and race. That order was overturned by President Donald

Trump before it could be put into action. In Denmark, Germany, and the United Kingdom similar disclosure rules have recently been put into effect. Early evidence from Denmark suggests that pay disclosure has reduced the gender wage gap by 13 percent.[16]

Until the laws change or data from Hired.com applies to more jobs, we can work to change taboos and rules against sharing salary information. According to a survey done by the Institute for Women's Policy Research, most employees are discouraged or even prohibited from sharing wage information and that secrecy contributes to the gender gap in earnings.[17]

Pay disclosure may have some unintended effects; it can make it harder to get a raise. The employer is reluctant to raise one person's wage, as with disclosure that information will get out and then everyone else will want to be paid more—or morale will fall when coworkers learn about the pay discrepancies. Research by Professors Zoë Cullen and Bobak Pakzad-Hurson shows pay disclosure helps equalize wages but at a lower level.[18]

The need to treat people the same way is an example of a rule that gives negotiation power to one side. "I'd like to pay you $1,000 more but if I did it for you, I'd have to give the same bump to all ten others at your level; it would cost me $11,000, not $1,000, and that's not worthwhile."[19] I've been focused on looking at a negotiation in isolation. That's true for many situations, though it's less true in the case of salary negotiations. We turn now to see how rules and interactions across negotiations can shift the power dynamics.

Chapter 13

RULES AND REPUTATIONS

There's no law of nature that every pie has to be split 50:50. It is certainly possible to get more than half the pie if the other side isn't thinking in terms of the pie or there's something external to the negotiation that gives more power to one side.

The argument for an equal split arises because there is a fundamental symmetry between the two parties. Each side is equally needed to create the pie. Any argument one side can make, the other side can make equally well. But if there's something that breaks the symmetry, one side may be able to gain more than half.

Here I consider two possibilities. The first is when results from one negotiation spill over into another. We saw this just above in the case of a salary negotiation if raising one person's wages required the firm to raise pay for many others. This could be due to a legal rule that requires equal pay or a firm's concern that it would suffer a loss in morale or lose employees who discover they are being paid less than coworkers. Whatever the cause, the spillovers create an asymmetry in that $1 more for Bob might cost Alice $1 here and $10 elsewhere. Spillover effects also arise when parties care about their reputation regarding future negotiations. In these cases, the negotiation result has to be evaluated in a larger context, and that larger context can be different for the two parties, thereby breaking the symmetry.

A second way to break the symmetry is when one party can make an ultimatum. The side making a take-it-or-leave-it offer can push the other close to its BATNA and keep all the rest. While an ultimatum provides asymmetric power, it is less clear where the ability to make an ultimatum comes from. It must be something outside the negotiation. One potential source is a principled stand. In this situation, ultimatums play a different role: they can help one side get half the pie!

Reputations

It's ironic that a concern for fairness can lead to an unfair outcome. And yet the fact that Alice would have to treat other existing Bobs or future Bobs the same way means the cost of giving Bob an extra $1 is much more than $1. We've all heard: "I'd love to do this for you, but then I'd have to do it for everyone."

When you're in such a situation, I advise you to ask for things others might not want or where exceptions can be justified. In my case, when I moved from Princeton to Yale, I asked Yale to provide a second mortgage in the event my wife had trouble finding a new job in New Haven. We could afford the mortgage on our desired house with our two salaries, but it would be dicey with just one.* Even if Yale had to provide this offer to others, few would value it. Doing this once didn't mean they'd have to do it ten times. In other circum-

---

* Fortunately, my wife found a job before she moved and so we never needed the second mortgage. Even so, it meant we didn't have to worry about temporarily getting in over our heads.

stances, you can get around the equal treatment rule by asking for something where exceptions are justified. A sales rep who spends time on the road might ask the company to pay for a cell phone, while the accounting person can't make the same argument.

Outside the employment examples I've given—whether it be buying a domain name, a car, or Coca-Cola buying Honest Tea— the negotiations were of a one-off nature. The two parties were unlikely to interact again. This situation covers a large number of important cases, but there are clearly situations where one or both sides are concerned about their reputation. Even if Coca-Cola won't negotiate with Honest Tea again, it may care about its reputation for future deals.

This is different from the previous concern about salary spillovers. Let's say that whatever Alice gives Bob today won't have a direct impact on other Bobs or even future Bobs. Even so, Alice can earn a reputation for being a certain type of negotiator, and that reputation may change how others negotiate with her in the future. My view is that such reputational concerns tend to provide an additional argument in favor of splitting the pie.

There are three reputations a negotiator could acquire: (1) being a pushover; (2) being fair; (3) being unfair. How does the potential to build a reputation change what the party would otherwise be willing to do in a one-off negotiation?

Start with the case where Alice would be willing to accept an unfair deal in a one-shot situation. Even so, she might say no because she doesn't want to develop a reputation for getting less than half the pie. She doesn't want others to see her as a pushover. Reputational concerns lead people to reject anything less than half the pie.

In the case where Alice gets half the pie in a one-shot negotiation, the reputation she creates is simply reinforcing the behavior she is already doing. It makes a fair split easier to achieve in the future. And it may help her find future negotiation partners. People want to do deals with other people who will treat them fairly. Here, too, reputational concerns reinforce the incentive to split the pie.

There is a potential counter. Alice might be willing to do an even split in a particular case but rejects it because it might cause her to lose a reputation for being tough. For this to hold, Alice would have to want such a reputation, in spite of the fact that it may lead others to avoid doing business with her.

Our final case arises when Alice could end up with more than half the pie in a one-off negotiation. Alice might decide not to take more than half in order develop a reputation for being principled and fair. She doesn't take the lion's share because she is concerned others wouldn't then want to do business with her in the future. In these situations, reputation concerns again push the result toward an even split of the pie.

Of course, if the person values a reputation for being tough, even being unfairly so, and all that comes with it, that can push the deal away from splitting the pie. While there are certainly examples of negotiators who seem to value a reputation for being unfair, such a reputation can lead to spectacular blowups and to people not wanting to partner with them (if they can avoid it).

On balance, I believe reputational concerns lead people to reject getting less than half and not to insist on getting more than half. Indeed, the ideal reputation would seem to be one for acting fair and splitting the pie.

Take It or Leave It

The rules of a negotiation can create power. The most obvious example is when one side can make an ultimatum to the other. The side able to make an ultimatum can capture most of the pie and leave the other side with something just enough above their BATNA to say yes.

Let's go back to Alice and Bob with 12 slices of pizza to split up. Absent an agreement, Alice gets 4 slices and Bob gets 2. Were Alice able to make an ultimatum to Bob, she could offer him 3 slices, which is 1 better than his BATNA, so he should accept. This leaves her with 9 slices, which is better than the 7 slices Alice gets under an equal split of the pie.

Even here, I advise caution. An ultimatum might backfire if it is too lopsided. If Alice only offers Bob 1 slice more than his BATNA, he might say no out of spite. He only stands to lose the 1 extra slice he's been offered. Meanwhile, Alice stands to lose 5 slices, as she would fall from 9 back down to 4 if there's no deal. Perhaps it would be safer for Alice to offer Bob 4 slices, which is 2 more than his BATNA. That leaves 8 slices for Alice, one more than when they split the pie.

A single take-it-or-leave-it ultimatum is hard to accomplish. Bob could come back to Alice with a counter ultimatum: "I'll give you 5 slices. Take it or leave it." Alice should take it as the offer is 1 better than her BATNA.

It isn't clear why either side has an ability to make an ultimatum to the other. One side can claim they've made their best and final offer, but it isn't believable. Indeed, when Alice makes an ultimatum demanding 8 slices, she has a lot more to lose than Bob if she walks away. (She'd lose 4 and he'd lose 2.) Why is she the one walking away if Bob says no? Alice can try walking away but Bob can wait for her to return.

While it is hard to make a forever ultimatum, negotiation protocols can create the potential for a short-term ultimatum. Consider, for example, a protocol that has each side take turns making an offer or counter to the other. The negotiation continues until one side accepts the other's proposal. In some situations, one side can counter right away, while in others, there is a built-in time lag between offers and counteroffers. That delay will typically be costly, and the cost might be different for the two parties. In effect, the party making the offer can make a short-term ultimatum—they can capture how much the pie shrinks from the built-in delay.

To see how this works, we have Alice and Bob looking to divide a $50 pie. Every day they don't agree the pie shrinks, as might happen if there is strike or lockout, and this leads to missed sales. In this example, an offer can be accepted right away, but it takes a week to reject an offer and present a counter. During that week, the pie shrinks by $10.

The party making the offer has, in effect, the ability to make an ultimatum over the $10 that will be lost. If Alice gets to go first and she offers a $30/$20 split, by the time Bob can counter, there's only a $40 pie left. Bob might as well take the $20 for sure today than hope to split the pie in a week and get $20.* The short-term ultimatum provides a small edge, just the size of the lost pie. And, as discussed above, one shouldn't try to be too greedy in terms of getting that whole amount. Perhaps Alice should offer a $28/$22 split to give Bob a little bit more incentive to say yes right away.

Other rules might also provide an edge to one side, for example, the opportunity to go first and provide a number that serves as an anchor—more on this in Chapter 22. While rules have the potential to create advantages, in most negotiations there is no external rule-maker. Since neither side gets to set the rules unilaterally, it isn't clear that rules really confer power. The rules of a negotiation are whatever the two sides agree to.

In particular, default rules can be changed. Recall the CEMA example in Chapter 7. The savings on New York mortgage recording taxes paid by the buyer and transfer taxes paid by the seller lead to an 80:20 split in favor of the buyer. That's true, but there's nothing stopping the seller from insisting on a payment that restores a 50:50 balance. Changing the default division is just one more component of a larger negotiation over the pie. In this larger negotiation, there's no reason to think that the pie won't be split evenly.

The exceptions, of course, are rules that come from an external source, such as the law or regulations. In a union negotiation, management must negotiate in good faith and this rules out actions such as making ultimatums. In other cases, the law doesn't impact power inside the negotiation but shapes the BATNAs. A divorce negotiation

---

* You might be thinking Bob could counter with $15/$25 (where he gets the $25). But if Alice says no to that, the pie will shrink further to $30. At this point, Alice can ask for $20 and offer Bob $10. If Bob says no to the $10, the pie will collapse down to $20. At this point a $10/$10 split is Bob's best option. Otherwise, the pie will be reduced to $10 and Alice can make an ultimatum that leads to her getting all (or nearly all) of the last $10.

is done with the understanding that if the parties end up in court, state law determines the split. In the nine community property states, all property obtained during the marriage is divided 50:50. The other 41 states require an "equitable" distribution of property, so that the different needs and earning powers of the divorcing partners are taken into account.

The external source could also be a guiding principle. I started this discussion with the view that ultimatums could lead to an uneven division. But the more I think about it, the more I'm persuaded that ultimatums are best used to get an even split of the pie. In my own case, I am prepared to make an ultimatum to the other side that I want to be treated fairly. I won't accept an offer that gives me less than half the pie. They can make the same ultimatum to me and it will all work out: we split the pie. I haven't insisted on anything I'm not willing to accept myself.

My ultimatum is coming from a principle. If the other side can provide a principled reason for why they should get more than half, I'm willing to listen. If I've miscalculated the pie, I'm open to a correction. Because splitting the pie isn't arbitrary, the ultimatum has sticking power. I don't want to make even a small deviation as then I'm left with nothing to stand on. And since I've proposed an even split, both sides have the same amount to lose if they walk away.

Chapter 14

MULTI-PARTY NEGOTIATIONS

When there are more than two parties, negotiation gets complicated. One main reason is that the BATNAs are not clear-cut. They depend on how other negotiations play out. Because it's hard to pin down the BATNAs, it's hard to know what the pie is or how it's being split up.

With just two players, each party knows what they can do on their own if there's no deal. For example, Anju will buy a $5,000 CD and Bharat will buy a $20,000 CD. There's no other negotiation they need to consider.

We added Chiragh as a third party in our original example with Anju and Bharat, but we didn't make him an active negotiator. His standing offer to provide $5,000 if he were paid 3 percent interest improved Bharat's BATNA. If Bharat didn't do a deal with Anju, he could make $600 working with Chiragh. (As a result, the pie that Anju and Bharat could create fell from $300 to $100.) The potential to do alternative deals changed the BATNAs. But why should Chiragh stick with a 3 percent interest rate when Anju undercuts him? Chiragh should be part of the negotiation.

In this chapter, we look at multi-party negotiations where all the players are active. In that case, the terms of a deal between Chiragh and Bharat depend on the best deal Bharat could strike with Anju, which, in turn, depends on what Chiragh offers, and also on what Anju and Chiragh could do together. Everything is interconnected. To cut through the tangle, we take a step back and return to the BATNAs. What will each player end up doing if they can't reach a deal?

With three active negotiators, if there's no three-way deal, the end result is likely to be some two-way deal. The BATNAs depend on which two-way deal will happen and how the spoils will be divided up in that two-way deal. To understand the BATNAs, we have to figure out how a different set of negotiations will play out.

We understand how two-party negotiations play out: the parties split the pie. The open question in a three-party negotiation is which of the two-party deals will arise in the event of a breakdown. That arrangement determines the BATNAs. It is a game of musical chairs in that the two-party fallback deal must leave one person out. And no one wants to be the one left out and end up with no deal.

Some might be tempted to leave out the person, say player A, if they are the one who refuses to accept the three-way deal. But A might just be responding to an unreasonable offer from B or C. We don't look to assign blame if a deal doesn't happen. Instead, we look to see who is most likely to pair up with whom.

You might wonder if this could all be worked out in advance. That's unlikely. We shouldn't expect people who can't agree on a three-way deal to reach alignment on who will pair up in the absence of a deal. It isn't just that each person doesn't want to be left out. Each party has its preferred result if the three-way deal falls apart. Party A might want to join up with B, while party B might want to join up with C.

That doesn't mean anything goes or that the parties should expect pairings to happen at random. Some pairs are more likely than others to form. For example, if both A and B want to join with C, then C would be the one who picks. Parties A and B can anticipate who

C will want to join with. Say that's B. The negotiators should expect that if a three-way deal falls apart, the BC pair is the most likely to arise, followed by AC and then by AB.

With four or more players, the situation is similar. If the parties can't reach a four-party agreement, the BATNAs are likely to be one of the three-party deals. As before, we have to consider which one. But at least we know the answer for each case. If we can solve the three-party agreement based on two-party deals as the BATNAs, we can solve the four-party agreement using the three-party solutions as the BATNAs.

No matter how many parties are involved, the big picture remains the same: the point of a negotiation is to beat your BATNA. When you enter a negotiation, your starting point should always be what will happen if you don't reach an agreement. Absent that information, it is hard if not impossible to know if you are getting a good deal or not.

Just like in two-party negotiations, the parties are still splitting the pie. The only difference is that the parties doing the splitting are now (a) the group that forms if things break down and (b) the person left out. The pie is how much profits or savings can be created if that left-out person joins in.

Even if it is hard to pin down exactly which group will form, we can look at each possible outcome and split the pie on a case-by-case basis. That helps the parties narrow down the range of possible outcomes. In addition, the parties can take a weighted average across these scenarios to come up with an expected value for how the pie will be split.

I don't want to get too abstract. I'll go back to our example of airlines sharing a runway to illustrate how we go about coming up with a set of scenarios and the solutions that go with each one.

The Runway Redux

Several airlines will save money if they share a common runway. In the original example we had two airlines, A and B. Now we add airline C. Airline A needs a 1km runway, Airline B needs a 2km runway, and Airline C needs a 3km runway. As before, a one-kilometer runway costs $5 million, a two-kilometer one is $10 million, and a three-kilometer runway costs $15 million.

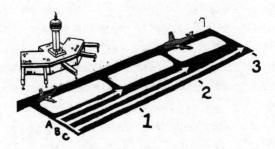

The three airlines can save $15m by sharing one long runway. A shared runway costs $15 million compared to a price tag of $30 million for three separate runways. Our challenge is to figure out how much each party should pay for the shared runway.

Let's start with a guess. If we think back to the logic of the two-airline case, it seems clear that C should pay the full cost of the last leg that it alone uses. The cost of the middle leg should be split evenly between Airlines B and C. Does that mean the cost of the first leg should be split three ways between A, B, and C? As we will see, that is one reasonable option. There's also a reasonable justification for A paying half the cost of the first leg, where the other half is split between B and C.

To figure which solution is more reasonable and why, we need to understand what will happen if the airlines can't agree on a three-way deal. I want to propose two possible scenarios.

Scenario 1. Absent a three-way deal, the two-way partnership that leads to the greatest savings is the one that will arise. That's Airlines B and C.

Scenario 2. Absent a three-way deal, each potential two-way partnership forms with equal chance. The potential partnerships, AB, AC, and BC, each arise with chance 1/3.

These two scenarios are the extremes of what might happen, and I expect the truth will lie somewhere in between. I think more profitable partnerships are more likely to form. Scenario 1 takes this all the way to the limit where only the most profitable partnership forms. Scenario 2 is the other extreme: the more profitable partnerships are not given any extra weight and each pairing is equally likely absent a three-way deal.

The negotiation in scenario 1 is not too hard to analyze. Absent a three-way deal, Airlines B and C come together. This makes sense in that each airline is the other's most preferred partner. Together they can save $10 million, double the savings if either partnered with A. Airlines B and C split the $10 million savings, 50:50. That is their BATNA. For Airline A, the BATNA is paying $5 million for its own landing strip.

Next comes the negotiation between A and the BC coalition. You can think of B and C as having conditionally formed this backup deal and are now negotiating to improve upon it. Bringing A on board adds $5 million more savings. That's the pie. In the negotiation between A and BC, I think it is more reasonable to think of BC as a single entity than two separate players. Thus, we stick with splitting the pie evenly. A gets half and BC together get the other half. Inside the BC pair, the two of them split their half evenly.

How much does everyone pay?

PARTY	HOW MUCH THEY PAY	TOTAL
A	50% of $5m	$2.50m
B	25% of $5m + 50% of $5m	$3.75m
C	25% of $5m + 50% of $5m + 100% of $5m	$8.75m
Combined		**$15.00m**

The total adds up to $15m, the cost of the 3km runway shared by all three. Airline A pays half the cost of the first leg, while B and C split the cost of the other half. Airlines B and C split the cost of the midsection 50:50. Airline C pays the full cost of the last segment of the runway that it alone uses.

The reason why the cost of the first leg is not evenly split three ways is that A is negotiating with the BC pair, which acts like a single unit. Each side feels entitled to half the $5m pie. Were A to pay only one-third of the cost, the BC pair would find this unreasonable. Airline A would be gaining two-thirds of the pie it creates (paying just $1.67m) and come out well ahead of BC. When Airline A pays half the cost, it has the same gain as the BC pair.

At this point, we have a potential result for the three-party negotiation. It's the second of the answers we guessed at the start. Now we understand that answer is based on the belief that Airline A would be the one left out of a two-way deal if things fall apart. This would seem to be the most likely outcome, as there's nothing A can do to stop B and C from coming together if the three-way deal falls apart.

Scenario 2. This scenario has more calculations since there are three possible results if the three-way deal doesn't happen. We treat each possible outcome symmetrically. Each of the three possibilities has an equal (one-third) chance of arising.

2.1   BC come together and A is left out. Then A bargains with BC.

2.2   AC come together and B is left out. Then B bargains with AC.

2.3   AB come together and C is left out. The C bargains with AB.

Case 2.1 was the one we just covered in scenario 1.

Under case 2.2, AC first come together. They are only able to create $5m of value since the only overlap is the first leg of the runway required by Airline A. They split that savings 50:50. When Airline B then joins, no additional runway needs to be built (as a 3km runway has already been constructed for C). Airline B joining the AC pair creates a $10m pie since B saves the cost of building its own 2km runway. Airline B should get half the pie, which implies B contributes $5m toward the 2km runway it uses. The question is how A and C split up the other $5 million. This time, the answer is not 50:50.

I think it helps to think of that $10m savings in two parts, a $5m savings associated with the first leg and a $5m savings associated with the second leg. There is no sense in which Airline A has any claim to the savings on the second leg. It is contributing nothing to the cost. Airline A should get its half share only on savings associated with the first leg and no share on the savings associated with the second leg. Airline C, who paid for the full cost of the second (and third) leg, gets all the savings associated with the second leg.

When B joins AC, B saves 50 percent of $10m. The other 50 percent of $10m or $5m goes to AC:

A saves 50% of $2.5m
C saves 50% of $2.5m + 100 percent of $2.5m

The first $2.5m in savings given to AC is associated with the first leg and is split evenly between A and C; the second $2.5m is the share of $5m savings given to AC associated with the second leg and it all goes to C.

Altogether, in case 2.2, A pays half of the first leg based on its BATNA, but then gets half of that back when B joins. B pays $5m (and thus saves $5m). Airline C, like A, initially pays for half the cost of the first leg and all the cost of the next two, but then gets back half of its outlays on the first two legs when B joins.

PARTY	HOW MUCH THEY PAY	TOTAL
A	$2.5m – $1.25m	$1.25m
B	50% of $10m	$5.00m
C	$2.5m + $5m + $5m – ($1.25m + $2.5m)	$8.75m
Combined		**$15.00m**

Under case 2.3, the result ends up being very similar to case 2.2 with the roles of B and C reversed. When Airline C joins the AB pair, the savings are still $10m and Airline C can use the existing 2km runway but has to build out a $5m extension that it alone pays for. As in case 2.2, A ends up paying half the cost of the first leg but then gets half of that back when C joins. Airline B pays the other half of the cost for the first leg and $5m for the second leg, and then gets half back on both legs when C joins. Airline C creates $10m of savings by joining AB, of which it keeps half.

PARTY	HOW MUCH THEY PAY	TOTAL
A	$2.5m – $1.25m	$1.25m
B	$2.5m + $5m – ($1.25m + $2.5m)	$3.75m
C	50% of $10m + $5m	$10.00m
Combined		**$15.00m**

All that is left to do is combine the three potential cases.

PARTY	BC VS. A	AC VS. B	AB VS. C	AVERAGE	EXPLAINING THE NUMBER
A	$2.50m	$1.25m	$1.25m	$1.67m	= 1/3 $5m
B	$3.75m	$5.00m	$3.75m	$4.17m	= 1/3 $5m + 1/2 $5m
C	$8.75m	$8.75m	$10.00m	$9.17m	= 1/3 $5m + 1/2 $5m + $5m

I've rewritten the Average column in a way I think better illustrates the intuition behind the results. All three airlines split the cost of the first leg. That is the 1/3 of $5m in each row. Airlines B and C split the cost of the second leg—the 1/2 of $5m in the second and third rows—while Airline C pays the full $5m cost of the third leg.

This is the first answer we guessed. Now we understand that answer is based on the belief that any two-way partnership is equally likely if things fall apart.

The difference between scenarios 1 and 2 comes down to what each party pays for the first leg. Airline A pays less under scenario 2 since it has a better BATNA. It is less likely to be left out. Since it is an equal player in terms of the BATNAs, it pays only one-third of the total. In contrast, in scenario 1, Airline A is sure to be left out if no three-way deal is struck. This puts A in a worse position and leads to its paying half the cost of the first leg.

The bargaining result should lie somewhere in the range between scenarios 1 and 2. The reason there is no single answer is that the result depends on what the participants expect to happen in the event of a breakdown. It seems reasonable to expect that more valuable coalitions are more likely to form. Just how much more likely is something the participants will have to judge for themselves.

Even if no one knows exactly what will happen if the parties fail to reach an agreement, that doesn't mean they should throw up their hands and give up. They can expect Airline A will pay between 50 percent and 33.3 percent of the cost of the first runway segment, the range between scenarios 1 and 2. The more likely they think the high-value players will come together, the closer the answer will be to scenario 1 and 50 percent. The more likely things will be a free-for-all, the closer the answer will be to scenario 2 and 33.3 percent. If someone proposes a solution outside this range, at least one party has a logical reason to object.

To resolve the uncertainty, I've seen people start the negotiation with a plan for what will happen if things break down. In the context of the airline case, Airline A might open with something like:

> *I know we will reach a great deal, but just in case, we don't want to end up with nothing. Can we agree that if we don't agree then we'll pick two names out of a hat to do a two-way deal?*

You should be wary of agreeing to a "no-deal" deal. I concur that the parties shouldn't end up with nothing, but this clever person has picked the no-deal scenario most favorable to their position. Were I representing Airline B or C, I would make a counterproposal and suggest that in case no deal happens, B and C get together. My caution is to be careful what you agree to in the event of no deal. You might think it's always smart to have a better backup in case no deal happens. True, but that better backup ends up determining *all* the BATNAs and hence what will happen in the three-way deal.

The solution presented in scenario 2 might have been your first guess as the answer when there are three or more parties. It seems like the natural generalization of the answer presented in Chapter 9. Each party pays an equal share of the part of the runway it uses. In law this is called the Reaches method. In economics, this is the result of the Shapley value, a solution to multi-person negotiation problems developed by Lloyd Shapley (for which he was awarded the 2012 Nobel Memorial Prize in economics).

I, too, think it is a reasonable solution, but not the most reasonable one. Although there is something that seems fair about each party splitting the cost equally of what it uses, I don't think this is the most likely result. Among the potential reasonable solutions, it gives the biggest possible gain to the weakest parties. Behind the answer is the implicit assumption that Airline A is just as likely as B or C to be part of a two-way deal if the three can't come to an agreement.

If you think that in this situation B and C are likely to pair up first and then negotiate with A, then Airline A would end up paying half the cost of the first leg. While I might not want to admit it, even if I were Airline A, I'd put my money on B and C getting together if we didn't reach a three-way deal.

Sharing a Pipeline

The runway example is based on a real case. Five property developers built a shared pipeline to bring municipal water from Calleguas (a bit north of Los Angeles) to their new developments of nearly 20,000 acres in the Simi Hills. Just like a runway, the Lindero feeder pipeline and the five developments were laid out east to west. The cost of the pipeline was substantial, about $4.3 million. Thus, the savings from coming together were also large as the five developers shared one pipeline rather than build five separate pipes. The five property developers landed in court when they couldn't agree on how to share the costs or, more precisely, when they couldn't agree on how they had agreed to share the costs.[20]

One camp thought they had intended to use the "straight capacity method." Each party pays an amount proportional to the capacity they employ. If one developer has twice the land, plans for twice as many houses, and requires twice the capacity, that party pays twice as much. This approach divides the cost of the pipeline equally across each planned house.

A second approach, favored by the named plaintiff American-Hawaiian Steamship Company, is the "alternative-facilities method." Here, each party shares the savings in the same proportion. For example, everyone saves 30 percent compared to going it alone.

A third camp argued for the "Reaches method." The idea here is that parties only share the cost of the pipeline they use. The pipe from Calleguas to developer #1 is split equally among the five. The next length, from developer #1 to developer #2, is used by developers 2, 3, 4, and 5 and thus the cost is split four ways. And so on. The last segment of the water pipe from development #4 to #5 is only used by developer #5. There is no reason for the other developers to share in this cost. Thus developer #5 is solely responsible for the cost of the last leg. This is the perfect analogue to the runway situation in scenario 2. Each airline pays an equal share of the cost of the runway it uses.

I'll pick some rounded but realistic numbers to illustrate the three alternatives. To keep things simple, I'll limit the situation to three developers. Let's say the cost to build out to developer #1 is $1m, to developer #2 is $2m, and to developer #3 is $3m. Like the runway example, the route to develop #3 goes right past developers #1 and #2.

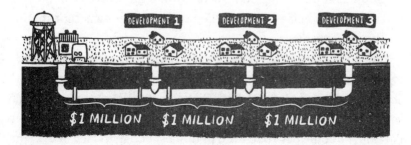

If they share the same pipe, all three can be served at a cost of $3m. Were they to build three separate pipes, the cost would be $1m + $2m + $3m = $6m.

I don't know how many units each developer was planning on building, so I can't tell you the outcome of the straight capacity method. But if each one was planning on the same size development, the total cost would be split evenly, $1m to each.

That makes very little sense to me. The first developer is paying the same as if it went alone. That should set off alarm bells. The reason it makes so little sense is that the price tag that ends up getting split three ways depends on a pipeline that goes past developer #1's land and so developer #1 gets stuck with part of the bill for something that should fall squarely on developers #2 and #3.

Under the alternative-facilities method, the parties share in the savings in the same proportion. The cost of going alone is $6m and working together is $3m. If each party were to save the same percentage, each side would pay 50 percent of its cost of going solo:

Developer #1 pays 50% of $1m = $0.5m
Developer #2 pays 50% of $2m = $1.0m
Developer #3 pays 50% of $3m = $1.5m

This also makes very little sense to me. Developer #3 is getting a share of savings on costs associated with the third leg of the pipeline that it alone uses. It alone should be responsible for those costs. Under the alternative-facilities approach, developer #3 only pays $1.5m. Since I think developer #3 is entirely responsible for the last leg, this implies it is contributing only $0.5m toward the $2m cost of the first two legs. That's half as much as the $1m developer #2 is contributing for the same two legs.

Indeed, the cost to developer #2 is so high it exceeds what it would pay under either scenario 1 or 2 from the runway case. Under both scenarios, developers #2 and #3 split the cost of the second leg, which comes to $0.5m each. The worst scenario for developer #2 is when developer #1 only pays one-third of the cost of the first leg or $0.33m, leaving $0.33m for each of #2 and #3 to pay. Thus, even in the worst scenario, developer #2 only pays $0.83m. That's why I think the alternative-facilities method offers an unreasonable answer.

The lower court settled on the Reaches method as the one most consistent with their original agreement to share the costs "on a pro-rata basis of installed capacity of said line."

Developer #1 pays 33.3% of $1m = $0.33m

Developer #2 pays 33.3% of $1m + 50% × $1m = $0.83m

Developer #3 pays 33.3% of $1m + 50% × $1m + 100% × $1m= $1.83m

The Reaches method is the same as scenario 2. Unfortunately, our story has a less happy ending for developer #1. Upon appeal, the higher court decided that the straight capacity method was most consistent with the original intent.

The examples I've used to illustrate the three-way negotiation are a bit too simple in one specific way: the runway or pipeline is a straight line. There's no cost of a detour or need to make the runway extra durable to handle the extra load. I've written an online appendix that shows how to handle those more complicated cases. (It will likely appeal to those who really like math.) You can find the appendix at SplitThePieBook.com.

Saving Bottle Costs Redux

In the examples with airlines or pipelines, the potential partners all came together to avoid duplication and thereby created the biggest pie. No one was left out. Here we consider a different type of multi-party negotiation, one in which a buyer negotiates with multiple sellers (or a seller with multiple buyers or even multiple buyers negotiating with multiple sellers). In these situations, not everyone is needed to create the biggest pie. The buyer can play different sellers off against each other to determine who gets left out. Those left out end up with their BATNA. That doesn't make them irrelevant—they play an important role in changing the terms of the deal that happens.

We'll go back to the negotiations between Coke and Honest Tea over bottle costs. Recall that Honest Tea was paying 19¢/bottle and Coke's costs were 11¢/bottle. This created a pie of 8¢/bottle.

Here we add Pepsi to the picture and assume it has costs of 15¢/bottle. If Honest Tea can play the two against each other, the bottle price will keep falling until it hits 15¢. At that point, Pepsi can go no lower and drops out. That doesn't mean that Coke wins the bidding at 15¢.

Once Pepsi drops out, there's still another 4¢ of savings to be negotiated. Coke can bring the price down from 15¢ all the way to 11¢. That's a pie to be split between Honest Tea and Coke. In that negotiation, the price would be 13¢.

So far, Pepsi only has a backstage role in the negotiation. It is as if Honest Tea's BATNA is to go to Pepsi and have them provide bottles at their 15¢ cost. But Honest Tea might have to negotiate with Pepsi if it doesn't reach a deal with Coke.

We can use the approach just developed to look at runway cost-sharing to reexamine how the negotiations would play out when all three parties are active. Instead of A, B, and C, it makes more sense to call our parties C, P, and H for Coke, Pepsi, and Honest Tea. We'll do everything on a per-bottle basis.

If all three parties come together—denoted by C-P-H below—the savings are 8¢. The savings are also 8¢ if just Coke and Honest Tea come together, indicated by C-H below. Here's a list of savings depending on who comes together:

C-P-H	8¢
C-H	8¢
P-H	4¢
C-P	0¢

While it seems strange to think of a three-way agreement between Coke, Pepsi, and Honest Tea, what that really means is they agree on how to divide up the 8¢. At the end of the day, it will be Coke supplying the bottles to Honest Tea. Pepsi might still make something for helping to bring the price down.

As before, we are in scenario 2 and there are three possibilities in the event there is no three-way "agreement."

2.1   Coke and Honest Tea get together with Pepsi excluded.
2.2   Pepsi and Honest Tea get together with Coke excluded.
2.3   Coke and Pepsi get together with Honest Tea excluded.

Case 2.1 is straightforward and the most natural. Coke and Honest Tea can create the full 8¢ pie just with the two of them. They split this pie. Pepsi then has nothing to add and so gets zero.

COKE	HONEST TEA	PEPSI
4¢	4¢	0¢

Case 2.2 has Pepsi and Honest Tea coming together as the backup. They split the 4¢ pie they create together. When Coke joins, it brings another 4¢ of savings. Coke gets half and Honest Tea gets the other half. The reason Pepsi doesn't get any more is that it only brings 4¢ of savings to the table. Unlike Honest Tea, who is needed to create the remaining 4¢, Pepsi is not necessary. Pepsi is like Airline A and is only entitled to savings on the first leg of the runway. After Coke joins the result is as below:

COKE	HONEST TEA	PEPSI
2¢	4¢	2¢

The potential for Pepsi to be a backup explains why it might make some small amount of money in a three-way agreement.

Case 2.3 has Coke and Pepsi getting together as their BATNA. The two of them can't create any savings by themselves. Their BATNA is zero. Note that when Coke and Pepsi are together this doesn't mean they are colluding. In fact, their being together creates the biggest opportunity for Honest Tea to play one off against the other.

When Honest Tea joins, it doesn't have to split the entire 8¢ with Coke and Pepsi. The reason is that Coke is only bringing 4¢ to the table (the additional gains it has over Pepsi). Honest Tea splits that 4¢ with Coke. Pepsi doesn't get any of it as Pepsi brings no value on its own other than lowering Coke's value. Honest Tea gets half of the 4¢ it splits plus the full 4¢, for a total of 6¢.

COKE	HONEST TEA	PEPSI
2¢	6¢	0¢

Let's look at our original two scenarios again. Scenario 1 has the pair that creates the most value get together in the event of a breakdown. This is case 2.1 here: Coke and Honest each get 4¢.

Under scenario 2, all three cases are equally likely. We take the average of the three cases:

COKE	HONEST TEA	PEPSI
8¢/3	14¢/3	2¢/3

Honest Tea gets a bit more than half the savings. It always gets at least half the savings, but it can sometimes leverage the presence of Pepsi to strike a better deal with Coke.

There is one surprising point I'd like to highlight. One might think the ideal scenario is to be included in the two-person pairing rather than be left out and have a BATNA of zero. But, as this example shows, Honest Tea does the best in case 2.3 when it is the one excluded. The reason is that the pair it's negotiating with also has a BATNA of zero, and there's an internal competition that means neither of the pair brings much value to the table. As a result, Honest Tea keeps all the savings created by Pepsi and then half of the additional savings created by Coke. This is the same outcome as in the example we started with, where Pepsi played a backstage role.

Chapter 15

WHAT IF YOU ARE BEING USED AS A PAWN?

I've made the case that power is equal in any two-party negotiation. That result doesn't extend to situations where there are three or more parties. In particular, one of the parties can find itself being used as a pawn. The person is used to help someone else get a better deal and doesn't get anything in return. That happened to Pepsi in case 2.3 in the previous chapter.

The best illustration I know of this took place in 1986 when Holland Sweetener built a $50m plant to produce aspartame, the generic version of NutraSweet. Holland Sweetener built the plant anticipating the expiration of Monsanto's European patent on NutraSweet. Coke and Pepsi were eager to have competition in the market. They told Holland Sweetener how unhappy they were with Monsanto and encouraged Holland Sweetener to enter.

What happened after Holland Sweetener entered? Monsanto cut its prices by two-thirds and kept all of Coke's and Pepsi's business.[21] That saved Coke and Pepsi some $200m over the life of the new contract. As for Holland Sweetener, it managed to capture the business of Diet Squirt, which is worth just about what it sounds like. Holland Sweetener had no chance to earn back their investment in the plant.

For all their stated unhappiness with Monsanto, what Coke and Pepsi really wanted was good old NutraSweet at a much better price. They couldn't have done that without having an alternative. Holland Sweetener's generic aspartame was the same chemical but didn't have the brand value. It was good enough to provide a credible threat if Monsanto didn't cut its price, but not good enough to win over NutraSweet.

This outcome was entirely predictable. Indeed, I would be surprised if you haven't found yourself put in the position of Holland Sweetener. In dating, someone seems to be interested in you but is really using you to get their current romantic interest to up their game or make a greater commitment. At work, someone seems interested in a job at your company but is really using you to get their current employer to up their salary or get a promotion.

I admit to having played this game—not in dating, but when buying a house. After locking in a mortgage rate with Bank of America, interest rates fell quite a bit in the summer of 2019. Since I had locked in the rate, my number didn't go down. But as rival lenders were offering lower numbers, I got a new offer at the current lower rate. Only at that point did Bank of America come down and match the better bid. Sure, I could have gone with the "Bank of Holland Sweetener," but I had all the paperwork, appraisals, and income verification already done. I liked my current lender, just not the rate.

What do you do when you think someone is putting you in a Holland Sweetener position? Someone asks you to bid on a contract. You know there's an incumbent supplier who is likely to keep the business. Your quote is there to keep the supplier honest.

It's a lose-lose proposition. If you don't respond to the request, you have no chance of getting the business. If you do respond, you end up doing a lot of work that mostly helps the customer. The most likely result is you end up with squirt.

There is a solution to this conundrum: get paid to negotiate. You may not be able to get any slice of the pie in the actual negotiation. What you can do is change how the other players divide up the pie. That can be worth a great deal to the player who gets more.

Here's what Holland Sweetener should have done. Prior to building the plant, they should have gone to Coke and Pepsi and insisted on getting a long-term contract conditional on building the plant.

You are currently paying $90/ton. Can we agree now that once our plant is up and running, you'll buy 1 million tons at $50/ton from us?

If Coke and Pepsi had said no, that would have been a very useful warning sign. Why should Holland Sweetener expect to get a contract with Coke and Pepsi after they build a plant if they can't get one now?

At the end of the day, Holland Sweetener lost so much money that it had a credible case for shutting down the plant. At that point, it went to Coke and Pepsi and said that it would exit the market absent a long-term contract. Coke and Pepsi realized that would put them back at Monsanto's mercy, and so they agreed. Holland Sweetener got paid to stay. It would have been far better to have been paid to play.

When I say get paid to play, I don't generally mean cash or even an advance contract. There are lots of ways of getting paid. You can ask for more information or access to key decision makers.

For example, if you are asked to bid on a supply contract, you may want to talk to the engineer in charge of quality, not just the procurement person. The procurement person is rewarded for getting a lower price. If you have something else to offer, such as better reliability, figure out who cares about what you have to offer, and ask to connect with them. Ask that person about their KPIs (Key Performance Indicators) so that you can design your offer to help them achieve their goals. If the buyer expresses no interest in helping you make these contacts—and therefore make a better bid—that is telling you right up front you have little chance of success and are most likely being used as a pawn.

In my world of academia, there are two types of raises. There's the regular 2 percent cost-of-living annual increase. Then there's the big raise when you have a competing outside offer. (Of course, sometimes the dean says: that's a great offer, I would take it if I were you.) To get a big raise, faculty have been known to shop an offer.

Let's say that Professor Cash expresses an interest in coming to Yale and we'd be excited to have her join our faculty. If we don't make Cash an offer, there's no chance of Cash coming. At the same time, we don't want to go through all the distraction and effort required if all we are doing is helping Cash get a pay raise.*

We can start by asking Cash why she thinks New Haven and Yale are better than her current location. Pretty much everyone can come up with a reasonable story about why they are unhappy, and why they want to move. Even so, most people's unhappiness with their current employer can be fixed with a big pay raise, and just such a pay raise will likely happen in response to our job offer. How can we determine who really wants to move?

In theory, one could ask the candidate to accept a conditional contract. Just like Holland Sweetener should have asked for a contract with Coke conditional on building a plant, we could ask for a conditional employment contract. Were we to offer you this salary, research support, and teaching load, would you agree to accept? In fact, this is how offers are made at the Questrom School of Business at Boston University.

The Questrom approach serves several purposes. It prevents them from going through all the effort only to discover that the can-

---

* In academia, making a tenure offer requires a huge amount of work. We ask a dozen scholars to evaluate the candidate's research contributions. There is a committee report, a faculty vote, and a provost committee.

didate has salary expectations that won't be met. Equally important, it forces the candidate to make a commitment to Questrom. There is an expectation on all sides that when the official offer does come through the candidate will say yes.

This makes it much harder to use Questrom as a Holland Sweetener. You can't go to your dean and say "I have an offer of $X from Questrom—now please give me the raise I deserve." You don't get something to show your dean until you've already accepted the Questrom offer.

Of course, an agreement to move jobs is not a binding contract. And just as I renegotiated my locked-in rate with Bank of America, the job candidate could renegotiate the terms with Questrom should a better offer arise before the deal is inked. That said, the prenegotiated contract goes a long way to demonstrating commitment on the candidate's part.

There are other ways for the candidate to demonstrate commitment short of agreeing to a conditional contract. Yale Law School typically insists the person come visit for a semester before they make someone a senior offer. That's a big commitment to make if you're only using them to get a salary increase.

Just as I want you to be cautious about being used as a negotiation pawn to help someone get a better deal, I want you to think about how you use others to help you get a better deal. When someone improves your BATNA, that gives you a leg up, but it doesn't help them. As a result, they may not have sufficient motivation to improve your BATNA as much as you'd like them to.

We expect people to provide this type of competition for free. If you want them to go all out, look for ways to compensate the parties that increase your BATNA. You can share in some of the gains they make possible. You can provide them with access to information or people. You can make sure they win some part of the business.

Imagine that Holland Sweetener was promised 10 percent of the savings they made possible. That gives them an extra incentive to lower their price. A lower price boosts their chance of winning and also boosts their profits when they don't. The more they know there is something in it for them, the more likely they will be to participate and the harder they will compete. In short, we can do a better job improving our BATNA if we do more to reward those who help us do so.

PART IV

HOW TO GROW THE PIE

I've talked about the pie and the principle of dividing it equally. In many of the examples, the pie was fixed in size—like the pizza with its 12 slices. It is better to think of the pie as something that can be made bigger or smaller, depending on what the negotiators do.

Poor negotiators see everything in terms of dividing the pie and frame everything as zero-sum. When the other side makes a request, the natural answer is no. If the other side is getting more, you must be getting less. Good negotiators work to make the largest pie possible. That way each half is as big as possible.

If you don't want to imitate poor negotiators, does that mean when the other side asks for something you should say yes? Actually, yes. But that doesn't mean you should just say yes and get nothing in return. And it doesn't mean you should pay more in terms of cash.

Chapter 16 explains why you want to give the other side what it is they want. The reason isn't to be nice or generous. If they get what they want from a deal, you will be able to get what it is that you want. It doesn't matter how many issues you win or lose. What matters is making sure that the side that cares the most wins—and compensates the other side. These "Smart Trades" are how you grow the pie. This is where empathy and allocentrism come to the fore.

Chapter 17 introduces the Zinc-It case. We use this extended example of a scientist selling his technology to put the ideas we've covered into action. The chapter offers a collection of negotiation transcripts and provides a debrief of what went right and wrong.

In Chapter 18, I share the lesson of making the other side's case. This is central to demonstrating you understand their perspective. People think the reason they aren't getting their way is that they haven't been heard or understood. So they keep arguing. They think if only you could see things through their eyes, you would change your mind. By presenting their position, you demonstrate you do indeed appreciate where they are coming from. The fact that you've chosen a different outcome isn't from a lack of understanding; it is because there are other factors you judge to be more important. The moral: The other side can't always get their way, but they can always be understood. You need to show your understanding.

Since the ideas of the pie are new, you will have to sell them. Chapter 19 offers some advice. When bringing new ideas back to the boss, it is helpful to employ conditional agreements: here's the agreement you asked for, and here's an option I think works even better and that the other side has also agreed to if we want to go that way. Rather than say no, figure out what it would take for you to say yes and ask for it. If they say no, you are no worse off. But they might say yes. And if you want the other side to go out on a limb for you, say "Yes if" rather than "No unless." The other side wants to know that if they make the stretch, they'll succeed.

Chapter 16

GIVE THE OTHER SIDE WHAT THEY WANT

You read that correctly: you want to give the other side what it is that they want. All too often, negotiators spend their energy arguing with the other side, trying to give them less than what they are asking for. I'm not saying just open up your wallet and give away the store. If you can find a way to help the other side get whatever it is they want, that's the best way to get what you want.

I learned this lesson from Cade Massey. Cade is a proud University of Texas Austin Longhorn. He is a football fanatic who also happens to have an MBA and PhD from the University of Chicago.[22] Together with Nobel laureate Richard Thaler, Cade showed that NFL teams way overvalue the top-ranked draft picks.[23]

Academics have long suspected that people are far too confident when making decisions. Most of these conclusions come from experiments in the lab. Do experienced professionals fall in the same trap? Yes, indeed. In the case of the NFL, the size of the mistakes is measured in the millions and in Super Bowl titles. Teams give up four second-round picks to get the top choice in the first round. While the top pick does better on average, four second-round picks give a team a much better chance of getting a Pro Bowl star. And they cost a lot less! (Even the four of them combined.)

When Cade isn't thinking about football, his day job is being a professor at Wharton, where he teaches influence and negotiation. Before that, we taught together at Yale, where he helped catalyze many of the ideas in this book.

Cade wanted to know what led to success in negotiation. He began by asking successful negotiators what they thought was the reason for their success. And he asked people from a truly wide range of industries.

Cade started with Joe Lemley, a friend of his dad's. Joe traded cattle, cars, ranches, whatever. His only two tools were a phone and an ashtray. Joe's answer was simple:

If you can figure out how to give the other guy what he needs, or better, what he wants, you can get just about anything from him.

Next up was a successful venture capitalist:

We try to figure out what the [entrepreneurs] want, and how to give them as much of that as possible, so we can get what we want.

A pattern was beginning to emerge. Greg Berlanti, the showrunner of the *Everwood* series, was quoted in the *Wall Street Journal*:

I know it sounds so unartistic, but if I can give them [the network] what they want, then I can do what I want.

The reason to give the other side what they want is not to be nice or generous. It's because it is in your interest. If the other parties are getting what they what, they will be motivated to reach an agreement. To get what you want, it helps if the other side is motivated to do a deal.

This has an important follow-on implication: You need to understand what it is that the other side wants. It doesn't help to give the other side what it is that you would want in their shoes. You need to figure out what they actually want.

A Seafaring People

We can see how this plays out (or doesn't play out) in the following negotiation. Michael and his spouse are selling their gasoline station with the goal of using the proceeds to fund a multi-year sailing trip around the world. Michael is naïve in that he bases the price of the station on the cost of the trip and not upon the market value of the station. This seriously annoys the buyer. At one point, she says, "So, your business proposition is that you would like our company to fund your sailing trip."

As you read the transcript below, think about the mistakes being made. (You can watch a reenactment of the negotiation at the book's website, SplitThePieBook.com.)

Meghan [buyer]: I'd like to talk about buying your station.

Michael [seller]: Okay, I guess I'll tell you, so you understand where I'm coming from. I've spent twelve years building this business, and we're getting to the point where my wife and I, we're working eighteen-hour days. My wife is on the verge of a nervous breakdown. We want to take a trip and we would like to cover the expenses of that trip.

That's going to come to $488,000. That's the bare minimum I can accept to do this deal. I can't accept less because that's what it's going to cost to go on this trip. I've sunk $50,000 into a boat, we sold our condo, and that $50,000 is gone. It's in the boat and I have to continue making payments.

Meghan: You said a boat?

Michael: Do you want to see pictures of the boat?

Meghan: No, no, that's okay.

Michael: I have some pictures . . .

Meghan: Would you be willing to accept $400,000?

Michael: That's not enough. I think where we can negotiate maybe is that I have an additional boat payment that is upcoming.

Meghan: How are you saving for this boat? There are less expensive forms of travel than a boat.

Michael: [laugh] We're a seafaring people.

Meghan: Seafaring?

Michael: I think where we can negotiate is we have additional expenses that are upcoming. We have a boat payment of $230,000, and then we have payments of $68k, $75k, and $40k down the line, so if we could maybe space it out, we can work on when—

Meghan: So, your business proposition is that you would like our company to fund your sailing trip?

Michael: [laugh] Well, what I do—

Meghan: Because I'm not sure why I should care.

Michael: —what I do with my money is what I do with my money. I'm laying my cards on the table and I would like for you to reciprocate in some way. I feel we could work better if I knew a little bit more about where you're coming from, and that's why I told you all that.

Meghan: We have more flexibility. We could buy your station, we could buy elsewhere, we could pick up something new, we could get something old and fix it up. We don't have to be in this area at all. Considering our expertise in the field and our ownership of the other two stations, I think we've given you a pretty fair offer.

Wow. That did not go well. I couldn't make this up if I tried. There's plenty to criticize.

Michael has verbal diarrhea. He gave away too much information. He waited too long before asking for reciprocity. He based his price on noneconomic arguments. That's all true. But the two sides ended up with no deal. Who should we blame for that?

I think the root cause of the failure was the buyer's lack of caring. At one point Meghan says: "Because I'm not sure why I should care." This is the critical mistake. It explains why the two sides end up with no deal.

If you were a buyer, would you like to go up against Michael? While he doesn't always make rational arguments, he's an open book. This is a great person to negotiate with. Michael was very clear what he wanted; he wanted to take a sailing trip around the world. Meghan didn't care about giving Michael what he wanted.

Why should Meghan care? The price of the station bears no connection to the cost of a sailboat.

Here's the reason to care. What happens if Michael gets to take his desired trip around the world? He'll sell the station and Meghan will get what she wants. If Michael gets what he wants, Meghan can get what she wants.

Just because you care doesn't mean you pay more. It means you work hard to see what you can do to help the buyer achieve his objective. If Meghan had been more curious about the trip, she would have learned that Michael budgeted $75,000 for a reserve fund to cover living costs when he returns. Meghan thinks Michael is a great manager and would be happy to offer him a job upon his return. With a job in hand, Michael doesn't need the reserve fund or, at least, doesn't need a $75,000 reserve fund.

The solution here reminds me of a negotiation over the division of an orange, an example from an exercise developed by Robert House and made famous in *Getting to Yes*.[24] One side only wants the juice and the other only wants the peel. But they don't know this and so each asks for the whole orange. The two sides need to share information about their preferences in order to find a better way to split the orange than just dividing it in half. In our case, the seller has a problem—lack of a job upon return—that is solved by a reserve fund. A waiting job is a better way to solve the problem. The seller hasn't considered this possibility and thus hasn't asked for it. Just as the two parties with the orange need to talk about what they each want the orange for, here the two sides need to share information about their plans and their needs in order to find the job solution.

Meghan might discover other problems Michael has that she can solve. When Michael and his spouse return from their sailing trip, all their assets will be tied up in a boat. They'll need to sell the boat, but don't want to have a fire sale. Meghan's company shouldn't buy the boat; that's not their business. But her company could provide a short-term loan backed by the boat. This would give the couple more time upon their return to sell the boat and thereby get its full value.

The job and the loan are two ways to grow the pie. With those offers on the table, Michael can now start tasting the pie. He will want to do a deal.

The situation is different from the orange in a very important way. When Michael gets the job offer, the price of his station comes down. That's another reason to care.

Let's say that the market salary for a station manager is $50,000. What is a job worth? Not $50,000. If Michael cuts the sales price by $50,000 to get a job paying $50,000, he is working for "free" for a year. Think of it this way: How much should Michael pay to have a $50,000 job waiting for him upon his return?

Maybe $20,000. He saves the risk of a few months of unemployment and has greater peace of mind. That's the additional pie. There may even be some additional pie to Meghan: Michael is a great manager and good managers are hard to find. Call that value $5,000. This combined $25,000 is extra pie to be split.

When someone asks for something in a negotiation, people say no because they think it is about dividing pie. When it is simply asking for more money, that's true. When you can give them something they want other than cash, that's how you create pie.

What should Michael have said? We'll talk more about what to reveal in Chapter 21, but for now we can say that it was fine for him to talk about wanting to take a sailing trip around the world. That doesn't reduce the value of the station. Doing so, especially if the buyer is empathetic or at least curious, could naturally lead to conversation about what the seller plans to do after the trip. Is he planning to retire? No. What is he planning to do? Would he like to work as a station manager?

Michael should not have been so quick to reveal his bottom line and he shouldn't have based the price on the cost of the trip. He did one thing right: he was clear about what he wanted.

There is a risk to what I preach. If you let the other side know what you want and they give it to you, you will likely have to give something back, often via a lower price. Let's say the offer of a job leads to a $25,000 bigger pie. To split the pie, the seller should take a $10,000 lower price reflecting the $20,000 benefit of the job and the buyer should pay $2,500 more reflecting the increased value from having a great manager. The net effect is a $7,500 lower sales price.

This price adjustment sometimes leads people to pretend what they are getting is worth less than it is in truth. If the job offer is only worth $12,000, the seller only has to give back $6,000, not half of $20,000 or $10,000. The problem is that if you hide or degrade the value of what it is you want, you may not get it. Remember, if you split the pie, you get to keep half of what you create.

I am a big believer in symmetry. Just as you want to give the other side what they want, you don't want to take something they don't want to give up. I discuss this later in this chapter in "Smart Trades." If the other side really doesn't want to do something, it is likely that action would destroy pie. Don't make that part of the deal.

People may be hesitant to tell you what it is they really want. They are often more willing to tell you what they don't want. This is equally useful information. Learning about the dislikes helps you discover the likes. Finding something the other side really doesn't want to give up tells you it is important to them. The way they express this is via the no rather than the yes. Getting to no is a great way of getting to know the other side.

Hoop Dreams

After two years of on-and-off meetings, the 2011–12 basketball season was in grave jeopardy. The preseason had been canceled and then opening day was lost. So was the rest of October and November. Pretty soon, there would be no season. A labor dispute cost the full 2004–2005 hockey season and it was looking like the NBA might follow suit. What allowed the NBA and the National Basketball Players Association to reach an agreement was figuring out what each side really wanted and giving it to them in a creative way.

Professional sports are a business, but one quite unlike most other businesses. No one buys tickets to watch Coke compete with Pepsi. If Coke makes better beverages and captures all the market, that's competition at its best. In contrast, if one sports team handily beats all its rivals, there is less excitement and suspense in watching the game. Fans of the dominant team might be gratified with all the wins, but fans of the other teams will tune out. There goes the pie.

To make a big pie in sports requires competitive balance across the teams. That's why most sports leagues take actions to limit the extent of inequality among teams. Examples of balancing actions include giving better draft choices to teams that finish at the bottom of the standings; capping the number of players on a team's roster; and restricting the amount that teams can spend to acquire talent.

It wouldn't be fair if one team could have 30 players on its bench while the rival only had 15. That's not controversial. Would it be fair if one team could have twice the payroll and thereby attract better talent? Sure, some teams have had a high payroll and a poor record, but that's the exception, not the rule.

The NBA believes that maintaining a healthy competitive balance among teams is essential to growing the largest pie. That led the owners to seek a hard salary cap for each team. This was not an easy sell. Each player wants his team to do everything possible to win. (The fans feel the same way.) And the players don't like the fact that a team salary cap means that if one of their teammates gets paid more, there is less money left under the cap to pay the rest.

One dimension of the collective bargaining was over the ground rules—everything from team salary caps to drug testing—designed to expand the pie.[25] This was all done in the shadow of a negotiation over a single number, the revenue share that determines how that giant pie would get divided up. Under the prior bargaining agreement, the players collectively were paid 57 percent of "Basketball Related Income" or BRI. This is a formula that starts with total television, arena, and other basketball-related revenue and then subtracts agreed-upon expenses.

If you read that Stephen Curry has a $40.23m salary, that isn't exactly right. To figure out Curry's actual take-home pay, you add up the salaries of every player and see how that compares to the players' share of BRI. When the players' share was 57 percent and the salaries added up to 60 percent of BRI, every player took a 5 percent haircut, and that brought the salaries back down to 57 percent. Conversely, if the salaries only added up to 50 percent of BRI, everyone got a 14 percent pay increase to bring the total back up to 57 percent. No matter what the contract salaries added up to, the owners were on the hook for no more and no less than the players' share of BRI.

From the owners' perspective, a 57 percent share was too high. By their count, they had jointly lost $300 million in the prior season—which comes out to an average $10m loss per team. Twenty-two of the thirty teams were in the red. The owners came into the negotiation wanting to stop the operating losses.

The players naturally wanted to get as much of the revenue as they could. Without them, there's no game. After the negotiations broke down and the owners instituted a lockout, we saw that there's also no game without the owners. (A few players went off to Europe, but that was far from attractive for most.)

By late November, the negotiations were tense. The players had dissolved their labor union as a way to threaten antitrust action. The NBA had canceled the season through December 15. Each day lost was costing both sides millions. The two sides were close. The owners had come up to a 50:50 split of BRI and the players had come down to a 51:49 split.[26] Neither party was willing to make the last concession needed to reach an agreement.

The two sides had done their best to create a large pie. While there wasn't a hard cap on what each team could spend, the owners and players had worked out a series of taxes that penalized teams for spending well above the average. But the inability to agree on a division was leading to no pie at all.

The solution that broke the deadlock was a payment rule that adjusted the players' share based on the actual revenue received relative to the forecasted amount. The final deal was:

Total Player Salaries =

50% of Forecasted BRI + 60.5% × (Actual BRI − Forecasted BRI)

The share was capped above at 51 percent and below by 49 percent.

The way to reach an agreement is to give the other side what they want (so as to get what you want). The players were determined to get 51 percent of BRI. If total revenue ended up being more than forecasted, the owners could afford to be more generous. The players would get 60.5 percent of the upside. That allowed the players to get what they wanted. If revenue was 10.5 percent or more above forecast, the players would get their full 51 percent.

If the revenue results were less than forecasted, the owners wouldn't have to pay more than 50 percent and could go down as low as 49 percent. With that sliding scale, the owners wouldn't lose money at the targeted forecast or even if revenue slightly missed its target. The owners got the downside protection they wanted, and the fans, owners, and players got their season.

The two sides reached a contingent agreement that helped both sides deal with an uncertain pie. As things turned out, revenue was more than 10.5 percent above forecast. The players got their 51 percent and the owners made more money, too. The agreement worked so well that when it came time for renewal in 2016, both sides stuck to the formula without the need for a disruption.

Smart Trades

If the other side is getting what they want, does that mean you should get what you want, too? The answer is yes, though with a bit of a caution. You have to be careful with what is meant by what you want.

When I went to buy a Chevy Bolt, there were three specs I cared about: year, color, and packages. It was late in 2019 and I wanted one of the 2020 models. The two model years were nearly identical, but I figured the 2020 model would hold its value a bit better. I wanted the Cayenne Orange metal paint. And I didn't want the $595 infotainment package.

I ended up with a 2019 Kinetic Blue Bolt with infotainment. Does that mean I lost the negotiation because I didn't get what I wanted on any of my three goals? Not at all. The dealer cared more than I did about each one and thus I did better by letting the dealer win.

I began the process by calling a few dealerships to determine my options. Sadly, none of them had any 2019 cars in Cayenne Orange or without infotainment. I could get the exact car I wanted in a 2020 model. But the best price I could get was the dealer cost of $37,085 plus a $3,000 dealer profit.

Buying the perfect 2020 model year car turned out to be my BATNA. I wrote down the relevant factors in a table. The 2020 model year was worth an extra $1,500 based on its higher resale value and that amazing Cayenne Orange color. Thus, I started with a loss of $1,500 for the Premier 2019 model in blue. On the next line, I took into account having to buy the infotainment package on the 2019 car. The system was worth $295 from my viewpoint. Unfortunately, the infotainment package raised the price by $595. So far, I was $1,800 below my BATNA.

I negotiated a price based on cost plus dealer profit. GM had raised the dealer cost from $36,085 to $37,085 on the 2020 model. Going with the 2019 model saved me $1,000. The biggest difference was the dealer profit. The dealer was willing to accept a $500 profit on the leftover 2019 car compared to the $3,000 profit they required on one of their 2020 model-year allocations. That was a $2,500 gain.

	GAIN IN 2019 MODEL OVER 2020 MODEL
COLOR + MODEL YEAR	–$1,500
INFOTAINMENT VALUE	$295
INFOTAINMENT COST	–$595
REDUCED DEALER COST	$1,000
REDUCED DEALER PROFIT	$2,500
NET GAIN	**$1,700**

Taking everything into account, buying the 2019 model was $1,700 better for me than getting my perfect car. I lost out on color, infotainment, and model year because the dealer cared more than I did about those choices and made it up to me in price.*

In short, I won by losing. And so can you. When I say you should give the other side what it wants, by that I mean you should give the other side what it wants when it wants something more than you do. And they should pay you for that in terms of a better price. That is how you create pie.

Similarly, if you want something more than the other side, they should give it to you, and you should be the one paying for it. The person who wants it more is the one willing to pay more.

There is a temptation to keep score on who won which issue and then even out the wins. That is the wrong calculation. Provided money

---

* Did I split the pie with the dealer? I'm not sure. I was up $1,700 and they were up $500. While it looks like I was ahead, there may have been hidden dealer incentives based on total sales. Or, they could have ended up being really stuck with the car and having to sell it at a $1,200 loss; if so, a $500 profit was $1,700 better than their BATNA. The dealer also makes money on future servicing (assuming I go to them). I did manage to close the deal before Connecticut lowered its BEV tax rebate from $3,000 to $1,500. With the federal $7,500 tax rebate, the state $3,000 rebate, and the General Motors $750 educator discount, it was hard to say no.

can compensate the losing side, both sides can come out ahead. We turn to see how this works out in a house price negotiation.

Andy and Ben were looking to buy their first house. They found a well-maintained ranch house outside of Tucson with an asking price of $650,000. Taking into account the potential to find a better deal by searching more, they thought the ranch house was worth $620,000 and offered $605,000. After some back-and-forth, the sellers came down to $630,000 and the buyers came up to their $620,000 limit. The two sides were close but hadn't managed to reach an agreement. Neither was willing to move as each felt the price was equivalent to their BATNA.

At this point, they looked for some creative solutions to bridge the gap. Andy offered to bridge the gap if the sellers would throw in the living room and dining room furniture. He valued the furniture at $10,000, so he was willing to pay $630,000 with the furniture included.

The sellers appreciated the offer. They were downsizing and to them the furniture was only worth $6,000. It made sense to include the furniture in the sale, they said. The price, however, would have to go up to $636,000. Still no deal, though they were getting closer. The gap was now just $6,000.

It was Ben's turn to be creative. Was it possible to move up the closing date to August, in time for the start of the school year? The value of closing in August compared to September was $20,000, which meant they could increase their offer to $650,000.

While the owners preferred a September closing as they didn't yet have a new place to live, they figured if need be, they could put their items in storage. The extra value of closing in September compared to August was only $10,000 to them. That meant they were willing to close in August if the price were to increase from $636,000 to $646,000.

Now there was a $4,000 pie. The two sides were open with each other about the new valuations and closed the deal at $648,000. Before the creative solutions, they had a gap or negative pie of $10,000. The solutions created $14,000 of value and thus a net $4,000 pie that they split.

The buyers "won" on both issues: they got the furniture and an earlier closing date. The sellers equally "won" with the increased purchase price. Of course, the buyers would like to have gotten their way on both issues *and* not paid a higher price. This is no different than my trying to get the 2020 model year at the 2019 price. You can try, but . . . a more productive approach is to agree that the side that cares more wins and even things out with price.

In a sense, negotiation over who wins each issue should be like shopping in a store. You wouldn't buy something that costs $10,000 if the value to you is only $6,000. The same is true in a negotiation. You don't want to win on something that costs the other side $10,000 if the value to you is only $6,000. That's why the seller doesn't want to win on the earlier closing date or keep the furniture.

The difference between a negotiation and a store is there are no price tags. If the two sides are open with each other about valuations, it is as if they know the prices and can make the smart trades that increase the pie and avoid the poor trades that shrink the pie.

I want to consider one last wrinkle. What if the sellers had also wanted an earlier closing date and this was worth $10,000 to them? In that circumstance, neither side wants to wait until September. The only question is how the price should adjust. One view is that no adjustment is needed since both sides want the same thing.

The value of the $630,000 bid to the sellers is now $630,000 + $10,000 (closing date) − $6,000 (furniture) = $634,000 or $4,000 above their BATNA.

The cost of the $630,000 bid to the buyers is now $630,000 − $20,000 (closing date) − $10,000 (furniture) = $600,000 or $20,000 below their BATNA.

It's true that moving the closing date forward has made a deal possible at the prior offer of $630,000. It's also true that moving the closing date forward has made a deal possible at the prior asking price of $636,000. Just because both prices work doesn't mean we should pick one or split the difference. We want to split the pie.

At a $630,000 price, we have a $24,000 pie that is being split $4,000 and $20,000. At a $636,000 price, we have a $24,000 pie that is being split $10,000 and $14,000. To make an even split, the price must rise to $638,000 so that each side is $12,000 ahead.

The buyers value the earlier closing date at $10,000 more than the sellers and thus should increase their offer by $5,000 to even things out. If we start at the midpoint between the $630,000 offer and the $636,000 ask and add $5,000, we get to the $638,000 price that splits the pie.*

The reason to adjust the price is that neither the $10,000 nor the $20,000 gain exists unless the two sides reach an agreement on how to split it. This is no different than the CEMA case. Both the buyer and seller want the CEMA to take place. They have different gains based on the tax code. Under the default, the seller was only going to get about 20 percent of the gains. Here, absent a price adjustment, the seller would only get $4,000 of a $24,000 pie. The seller should hold out for half.

When only one side gets what it wants, it is easy to see why it needs to compensate the other side in order to split the pie. Even when both sides want the same thing, they may want it to a different degree. Absent compensation, the result is pie that's unevenly split. Both sides are still needed to create the pie. Money is the great equalizer and allows the two sides to split the pie.

---

* Before the change in closing date, the $633,000 midpoint price was $3,000 worse than no deal for both sides. The new closing date plus a $5,000 price adjustment is worth $15,000 more to each side, leaving both sides ahead by $12,000.

———

Chapter 17

WHAT IF THE PARTIES SEE DIFFERENT PIES?

It is typical for one side to be more optimistic than the other: a poker player thinks he will win the pot, while other players call his bet; an athlete thinks her team will win the championship, while the rival teams are equally confident; an entrepreneur thinks the business will be the next Amazon or Tesla, while potential investors are not so sure.

In these situations, it is tricky to calculate the pie because the parties see the pie differently. How do you negotiate when the parties can't agree on the basics? How do you split the pie if you can't agree on what the pie is?

One option we've discussed is to wait until the pie materializes. The parties don't have to agree ahead of time what the pie will be; they just need to agree in advance to split whatever pie arises. But if the two sides have different views about what the pie is likely to be, there's a better option.

I'll illustrate how divergent views can create a bigger pie. I do this via an extended negotiation example. In the Zinc-It (rhymes with trinket) case, an inventor is much more optimistic about a drug's chance of regulatory approval than is the potential buyer. As you read the case, think about how you would negotiate with such an individual. And if you were the inventor, what would you ask for?

Zinc-It

Ali Hasan had always wanted to be an inventor. In high school, he was a runner-up in the Intel Science Talent Search. He went on to study chemistry at MIT, before earning an MD from Tufts. Dr. Hasan's day job was radiation oncology in private practice, but weekends were a chance to experiment. His latest experiment was highly personal. Hasan's father was suffering from acid reflux, a condition that is both extremely unpleasant and dangerous, as it can lead to esophageal cancer. Hasan experimented with traditional medicines along with minerals, and settled on a compound made up of turmeric, barley grass, and zinc salts. This compound was added to calcium carbonate, the main ingredient in Tums, and compressed into a tablet.

After seeing dramatic benefits for his father, Dr. Hasan did a pilot study and used the data to obtain a patent on the use of zinc salts for acid reflux. The results were published in the *American Journal of Gastroenterology*. When the article came out, Hasan started receiving inquiries from companies looking to obtain an exclusive license to the patent. One company had plans to use the tablet as a competitor to Tums. The "Zums" team was not going to apply for Food and Drug Administration (FDA) approval; they would sell Hasan's in-

vention as a dietary supplement. Hasan was both surprised and pleased when Zums made a $20 million all-cash offer.

While this was a great option, as a physician and scientist, Hasan wanted the invention to have the credibility of a medicine, not a dietary supplement. That was not an option with Zums, who had no experience or interest in seeking FDA approval. Hasan had also been talking with another potential buyer of the license. The "Zinc-It" team had experience with the FDA approval process and was willing to pursue that approach. After some back-and-forth discussions with Zinc-It, the following five packages were being considered:

PACKAGE	UP-FRONT	BONUS (if FDA approval)	EXPECTED VALUES (see discussion below)
A	$25m	$0	$25m : $5m
B	$20m	$15m	$29m : $8.5m
C	$20m	$10m	$26m : $9m
D	$17m	$15m	$26m : $11.5m
E	$12m	$20m	$24m : $16m

Getting FDA approval would be a huge boost to sales, and Zinc-It was willing to commit to the process. If successful, the company expected to earn $120 million in profits over the life of the drug. If the FDA did not grant approval, Zinc-It would settle for the dietary supplement route, where its estimated lifetime profits would be $20m.

The Zinc-It team estimated that Hasan's compound only had a 10 percent chance of winning approval. Even after hearing Zinc-It's estimate, Hasan still believed the efficacy of the drug was so great there was a 60 percent chance it would be approved. The two sides fundamentally disagreed about the chance of FDA approval.

That also meant they disagreed about the pie and the value of each potential package. For example, the expected value of Package B to Hasan was $20m + 0.60 × $15m + 0.40 × $0 = $29m. There was a sure $20m up-front payment along with a $15m bonus that Hasan would get 60 percent of the time (and a zero bonus 40 percent of the time). For Zinc-It, the expected profit associated with offer B was $8.5m. When FDA approval didn't happen, which was 90 percent of the time, Zinc-It paid Hasan $20m up front and that was just covered by the $20m it made selling the zinc salt tablet as a supplement—so Zinc-It made nothing. In the other 10 percent of the time when the FDA did approve the drug, Zinc-It took in $120m and paid Hasan $20m up front plus a $15m bonus, leaving a net gain of $85m. A 10 percent chance of $85m was worth $8.5m. The numbers in the right-most column represent these calculations for all five offers.

Given the outstanding Zums offer, Zinc-It knew it couldn't buy the company with an offer worth anything less than $20 million to Hasan. That was the Zums offer and Hasan's BATNA.

Zinc-It's BATNA was continuing with business as usual. That meant Hasan could never get Zinc-It to pay anything above what it expected to earn from the deal. The drug's potential expected profits from Zinc-It's perspective (before paying Hasan) were

$$90\% \times \$20m + 10\% \times \$120m = \$18m + \$12m = \$30m$$

Zinc-It's expected profit would be the extent to which its contract with Hasan had an expected cost below $30m. Thus the $25m payment under package A leaves a $5m average profit for Zinc-It.

Those are all the background facts. There is no potential to go back and renegotiate Zums's $20 million offer to a higher number. And there are no other potential bidders. At this point, you should think about what you would ask for as Hasan and what you would offer as Zinc-It. What is the fair deal in this case?

Better than just thinking about your answer is to play it out. Before reading on, I encourage you to find a friend or colleague with whom to negotiate this case. If you don't have a partner, no worries: play out the negotiation in your head. Where do you expect to end up?

As you negotiate the case, I ask that you ignore risk. I fully recognize that risk is an important phenomenon. But there is enough going on that I want to keep things simple and focus on the different beliefs. Thus, I ask you to evaluate each option only by its expected value.

The case provides five different options to consider. For the start (say fifteen minutes if you play it out), please stick to these options. After that time, feel free to come up with new options. If you can reach a quick agreement on A–E, it's fine to move on to new options sooner. But if you haven't reached an agreement on A–E by fifteen minutes, consider adding new options into the mix.

The first step as you prepare is to calculate the pie. The different beliefs are what makes this tricky. As always, the pie is the extent to which the two sides beat their BATNAs. The BATNA for Hasan is a deal worth $20m and the BATNA for Zinc-It is the status quo profits. Any profits to Zinc-It from this deal are a gain over its BATNA. Rather than carry around Zinc-It's status quo profits in all our calculations, it is simpler to think of Zinc-It's no-deal profit as $0. Thus, the pie is the sum of Hasan's expected payoff and Zinc-It's expected profits from a deal compared to $20m.

For example, under option A, the two expected values are $25m + $5m = $30m, which is a $10m gain over their BATNAs. These expected values are from the right-hand column in the first table and are copied into the middle column in the next table.

If the two parties agree on B, the combined payoffs are $37.5m, which is $17.5m greater than the $20m payoffs under no deal. That $17.5m is the pie. In each case, we calculate the pie by adding up the expected payoffs under the agreement and subtracting $20m (to take account of the BATNAs).

PACKAGE	EXPECTED VALUES	THE PIE
A	$25m + $5m	$30m – ($20m + $0) = $10.0m
B	$29m + $8.5m	$37.5m – ($20m + $0) = $17.5m
C	$26m + $9m	$35m – ($20m + $0) = $15.0m
D	$26m + $11.5m	$37.5m – ($20m + $0) = $17.5m
E	$24m + $16m	$40m – ($20m + $0) = $20.0m

Here are a few quick observations. The pie is smallest under A and largest under E. The pie is the same under B and D. Hasan's favorite option is B, while E is best for Zinc-It. And both sides prefer B to A.

Having seen this case play out literally thousands of times, there are several different ways people approach the negotiation.

Play hardball: One side offers just a bit over the other side's BATNA.
Employ alternating removals: I'll take my favorite option off the table if you take your favorite off the table.
Plot the options: Use a graph to show which option best splits the pie.
Split the ex post pie.
Trade beets for broccoli: Give each side what it wants.
Go long: How far can you go?

Spoiler alert: if you are planning to do the negotiation, stop reading here and then come back when you are done.

Play Hardball

While I believe in the 50:50 split, you'll come across people who will try to get more than half—sometimes, a lot more than half. In the case of a deal based solely on an up-front payment, the potential range of up-front payments is $20m to $30m. Hasan has an offer of $20m, so he will never accept anything less. And if Zinc-It pays more than $30m, it would expect to lose money. At a $20m up-front payment, the whole $10m pie goes to Zinc-It, while at a $30m up-front payment, the whole $10m pie goes to Hasan. In option A, the $10m pie is split right down the middle. For Hasan, $25m is $5m better than the Zums offer, and Zinc-It expects to make $5m.

How should you respond if someone asks for more than half the pie? Everything with regard to the pie is perfectly symmetric. If the other side offers a 60:40 division of the pie in its favor, you can come back with 60:40 in your favor. For every offer there is an equal and opposite counteroffer. With apologies to *Annie Get Your Gun,* anything they can do, you can do equally.

And yet, there is an issue if you take up this approach too literally. Consider the following transcript from one negotiation. Hasan takes the flip to an extreme and gets himself in some hot water.

> **Zinc-It (buyer):** We should just cut to the chase.
>
> **Hasan (seller):** I agree.
>
> **Zinc-It:** I'm clear that Zums is offering you $20 million.
>
> **Hasan:** That is correct.
>
> **Zinc-It:** And we are prepared to beat that.
>
> **Hasan:** Excellent.
>
> **Zinc-It:** Yes, and our offer is $20 million and ten dollars ($20,000,010).
>
> **Hasan:** ???
>
> **Zinc-It:** Yes.
>
> **Hasan:** When you said beat that, I thought you meant in some sort of significant way.
>
> **Zinc-It:** I did. $20,000,010 is $10 more than you're being offered by Zums.
>
> **Hasan:** I'm not quite sure if that makes sense from a business perspective on our end of the deal. Having gone through the numbers I know your company is willing to pay $30 million. So,

if we use your logic, you should give us $29,999,990, which is exactly the same scenario in which you're putting—

Zinc-It: We should speak rationally about this $29 million, when you're only being offered $20 million by Zums.

Hasan: Well, okay, if we made a deal for $29,999,990, you're saving $10. Shouldn't you be willing to give up some—

Zinc-It: I think you're getting a little bit greedy when you ask for $10 million more than you're being offered by Zums.

Hasan: I think you're getting a little bit greedy.

Zinc-It: Okay, I'm out of here, thank you.

With that the buyer leaves the room.

One insulting offer was matched by an equally insulting offer the other way. When an offer is insulting, it works better to propose a hypothetical flip rather than an actual flip. If the pie is $10 million and someone offers you $10, rather than flip the offer and give them $10, flip the offer in a more hypothetical fashion:

> You've offered me $10 of a $10 million pie. I imagine that were I to propose you get $10 and I take $9,999,990, you'd be mighty upset. I wouldn't do that because that's not how I negotiate. But understand that the way I feel about your $10 offer is exactly how you would feel were I to offer you only $10.

I call this FFWW, shorthand for Fight Fire With Water. By offering only $10 the other side has lit a fire. You can fight back in kind with fire and offer them $10. That leads to escalation. When someone lights a fire, the smarter move is to put out the fire.

If you put out the fire and persuade the other side to split the pie, that doesn't mean you should agree on package A. It's a small pie. Because the two sides see the world differently, it is possible for both to do better: B, C, and D are all better than A for both sides.

Employ Alternating Removals

In practice, how do negotiators make decisions between a list of options? A common tactic is alternating removals: I'll get rid of this if you get rid of that. I'll take E off the table if you take B off the table. While such a procedure might be seen as fair, I should be clear up front: I think this is a misguided view. There is nothing fair about trading away options.

Here's an example where Zinc-It plays this game with Hasan and his lawyer.

Zinc-It: Let's work to get something off the table here. Let's make some progress and get to—

Hasan's Lawyer: Sounds like E is off the table.

Zinc-It: No, E is not off the table.

Hasan's Lawyer: We've both discussed that E doesn't work well for either of us so we should just try to—

Zinc-It: E may not be very good for you, but it works really well for me. If you want to cut something, I'll take E off if we can also take B off.

Hasan's Lawyer: No. No, no, no, no, no, absolutely not!

Zinc-It: I think we both need to make a compromise.

Hasan's Lawyer: B stays on the table.

Zinc-It: B can't stay on the table if you want—

Hasan's Lawyer: I think we should compromise and take E off the table.

Zinc-It: You're not listening to how this is disadvantageous for me.

Hasan's Lawyer: No, no, no. I hear what you're saying, and I'm saying we're not going to go that way. We're going to take E off the table. We'll leave B there.

Zinc-It: I don't think you really understand. I will not compromise on E unless you make a compromise on B. And that will leave us—

Hasan's Lawyer: You can reconsider because we're not going to do that.

Hasan (undercutting the lawyer): I think we can do that, I think we can do that.

Zinc-It: That's fabulous. Thank you. Finally, we have someone who is willing to make compromises for the better of this negotiation. . . . We're down to C and D.

This is what happens when people don't apply the pie. They come up with procedures that superficially sound fair but have no underlying principle behind them.

There's nothing to justify the idea that I'll take E off the table if you take B off the table. It sounds fair as each side is giving up its best option. The problem is that E is extremely lopsided, while B offers a near perfect split of the pie. Playing this game typically leads to D, which has the same pie as B but is split way in favor of Zinc-It.

Indeed, if the other party thinks you'll play this game, they'll add F, G, H, I, J, K, L, M, N, O, and P of terrible options from your perspective. Getting rid of these options in return for eliminating A, B, C, and D will be seen as fair. Actually, these were just decoys, and you'll end up with option E or maybe something worse. You'll end up somewhere in the middle of a set of bad offers that have been put on the table. There's nothing particularly fair about that.

The idea of procedural fairness is very powerful. You start a process and that process gains momentum. Each side makes concessions. The participants see this as reciprocity. Each side is giving up something. This reciprocity leads people to think the process is fair.

And yet, there is no true reciprocity. The concessions need not be equivalent. It makes no sense to give up a fair outcome to get rid of an unfair one. *It makes no sense to give up a fair outcome, period.* The parties are led to follow something they see as a fair process rather than seek a fair outcome. But there is nothing fair about the process or the result. The reciprocity in alternating removals is a mirage. Along with sacrificing fair outcomes, it creates incentives for people to game the negotiation by creating bad options they can later give up.

So far, I've emphasized what *not* to do. Let's turn our attention to some smarter moves.

Plot the Options

Looking at all the numbers can make one's eyes water. The two sides can go back and forth endlessly on the merits of B versus D. If the options are plotted on a graph, everything becomes much clearer.

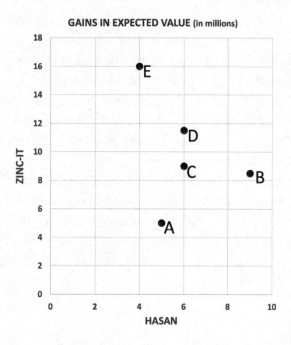

GAINS IN EXPECTED VALUE (in millions)

One sees that A perfectly splits the $10m pie. It is also clear both sides prefer B to A, so that pretty much makes A a nonstarter. Option E creates the largest pie, but the split is extremely uneven. Goodbye E. Hasan is indifferent between C and D, while Zinc-It prefers D. No reason to pick C. That leaves B and D.

The pie is the same size in both cases (at $17.5m). But as can be seen right away in the graph, the split in B is nearly 50:50, while the split is far more uneven in D. The graph makes a clear and compelling case for B. Zinc-It might not like the conclusion, but there is no effective counter. Once the five options are put on a graph, the fair result should be apparent to both sides. The negotiation can be wrapped up with little wasted time.

Up to this point, we have focused on negotiations over the five specified options. Once we are open to the idea of creating new options, there is the potential to create a much bigger pie

Split the Ex Post Pie

In this scenario, Hasan and Zinc-It agree to disagree. While they don't agree on the chance of FDA approval, they agree that it is worth an extra $100m in profits, which they split. They go with a $20m upfront payment (to match Zums) and a $50m bonus.

In the event there's no FDA approval, both parties gain nothing from the deal. Hasan makes the same amount as with Zums, and Zinc-It just breaks even. In the event the FDA does approve, both sides are $50m ahead.

That seems fair. But there's a problem. Look at the valuations at the time the contract is signed. Hasan thinks this contract is worth $20m + 60% × $50m = $50m, which is $30m better than the Zums offer. Zinc-It only profits when there's FDA approval; its expected gain is 10% × $50m = $5m. We have a large pie at $35m, and it is very unevenly split.

Trade Beets for Broccoli

What does an ideal contract look like?

To answer that question, first consider a negotiation between Ai-Ping and Bo-Lin over how to divide three scoops of beets and three scoops of broccoli. Ai-Ping likes beets more than broccoli, while Bo-Lin prefers broccoli over beets. The wrong answer is to give each party half the beets and half the broccoli. Since Ai-Ping prefers beets and Bo-Lin prefers broccoli, it would be far better to give all the beets to Ai-Ping and all the broccoli to Bo-Lin.

In the Zinc-It case, we have up-front payments and bonus payments. The situation is like beets and broccoli. Hasan values each dollar of bonus payment at 60¢ while Zinc-It treats the cost at 10¢. The ex post split gives only half the bonus to Hasan. We should give *all* the bonus to Hasan. Each extra dollar of bonus creates an extra 50¢ of pie.

We can see this in the original table. With no bonus, the pie is $10m. If the bonus goes up to $15m (as in option B), this creates an extra $7.5m of pie, bringing the total pie to $17.5m. If the bonus goes all the way up to $20m (as in option E), this creates an extra $10m of pie, bringing the total up to $20m.

How far should we go? Just as with beets and broccoli, we should take things to an extreme. The more bonus we give to Hasan, the bigger the pie. The pie is biggest if we give Hasan a $100m bonus for FDA approval! That would create a $60m pie.

Why stop at $100m? Besides the fact that it is a very big number, if the bonus becomes too large then Zinc-It won't want the project to be successful. If Zinc-It deliberately tanks the project, Hasan will get nothing. Thus, Hasan wants to ensure that Zinc-It still has some incentive or at least not a negative incentive to get FDA approval. Total profits absent FDA approval are $20m and they rise to $120m with approval. Approval adds $100m to profits. If Zinc-It pays anything more than a $100m bonus, they would rather see the project fail.

Perhaps we should cap the maximum bonus at something below $100m to ensure Zinc-It has a strictly positive incentive to get approval. For simplicity, we'll put the cap at $100m.

Now that we've figured out how to make the pie as big as possible, how do we split it evenly? The more Zinc-It pays up front, the more pie that goes to Hasan, and, conversely, the less Zinc-It pays up front, the more pie that goes to Zinc-It. If we give all the broccoli or bonus to Hasan, we should give Zinc-It all the beets, which means Zinc-It gets to keep all the up-front money

We can use an Excel sheet to calculate the gains to each side for different-sized bonuses. In all cases, the up-front payment is $0. We have used the lowest up-front amount so as to give as much of the broccoli or bonus as possible to Hasan. As can be seen from the chart, a bonus just above $70m, $71.4m to be exact, creates equal gains to the two sides.

BONUS	GAIN TO HASAN	GAIN TO ZINC-IT
$10m	– $14m	$29m
$20m	– $8m	$28m
$30m	– $2m	$27m
$40m	$4m	$26m
$50m	$10m	$25m
$60m	$16m	$24m
$70m	**$22m**	**$23m**
$80m	$28m	$22m
$90m	$34m	$21m
$100m	$40m	$20m

People have been taught that the fair solution is a compromise—to meet somewhere in the middle. In the case of options A–E, that would suggest meeting at C. Meeting in the middle is like giving both sides half the beets and half the broccoli. It is fair, but it leads to a small pie. The way to expand the pie is to take things to extremes. The case of a $0 up-front payment with a $71.4m bonus also splits the pie, a pie that's almost $46m.

Why do people have trouble seeing this? I don't mean the exact number $71.4m. I mean, why do people resist the idea of a large bonus? When people negotiate this case, many fail to consider a large bonus or even any bonus above $20m.

One obstacle that creates a blind spot is the fact that a large bonus comes with a small up-front payment. Many Hasans take the view that if Zums is offering $20m up front then any Zinc-It offer must also have at least $20m up front. The negotiators take the position that the Zinc-It offer must beat the Zums offer in *all* dimensions.

Is there any truth to this? No. Taking things to an extreme should make this clear. As Hasan, would you be willing to take $19,999,999 up front to get a $50m bonus for FDA approval? I certainly hope so. You are risking $1 on the downside to get a 60 percent chance of $50m. If you wouldn't take that gamble, you might not want to risk crossing the street.

If Hasan insists on getting $20m up front, the bonus that splits the pie is $14.3m. The expected value of that deal is only $8.6m better than his BATNA, compared to the $22.9m expected gain under the $0 up front with a $71.4m bonus. Putting on the blinders doesn't just hurt Hasan; the expected profit to Zinc-It also falls from $22.9m to $8.6m. An unexpected advantage of agreeing to split the pie is that the other side has a strong incentive to prevent you from making mistakes that hurt you (as your mistakes drag them down, too).

OVERCOMING OBJECTIONS

It isn't enough to come up with a creative solution to expand the pie. You also have to sell the idea to the other side. That means anticipating and overcoming potential objections, such as Hasan should never accept an up-front payment below $20m. The total value of payments to Hasan must exceed $20m to beat the Zums offer, but that doesn't mean the up-front payment has to exceed $20m. We return to the topic of preparing to overcome objections in Chapter 20.

Another common mistake is for Zinc-It to try to persuade Hasan that the true probability of FDA approval is closer to 10 percent than

60 percent. Imagine that Zinc-It had the power to magically influence Hasan's thinking—perhaps something akin to Mr. Spock's Vulcan mind transfer. What probability would it want Hasan to employ?

One hundred percent! If Hasan thought that FDA approval were a sure thing, Hasan would value bonus payments the same as cash. Zinc-It could pay Hasan with a bonus and get $1 of value at a cost of 10¢.

I'm not proposing Zinc-It lie to Hasan and pretend the true probability of approval is 100 percent. But there's no value in persuading Hasan that the chance of success is anything less than 60 percent. Indeed, Zinc-It would do well to adopt Hasan's probability. Zinc-It could say:

> We think this is a great opportunity and are prepared to give you a $71.4m bonus. With a 60 percent chance of approval, this is worth $42.9 to you, which is $22.9 better than your Zums offer.

Turning to Hasan, what probability would he want to place in Zinc-It's head? The answer is 0. The greater the chance of success, the more costly it is for Zinc-It to give Hasan the big bonus he wants.

Think about beets and broccoli. Remember that Ai-Ping likes beets and Bo-Lin prefers broccoli. It is not helpful for Bo-Lin to say to Ai-Ping:

> This broccoli is amazing. It's more like broccolini than your average broccoli. It doesn't get caught in your teeth. Great taste, less stringy, perfectly cooked with garlic and olive oil. You have to try it!

What happens if Ai-Ping tries it and discovers just how good it is? Ai-Ping is then less keen to give up the broccoli. That makes it harder for Bo-Lin to get all the broccoli. Bo-Lin doesn't have to pretend that the broccoli tastes bad. But it is not in his interest to talk it up.

Similarly, Hasan does better when Zinc-It thinks the chance of FDA approval is low while Zinc-It does better when Hasan thinks the chance of FDA approval is high. There is a caveat. If Zinc-It thinks the chance of success is so low that it has no interest in buying the business or investing, then there's no deal to be done. The ideal situation from Hasan's perspective is that Zinc-It is optimistic about the business, enough to be excited about investing, but not so optimistic that it is very costly to pay Hasan a big bonus upon success.

People mistakenly think that to get an agreement, the two sides must see the world the same way. In fact, seeing the world the same way makes it harder to reach an agreement. To the extent that Ai-Ping and Bo-Lin feel similarly about beets and broccoli, it is harder to divide things up. To the extent that Hasan and Zinc-It feel similarly about the probability of FDA approval, it will be harder to reach an agreement as all payments will be zero-sum.

It is best for both parties to stick with the original probabilities. In that case, a \$71.4m bonus seems to create the largest pie that is evenly split. But that isn't right.

If we go to a \$100m bonus, the pie expands all the way to \$60m. The problem becomes how to split it evenly. If Zinc-It pays Hasan \$20m up front in addition to a \$100m bonus, Zinc-It will make \$0 if the drug is not approved and also \$0 if it is. Thus Zinc-It's payoff is \$0. And that means Hasan is getting the full \$60m pie.

To split the pie evenly means that Hasan would have to move \$30m of pie over to Zinc-It. The smart way to do this is not by reducing the bonus (which Hasan values more than Zinc-It). The smart way is by reducing the up-front fee. To move \$30m over, the up-front payment has to be reduced by \$30m.

Hold on a second. If we start with \$20m up front + \$100m bonus and reduce the up-front number by \$30m, that means the contract is –\$10m up front + \$100m bonus. Hasan pays Zinc-It \$10m to get this deal.

I recognize there are two issues with the contract. First, Hasan may not have \$10 million to spare. Second, this contract puts all the risk on Hasan. It starts to strain credibility that Hasan is indifferent to risk.

Those are fair critiques. But don't lose sight of the big picture.

Hasan should be pushing for the biggest possible bonus and the smallest possible up-front payment. And if he has the funds—perhaps from his last successful invention—he might even want to go negative.

Go Long

I anticipate that some of you will think it is folly to imagine that Hasan or anyone else might come up with the money and pay Zinc-It to go through the FDA process. Who would do something that crazy and take such a big risk?

Who, indeed? Which brings us to my first book contract. At the time, I was a young assistant professor at Princeton University. When I was an undergraduate at MIT, one of my very first economics professors was Avinash Dixit. Now Professor Dixit was my senior colleague at Princeton. Avinash and I were teaching the undergraduate game theory course and it was a popular class. We decided to see if we could write a popular book on the subject. The result was *Thinking Strategically*.

We showed the manuscript to Drake McFeely, who was then an economics editor at W. W. Norton. (He went on to become president and chairman of the company.) Drake was excited about publishing the book. He wasn't so excited that he was willing to give an advance, but he did offer the standard 15 percent royalty contract.

I was very optimistic about the book's potential to cross over from textbook to the general interest category. I asked Drake if Norton could see its way to a 30 percent royalty rate. Drake explained that there were substantial up-front costs, ranging from copyediting, typesetting, printing, advertising, and sample copies to overhead costs (office rent, his salary). If he gave us a 30 percent royalty, he wouldn't expect to recover those costs.

I asked if Drake had an estimate of those costs. As luck would have it, Drake had made a spreadsheet budget for the book. The costs added up to around $70,000. With that, I pushed a bit further.

If Avinash and I were to cover the up-front costs, would Norton raise the royalty rate to 30 percent?

You can think of this as a lot like Hasan's contract with a negative up-front payment. Instead of the traditional advance, we would pay the publisher to cover the up-front costs. And just like Hasan pays to get a bigger bonus, we would get a bigger royalty.

Drake thought about it. At that point, Norton would be taking no risk. If the book was successful, they would make less money, but it would be worth giving up some of the upside to eliminate all the downside. Avinash had published some more technical books before and I hadn't published any books. And who knew if there would be a general audience market for game theory. Drake agreed.

Now came the moment of truth. I was very optimistic, perhaps even overoptimistic, about the book's chances. Avinash, wiser and more experienced, applied some game theory to the situation. The publisher should know more than we do about the book's chance of success. If they are willing to offer us this deal, we shouldn't take it. Avinash decided to go with the status quo. And with that, I followed suit.

As things turned out, Thinking Strategically sold over 250,000 copies in the United States and almost the same in seventeen translations. It was a number one bestseller in Israel—where game theory seems to be in the water. Had we taken the 30 percent royalty deal, it would have been worth over $1 million more!

I couldn't have come up with the $10 million Hasan needed to invest. But I could have scraped together my half of the $70,000. When Avinash said no, I could still have bought my half of the extra 15 percent. Norton would pay a 22.5 percent royalty. Avinash and I would split the first 15 percent and I would get the next 7.5 percent for my $35,000. Had I been able to find $70,000, I could have bought the entire extra 15 percent royalty.

They say you learn more from your mistakes than your successes. This was a dear lesson.

Although I missed out, the idea seems to be catching on. Michael

Lewis, the bestselling author of *Liar's Poker*, *The Big Short*, and *The Undoing Project*, has published all sixteen books he's written since 1999 with W. W. Norton. Why Norton? They are one of the few remaining independent presses. They have legendary editors such as Drake McFeely and Starling Lawrence. And Lewis gets to bet on himself: he gets no advance and splits the profit pie 50:50 with Norton.* That's what I call *The Big Long*.

---

* Splitting the profits improves incentives and thereby creates a bigger pie. With royalties all depending on profits, the author has an extra incentive to deliver a great book. So along with eliminating the risk of paying out a big advance and ending up with a dud, there are fewer duds. And there's less whining by authors. When author royalty is a share of revenue, the author just wants to maximize revenues while the publisher cares about profits. Thus, every author thinks the publisher hasn't spent enough to promote their book—which is, of course, true.

Chapter 18

MAKING THE OTHER SIDE'S CASE

At Yale, I teach the core negotiation course alongside Daylian Cain. Daylian has an unusual collection of interests. He is an expert on business ethics and he is also an expert poker player. Think about that.

Before turning to one of his negotiation insights, allow me to share a lesson from his research. Daylian is best known for his work on conflict of interest. You might think that when a conflict of interest arises—a doctor who gets paid if their patient enrolls in a medical trial or a real estate agent who represents both the buyer and seller—we want the person to disclose the conflict. What Daylian and his coauthors discovered is that disclosure can make the conflict-of-interest problem even worse.[27] The person, having disclosed the conflict, feels unburdened to act in a more self-interested manner. To make matters worse, the person now expects their advice to be discounted and thus exaggerates the advice. This wouldn't be a problem if the party on the other side of the disclosure took what they hear with a larger grain of salt. But receivers of biased information don't come close to providing the appropriate level of a correction, partly out of some sense of obligation to help the advisor who has earned their trust by disclosing that they will not necessarily be acting in their interest.

When Daylian is teaching executives how to negotiate, he has them think about negotiating with a young child who doesn't want to get out of a swimming pool. The parent says it is time to go home and the kid starts crying. The kid is crying for two reasons. First, the kid doesn't want to leave the pool. Second, and the point typically missed, the kid doesn't have the vocabulary or language skills to make his or her case. The kid is frustrated. The kid is thinking: if only I could explain why the pool is so great, I'm sure I could persuade my parent to let me stay another ten minutes. What comes out is: Waaah, waaah, sob.

Daylian's solution is for the parent to make the kid's argument.

I know that being in the pool is great. You can do somersaults. You can enjoy feeling weightless. I'd like to spend my entire life underwater, too. But, we have to eat at some point. You might not be hungry now, though you will be by the time we get home. And you aren't the only one coming home for dinner. That's why it's time to leave.

Here's the big lesson. We can't always get our way. But we can always be understood. What works for children also works well for adults.

People often argue and keep negotiating because they think: If only the other side better understood my position, I would get my way. Taking and presenting the other side's perspective demonstrates they are being understood even if they aren't getting their way. The fact that you've chosen a different outcome is not from a lack of understanding; it is because there are other factors you judge to be more important.

If you think A is the right answer but anticipate that the other side is in favor of B, make an impassioned case for B. Argue for B more eloquently than any B supporter. And then, just when the other side is ready for you to sign on to B, explain why A is really the better choice.

Those in favor of B have nothing left to say. All their arguments have been made, so there's no need to repeat them. Moreover, the reason they aren't getting B isn't that you don't understand their perspective. It is that there are other, more compelling reasons.

When you present the other side's argument, be sure to check you've gotten it right. The goal is to be allocentric and show that you understand their position. There is no better way to do so than to articulate the argument from their perspective. But you might not have gotten it right or you may have left something out. Take a pause and check. Just because you are making the argument doesn't mean you are agreeing with it. You want to get the argument down the way the other side would make it.

Chris Voss makes a similar point in *Never Split the Difference*. One of his goals is to get the other side to say: "That's right." When they say "That's right" it means you've demonstrated that you understand their position.

Let's take this approach to a negotiation example. In the Zinc-It case, there were five proposals on the table at the start of the negotiation, as recapped in the table.

PACKAGE	UP-FRONT	BONUS	EXPECTED GAINS	THE PIE
A	$25m	$0	$5m + $5m	$10.0m
B	$20m	$15m	$9m + $8.5m	$17.5m
C	$20m	$10m	$6m + $9m	$15.0m
D	$17m	$15m	$6m + $11.5m	$17.5m
E	$12m	$20m	$4m + $16m	$20.0m

Zinc-It prefers package E. Not only does package E create the biggest pie at $20m, it also leads to the greatest gain for Zinc-It at $16m.

Were I in the role of Hasan, I'd first make the case for and against E, and then pivot to B. I'd highlight B's flaws and then show why it's still the best option.

I certainly understand why you want to get E. It has the highest profits for you and the largest pie. But even in your shoes I would have trouble defending E due to the large imbalance in terms of how the pie is split. I couldn't defend getting 80% of the pie.

I also understand why you dislike B. It leads to your lowest payoff among the viable options. (We were never going to pick A as both of us prefer B.) Indeed, I, too, have a problem with B. It is unfair. The pie is $17.5m and I am getting more than half. We should each be getting $8.75m. Instead, I'm getting $9m and you are only getting $8.5m. I have no defense to offer. I wish there were a way to make it up to you.

But that is not an argument for D. Option D has the very same pie as B, but the split is even more uneven. Whatever problem I have with B is only magnified in D.

Having made this case, there is little if anything for the other side to say in response. Instead of defending his first choice, Hasan shows all its flaws. This has two effects.

First, it takes all the wind from the sails of those who prefer D. They don't have anything left to criticize about B. More important, it shows the other side that you appreciate their concern. While there are issues with option B, those issues don't justify picking option D where the same problems appear but only more so.

We have a natural tendency to defend our positions from attack and to denigrate the arguments of others. The more we do so, the more the other side thinks we don't understand their position and argues back. By acknowledging the valid points on the other side, we prevent the argument.

Some will fear that if you accept the conclusion that the other side has some valid points, you'll have to give in to their preferred result. No. You have to present compelling reasons why your preferred result makes more sense. If no such arguments exist, you'll be on the losing side.

Exposing your weakness is a sign of strength. It's scary to do. I'm not always successful at it even though I know it's the better way.

I've consciously tried to follow this approach in this book. I've given examples that might make you uncomfortable with the pie solution. The Ionity and CD examples are cases in point. I did this because I appreciate the arguments made by those who reject the pie. I want to show you those arguments (along with my compelling counters) because I believe that when you see both sides, you'll come down in favor of splitting the pie. Indeed, that is what I hoped to have accomplished in discussing all the "Yes, but . . ." objections in Part III.

Chapter 19

SELLING YOUR SOLUTIONS

As you follow the advice in this book, you will have to persuade people to do things differently. Up until now, we have focused on the logical arguments. Here we look at some of the psychological factors that will help you be more persuasive.

The common theme throughout is to be more allocentric and less egocentric. By allocentric, I mean more centered on others. Too often, people focus on why something is good for them and less on why it is good for the other side. I see this in job recruiting. The student has a long, prepared speech about why they want to work for company X; instead, I ask them to talk about why company X wants to hire them.

How to Make an Offer That Gets Heard

A great way to break a logjam and expand the pie is to develop a new option that turns out to be better for all sides. But it may not be enough to come up with a creative solution. You have to get the other side to open up to the new possibility. If you are not careful, the other side might not be receptive even if it is in their interest. To help your cause, when you present a new idea, begin with the part they will like. Focus on the pie while they are still listening.

I'll illustrate this point using an example from the Zinc-It case. To make a big pie, the ideal contract has a very large bonus alongside a small up-front payment. In the negotiation transcript below, the Zinc-It rep tries to sell this idea and fails spectacularly.

Zinc-It: I'm going to pay you no salary—

Hasan: I'm sorry. I find this a little bit insulting since we've been working—

Zinc-It: —and $71.4 million in bonus.

Hasan: We've been working off this figure so far and I think you are not hearing us or acknowledging us.

Zinc-It: I'm just throwing out this value.

Hasan: That's a hard no.

Once Zinc-It says "no salary," Hasan doesn't hear another word. It is particularly ironic that Hasan then says "you are not hearing us." Hasan is the one who isn't listening.

That's not too surprising. The no-salary part of the offer is not attractive to Hasan. It is what Zinc-It likes about the offer.

Zinc-It's mistake was to lead with what they liked, not what the seller would like. The low up-front payment allowed for a turbocharged bonus. By the time the buyer got to this, the game was lost. Imagine instead the following dialogue.

Zinc-It: I'd like to pay you a huge bonus.

Hasan: Really? How big?

Zinc-It: $71.4 million.

Hasan: Okay, you've got my attention.

Zinc-It: A $71.4 million bonus creates the largest possible pie and divides it equally. Of course, in order for me to pay this size bonus and still divide the pie equally, it has to come with a smaller up-front payment.

Hasan: How small?

Zinc-It: Well, actually, nothing up front.

That's better. Zinc-It got Hasan's attention with the big bonus up front. But Zinc-It might still lose Hasan with the bad news at the end. Let's see if the third time is a charm.

Zinc-It: I'd like to pay you a huge bonus.

Hasan: Really? How big?

Zinc-It: $71.4 million.

Hasan: Okay, you've got my attention.

Zinc-It: A $71.4 million bonus creates the largest possible pie. [Does some calculations and shows that the pie is $46 million.] If I pay you a $71.4m bonus, that is worth 60% × $71.4m = $43m, which is $23m better than your Zums offer. That's great for you.

Hasan: And what do you get?

Zinc-It: The pie is $46m. You are getting $23m, and I'm getting $23m, too. We are splitting the pie perfectly in two.

There's an old joke about a farmer who has a horse that can talk. He goes to show off the horse to a friend. What's 1 + 1, the friend asks the horse, but the horse just says neigh. What's the capital of France? Again, just neigh. After a few more failed attempts, the farmer hits the horse with a two-by-four. The horse says: Why'd you do that? The friend is amazed that the horse truly can speak. The farmer explains: Of course he can, but first you have to get his attention.

Let me assure you that no animals were harmed in the making of this joke. While the joke is nothing special, the punch line serves as a good reminder: you have to get the other side's attention. What can you say that will break through natural resistance and motivate the other side to hear your proposal? That is how to present your offer.

Just as job seekers need to convey why the company wants to hire them, you want to convey why the result is a win for the other side. In coming up with a win-win solution, focus on the second win, the win for the other side.

Write the Other Side's Victory Speech

This is an idea developed by William Ury, coauthor of *Getting to Yes*. If you want the other side to accept a deal, think about how they are going to sell it to their supporters and to themselves. Explain why they will ultimately be happy with the agreement.

Ury was involved in advising the Colombian government in their peace talks with the FARC rebels. He asked the government team to truly take the other side's perspective, starting with where the process might end up.

> *Start off by imagining, we've reached an agreement. And imagine that the FARC leaders . . . had to describe this agreement—give a talk to all their people, as they've just done this past week—in which they describe this agreement as a kind of victory for them. Not that it couldn't be a victory for the government as well. But it had to be something they could sell to their own troops and explain—look, we've been fighting for 52 years, and we're laying down our weapons. They can't say it was all in vain. And so, we worked backward from that speech. We even simulated that speech. I asked the President's brother to give that speech to us as if he were the guerrilla commander. Then we said, OK, how can we make it easier for them to give that speech. What are the key interests, what are the key needs, that they have?[28]*

Once you have an idea of what is a possible end result, you can work backward to figure out how to get there.

Permission or Forgiveness

One of the challenges with trying something new is that you don't always know if you have permission to experiment in this fashion. If you are the big boss, you can give yourself permission. For the rest of us, we may not be sure if we have the authority.

If you can reach the decision maker, you can find out. That may not always be practical. In these circumstances, people often think they have to choose between asking for permission and forgiveness.

Asking for permission means not acting unless you can get authorization.

Asking for forgiveness means acting without authorization and hoping that you made the right call.

There's a better alternative. The better option is a contingent agreement. You and your negotiation partner both agree that X is better than A, B, or C. But you are not sure you have the authority to do X. For example, are you really able to pay out a $71m bonus? To be safe, the two of you agree to the following:

We will do X if we can get permission to do so. Otherwise, we agree to do B.

No one ever got fired for presenting a contingent plan. You don't have to worry about incentives. You know that X is better if it is allowed and thus you have every reason to push for it. If the person with authority agrees, you proceed with X. Otherwise, you still have a deal with option B.

Better than a No

Sometimes you will find that there is no deal to be done. Or, at least, no deal you have the authority to do. In those cases, you can go back with a no. Better yet, go back with a conditional yes.

To keep things simple, say the most you are authorized to pay is $1,000. The seller has convinced you they won't sell for anything less than $1,150. And you think the item may be worth that much.

Just like we had the creative option and the standard one, now the creative option is the deal that exceeds your limit and the standard one is "no deal."

> *Hey boss. I tried to buy the first edition copy for $900. It was a no-go. The seller seems determined to get at least $1,150. She showed me an appraisal for $1,200. And that seems like the going price for first editions. I went to my limit of $1,000 and she didn't take it. So, I walked away.*

Instead of walking away, try this:

> *The seller is willing to sell for $1,150. I didn't commit to give her that amount. But she has signed a contract promising to sell it to us for that price over the next 48 hours. If you want to pay that amount, we have a deal. I can also go back and offer something between $1,000 and $1,150.*

If you're the boss, this is far better than no deal. You are free to turn down the $1,150 asking price, but if that is attractive, you are done.

It may seem peculiar that the boss was willing to pay $1,150 but didn't give the negotiator authority to pay that amount. It is quite common to give a negotiating agent limited authority. One reason to do so is that the person can then honestly say $1,000 is their maximum price. The boss couldn't honestly say the same if the cap is less than their true limit. For that reason, the seller would prefer to negotiate with the person who is setting the cap and not the person who has to abide by it.

Let's turn this around. Why would you as a seller ever give the buyer this free option? You've given the other side a commitment to sell at a fixed price. They didn't pay you anything for this option. Meanwhile, this limits your flexibility were someone else to come by with a better price.

In fact, the buyer has given you something. They have agreed to bring your case to their boss. Put yourself in the buyer's shoes. What is the worst possible outcome from their perspective?

The worst outcome is they go to their boss and say:

I couldn't do the deal at $1,000. I managed to bring the seller down to $1,150. Can I have authorization to go up to that amount?

The boss gives that authority. The buyer then goes back to you only to discover the new price is $1,300. This is the nightmare scenario. If they are going to go back and get permission to stretch their budget, they want to know they'll be successful.

What the buyer is offering the seller in return for the option is the ability to go over his or her head. It isn't money; it is time and attention.

As the seller, you would prefer to deal with the real decision maker, the person who doesn't have any artificial budget limit. But the person you are negotiating with has been assigned to you for the very purpose of keeping the two of you apart. If you want to go over their head, you may have to give them something in return. Giving the option is your payment for getting access.

This issue arose when Seth and I were selling Honest Tea to Coca-Cola. Coke had offered us an option to buy the company in three years at a pre-specified price formula. While they said they were proceeding with the intention to buy the company at the end of the three years, there was no guarantee they would exercise their option. We insisted that we be given a put—which was the ability to require them to buy the company.

In order to give us a put, the Coke negotiating team needed to get permission from the board of directors. The last thing they wanted was to go to the board, only to discover we weren't really interested in a deal or had raised our asking price. If we wanted them to go to the board, we had to commit to doing the deal at the agreed-upon terms. We were asking for a put and that was beyond their authority to give us. They wanted our commitment that if they got us a put, the deal was done. We said yes. They got us the put. We gave them the call. The deal was done.

We can also turn this lesson around. We've been saying that if you are the buyer and can't close the deal given your authority, ask for an option rather than walk away with no deal. But say that you are the seller. You see the buyer is walking away and you don't want to come down in price. You could just let the person walk. Instead, we suggest you offer the other side an option rather than have them walk away empty-handed.

> *I'm sorry we can't reach an agreement at $1,000. Rather than go back and tell your boss there's no deal to be had, we propose you go back and let your boss know we are prepared to give you a 48-hour option. If you hit our $1,150 price, the deal is yours. We are prepared to put that in writing.*

"Yes If" Rather than "No Unless"

The idea of giving away an option can be a very effective tool in a job negotiation. Let's say you've been offered a salary of $63,000. You'd like to see if you can bring the number up to $68,000. Some folks try the "I won't accept if you don't hit $68,000." That's the "No unless" approach. I'm proposing you try the "Yes if." You can say:

> *If you can hit $68,000, I am prepared to say yes right now.*

Just as we discussed above, this is giving the buyer—in this case the buyer of your labor—an option to hire you.

Let's be allocentric and think about the situation from the employer's perspective. They are wondering what you are up to. They know there are two different reasons you might be negotiating with them.

One is that you want to reach an agreement and work for them. The other is that you want to use them to get a better BATNA so that you can then get a better deal with your preferred employer. In the back of their mind, they are trying to figure out which camp you are in.

This takes us back to Chapter 15. The employer is worried they are being used as a pawn. Unlike Boston University's Questrom School of Business, they may not have the ability or foresight to get you to commit in advance before deciding if they will meet the $68,000. You can take the lead and make the commitment. That's what the "Yes if" does.

Once you do so, they'll go the extra mile. The negotiation process is time consuming and costly. They would rather close the deal with you than start over again and pay the cost of negotiating with someone else. In addition, the fact that they are negotiating with you means you are currently their first choice.

Again, think about the situation from their position. It's costly to go out on a limb for someone and make an exception only to have that person turn you down. There are only so many times the HR person can go upstairs and ask for special treatment. And if word gets out how much they are willing to pay a new hire, some of the existing employees may feel they are due a raise. A firm might be willing to pay these costs, but only if it's confident it will get something in return, namely getting to hire you. Your "Yes if" gives them the confidence they need.

When you say "I won't accept if you don't," that leaves open what will happen if they do meet your conditions. You might not accept. This doubt in the employer's mind limits how far they are willing to push on your behalf, especially if they've been burned in the past. They may also infer something from the fact that you didn't say "Yes if." Once you say "Yes if" they know what they have to hit to close the deal.

Of course, there is a cost associated with saying "Yes if." If they meet your terms, you are supposed to say yes. If there were no cost associated with making this statement, it wouldn't convey the same information. If you aren't sure you're willing to accept if they meet your request, you shouldn't make this offer. Rather than go back to "No unless," you should think harder about what it would take to get you to "Yes if." What are the terms they could offer that would lead you to accept? Propose those terms. Or, if your main goal is to improve your BATNA, then appreciate that what you don't say may lead them to understand what you are up to.

PART V

NEGOTIATION MECHANICS

Sadly, you are going to negotiate with people who haven't read this book. It's sad for you because that will make your life more difficult. (Sad for me as that's a missed book sale.) The solution isn't to give away your copy. The solution is to start the negotiation with a conversation about how you'd like to negotiate.

The irony is that the way typical negotiations go isn't just bad for you, it is also bad for them. Just as you want to take the driver's seat if the car owner isn't sober, you want to steer the negotiation to a safer and more productive path when the other side employs the traditional approach.

I want to prepare you for how to sell the pie approach. For starters, you should be prepared for the likelihood that the other side won't be expecting the pie. You have to do more than introduce the idea—you will want to anticipate the objections so that you can preempt and counter them. That's what I've been doing throughout the book. In answering the "Yes, but" responses, I've been trying to anticipate and counter the objections people bring up. You'll want to anticipate the potential objections that apply in your specific case. And you'll want to explain what the pie is in your specific negotiation.

I'm not a fan of the winging-it school. The prep work discussed in Chapter 20 emphasizes the value of taking the other side's perspective. How will they see the pie and how will they respond to your arguments? The better you understand and communicate their perspective, the better you will be at selling your perspective.

Chapter 21 discusses what to reveal and what to keep hidden. I don't advise laying all your cards face-up on the table. Nor should you keep all your cards close to the vest. To create a pie, negotiators need to share information. Sharing means asking questions *and* answering them. All too often, people keep things hidden or tell white lies to avoid answering the question. I explain how to answer questions without putting yourself in a weak position.

I also want to prepare you for how to create and capture pie in more traditional negotiations for when you find yourself stuck in that situation. Most of Chapter 22 is based on debriefing negotiation transcripts in which the participants haven't adopted the pie approach. I discuss tools people use to capture more of the pie, and how not to destroy pie in the process. As you will see, there are plenty of land mines. You can say the wrong thing or not say the right thing. More often, you will have to deal with people on the other side who make your life difficult. I offer some suggestions for how to keep things on track.

Chapter 22 provides guidance on how to present an opening offer, when to respond in kind and when not to, how to negotiate with jerks, and, equally important, how not to become one. I discuss the value of anchoring and making precise bids, and the danger of going overboard with these strategies. We are taught the value of reciprocity, but reciprocity works two ways. There is a tendency to respond in kind when the other side is being obstinate. You don't want to escalate and fight fire with fire. You want to put out the fire. The way you negotiate should reinforce the idea of the pie and sell it to the other people at the table.

Chapter 20

PREPARING FOR A NEGOTIATION

Prussian general Helmuth von Moltke (1800–1891) said no battle plan extends with certainty beyond the first encounter with the enemy's main strength. Mike Tyson famously shortened this to everyone has a plan till they get punched in the mouth.[29] That doesn't mean you shouldn't plan. Quite the contrary. It means you need a series of flexible plans.

There are some obvious ways to prepare. You want to have your numbers done in advance so that you are not having to do calculations on the fly. In the Zinc-It case, for example, you should come in with a spreadsheet that calculates the payoffs for both you and the other side. It isn't enough to know how good the offer is for your side. You also want to know (or at least estimate) how well the other side is doing. To split the pie requires having a view of what the pie is. The spreadsheet should show the pie along with its division: how much each side is beating their BATNA. You want the spreadsheet to be flexible so that it can easily adapt to new offers.

You want to plan for what could go wrong—in particular, what happens if there's no deal. That means understanding your BATNA and that of the other side. This typically involves doing research (such as determining the ICANN dispute process or a landlord's legal obligation to find a new tenant) as well as finding alternative negotiating partners (such as Zums). If you don't know the BATNAs, you aren't prepared to split the pie.

Plan for how the other side will object to your proposal or even your ground rules. What is the other side likely to propose? A starting point is to consider what heuristic approach works most in their favor. How will you counter a proposal to split the gains in that fashion? You want to be prepared to show the potential flaws in other solutions.

Let's go all the way back to our 12-slice pizza example. Alice's BATNA is 4 slices and Bob's is just 2 slices. Bob should anticipate that Alice will ask for a proportional split, 8:4. Thus Bob should be prepared to show why proportional division doesn't make sense in general and, in particular, when one of the BATNAs goes to zero. Alice should anticipate that Bob will ask for an even 6:6 split. She should be ready to explain why that doesn't work if either of the BATNAs is 7 or more and thus why it can't be a general solution.

QUICK TEST

Bob proposes a 6:6 split. He argues as follows: Getting half the total is far better than the four slices you'd get if there's no deal. Since this beats your BATNA, your BATNA is now irrelevant. How would you respond as Alice?

I'd say: You're trying to bamboozle me into ignoring the pie. I don't evaluate a deal by how much you and I end up with. I evaluate a deal by how much we each beat our BATNAs. Yes, I'm up 2 slices compared to no deal, but you're up 4 slices. That's not fair. Let's focus on the 6 slices that make up the pie.

A particularly effective tool is to show how the other side's proposed approach would hurt them if the numbers were different—that's what Anju did to show Bharat the problem with proportional division in the case of the shared CD. Or show how their approach breaks down as the numbers become extreme, as was the case with the 2,000:1 split of savings between Coke and Honest Tea. We've talked extensively about how to counter objections to splitting the pie. My point here is to be prepared. You want to have the examples relevant to your situation at the ready.

Preparation work goes beyond planning to sell the pie. You also have to consider how you will expand the pie. What questions will you ask and what information will you volunteer? How can you make an offer that gets heard?

When it comes time to make the presentation, be flexible. Be sure you understand their objections, not just the objections you would have made. Confirm you have it right. To overcome objections, make the objections yourself. This demonstrates your understanding and allows them to hear your counterarguments. End by presenting their victory speech.

There's nothing new here. But again and again, I see people being surprised and unprepared for how the negotiation plays out. They come in with an opening proposal and an end goal. What they don't have is a set of contingency plans for when the other side objects. You now have all the tools you need. You just need to plan for what could go wrong.

When I teach the Zinc-It case, I give all the parties the same set of instructions. Every so often, someone ends up getting sick and one of the students has to take on a different role. That student generally does extremely well.

In hindsight, the reason is obvious. The student who switches roles, say from buyer to seller, is especially well prepared to adopt their prior buyer's perspective when acting as a seller. They can make the other side's arguments and counter them as well. The ideal way to prepare for a negotiation is to imagine that you are representing the other party. You might even want to do this first, before you start thinking about your role.

Putting yourself in others' shoes is hard. One of Herb Cohen's expressions explains the challenge: we don't see things as they are, but as we are. To be allocentric, you have to move away from seeing things from your perspective to seeing things from the other side's perspective to ultimately seeing things from both perspectives.

The Dog Bite

I've picked the next case to illustrate how one plans ahead. The focus is less on the pie than on playing out the negotiation. The numbers might seem small, but not to the student who recounted the story below.

> *My husband got bit by our neighbor's dog. Actually, it wasn't the neighbor's dog. The neighbor was dog-sitting and they let the dog go off-leash. We live in a multi-family house. This dog dashed into our apartment and attacked our dog. When my husband jumped in to protect our dog, he was bit, too. The neighbor produced a rabies card, but it was all in German and I don't read German.*
>
> *Of course, we went straight to the hospital Urgent Care. After getting my husband patched up along with some antibiotics, we next went to the vet who took care of our dog. When we got home, I did some research on rabies. It can be fatal! There's only a small window in which you can get the shot. As a precaution, we went back to Urgent Care, and they gave my husband a rabies shot.*
>
> *I thought everything was fine until we got the bill: $32,000!!!!! Thank god we had insurance. We did have to pay a $2,000 deductible. Add the vet cost and we are out $2,500 (plus the pain, trauma, and lost time). We are meeting with the neighbor tonight to discuss compensation.*

How would you prepare for this negotiation? Let's start with what could go wrong. Perhaps the dog owner doesn't have any legal liability. That could be a knockout punch. Perhaps my student didn't follow medical guidelines. That's a blow best dodged by preempting it if need be. Perhaps the dog was vaccinated for rabies. That's what you believe to be the case, but you should confirm.

This suggests three factual elements to the preparation: (1) research the law, (2) obtain a copy of the dog's rabies vaccination form, (3) determine the medical guidelines. Once you've gathered the relevant facts, you can better figure out what you should ask for and how the other side will respond.

Here's what some quick research revealed.

The law: Different states have different statutes regarding dog bites. In some states, the dog gets a pass on its first bite. Until then the owner doesn't know that the dog could be dangerous. Connecticut is a no-bite state. The owner is liable even on the first bite.[30]

The dog's vaccination report: Upon later inspection, the word "rabies" was on the form in addition to the German.

CDC guidelines: "Rabies is a medical urgency but not an emergency. Decisions should not be delayed. . . . Decisions to start PEP [a combination of human rabies immune globulin and a rabies vaccine] will be based on your type of exposure, the animal you were exposed to, whether the animal is available for testing . . ."[31] The North Dakota Department of Health summarizes the guideline in a useful flowchart. Based on the heath guidelines, the recommendation is to quarantine and observe the dog for ten days and proceed with PEP if the dog shows signs of rabies (or dies).

Now we have the law, the vaccine report, and the medical recommendation. The good news is that the owner is liable. If there's no agreement, the BATNAs for both sides are going to court, and the dog owner will lose.

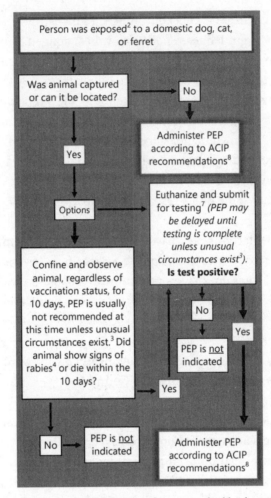

Person was exposed[2] to a domestic dog, cat, or ferret

Was animal captured or can it be located? → No

Administer PEP according to ACIP recommendations[8]

Yes

Options → Euthanize and submit for testing[7] *(PEP may be delayed until testing is complete unless unusual circumstances exist[3]).* **Is test positive?**

Confine and observe animal, regardless of vaccination status, for 10 days. PEP is usually not recommended at this time unless unusual circumstances exist.[3] Did animal show signs of rabies[4] or die within the 10 days?

No → PEP is <u>not</u> indicated

Yes

No → PEP is <u>not</u> indicated

Yes

Administer PEP according to ACIP recommendations[8]

North Dakota Dept. of Health flowchart, https://www.health.nd.gov/diseases -conditions/rabies/rabies-faqs

What might the dog owner say in their defense? The owner could point out that my student panicked and made a bad situation worse. She was told that the dog had been vaccinated and the vaccine report confirmed this. She had been shown the report at the time and had she spent even a minute more looking at it would have seen the word "rabies." Even if she hadn't known the dog was vaccinated, medical guidelines suggest watching the dog for ten days before getting the PEP shots.

These are legitimate points. You want to be ready with a response.

While I made mistakes, the root cause of the problem was your dog. The dog should never have been allowed to come into our apartment and should not have bitten my husband and our dog. While I appreciate the medical recommendations, we didn't want to take any chances: rabies is fatal.

While the dog owner won't want to hear there's a $3,000 bill to pay, this can be presented as a victory speech. Even if the owner is only 50 percent liable, they could have been stuck with a much higher bill.

You are very fortunate we have insurance. Otherwise, we would be holding you responsible for the full $32,000 cost. Instead, we're only asking you for $3,000 to cover our out-of-pocket costs of $2,500 plus $500 for pain and suffering.

These are the main points I'd make. To really prepare, I'd practice by recruiting a friend to take on the role of the dog owner. I wouldn't ask just anyone. I'd ask someone who is a dog owner. It is easier for a dog owner to play the role convincingly. And I'd ask the person to fight hard. I don't need to prepare for someone who just says yes. I want to prepare for what to do after I've been punched in the face. In my student's case, she was well prepared, and the result was anticlimactic. The dog owner's insurance covered all their costs.

To anticipate how the other side will react, you can run the equivalent of a mock trial; call it a mock negotiation. The advantage of using friends and colleagues to help is that they don't have to unknow what you know. You know too much. The other side will evaluate your proposal based only on what they know. All too often, we focus on how we would respond, not how someone who doesn't know everything we know would respond.

Our next case shows just how hard it is to block out your view when you take the other side's perspective. If you can do so, that's your negotiation superpower: you will know what to offer and you will make what looks like an otherwise impossible sale. That's the story of George Perkins and Moffett Studio.

Moffett Studio

There's a famous historical negotiation over the use of a copyrighted photograph. Business school professors love to teach this case. Most of my colleagues portray the result as a shining example of how to negotiate well. I think they are half right. Here's the situation according to historian John Garraty.[32]

It is late in the fall of 1912. Teddy Roosevelt has split with the Republican Party and is running for president on the Progressive/"Bull Moose" Party. He is up against New Jersey governor Woodrow Wilson for the Democrats and the incumbent William Howard Taft for the Republicans. (There is also Socialist Party of America candidate, Eugene Debs, who ended up with 6 percent of the vote!)

One of the Progressive Party's most powerful campaign tools is Roosevelt's convention speech, his "Confession of Faith." The campaign wants to use that speech as part of a booklet to hand out in California, which was then a swing state. They are ready to print three million copies. A photo of Roosevelt and his running mate, Hiram Johnson, is set to be on the cover.

When campaign publicist O. K. Davis does a routine check of the printer proofs, he discovers things are not okay: no one has obtained copyright permission from Moffett Studio to use their copyrighted photographs. This is a big problem because copyright law at the time provided a $1/copy penalty to reproduce a photograph without permission.* There's a potential $3 million dollars at stake or $80 million in today's dollars! The publicist goes up the chain to the executive secretary of the Progressive Party, George Perkins, and asks what they should do. How much should they offer to pay?

---

* Ironically, the penalties were specified in the Copyright Act of 1909, signed by then president Theodore Roosevelt on March 4, 1909, his last day in office.

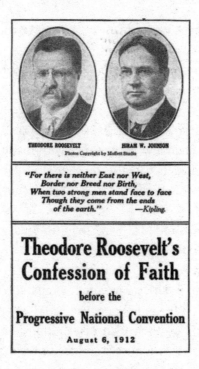

THEODORE ROOSEVELT   HIRAM W. JOHNSON
Photos Copyright by Moffett Studio

"For there is neither East nor West,
Border nor Breed nor Birth,
When two strong men stand face to face
Though they come from the ends
of the earth."   —*Kipling.*

Theodore Roosevelt's Confession of Faith

before the

Progressive National Convention

August 6, 1912

What would you do in this case? You need to print the booklets. Unlike the present, where it is easy to swap things out with digital production, there isn't time to come up with a new cover photo. In short, the situation looks desperate. Actually, it is desperate. People are shouting. They want your answer. Now.

It's hard to focus on the other side's perspective.

Perkins was an experienced businessman. He was a partner at J. P. Morgan and served on the board of U.S. Steel. Perkins quickly dictated the following telegram to Moffett Studio:

We're planning to issue an addition of three million copies of Roosevelt's speech with pictures of Roosevelt and Johnson on the front page. This will be a great advertisement for the photographer. What will you give us to use your pictures? Rush answer.

How would you reply as Moffett Studio if you had received this request and did not know the facts above?

Moffett came back with:

We've never done this before but under the circumstances, we'll give you $250.

Ten minutes later, according to Davis, the presses were running.

This story has been told many times with many embellishments. Sometimes the booklets had already been printed;[33] other times, we hear that Moffett was hard up for money, or that he was a Wilson supporter.

Deepak Malhotra and Max Bazerman use this story as the lead in their book, *Negotiation Genius*. The moral is George Perkins is one genius negotiator. As I said, I half agree.

The genius part is the preparation. Preparation starts by trying to understand the other side's perspective. Most people in Perkins's shoes would focus on their own desperation and not think about the value the Moffett Studio sees in having the campaign use their photographs. The fact that Perkins was able to be allocentric in that way was genius.

The place I part company with Malhotra and Bazerman is when it comes to Perkins's omission of critical information. In their telling, the campaign has already printed the booklets and thus they have to use the photo. Perkins conveniently left that out of his telegram. In doing so, he pulled a fast one on Moffett Studio.

Imagine the answer had come back: Will respond tomorrow.

At that point, Perkins might have to reveal the true situation. How would you then feel as Moffett?

If it were me, I would have felt I had been lied to—a lie of omission.[34] I would be quite uncharitable when it came to stating a price. Thus, separate from any ethical question, I think this is an unnecessarily dangerous strategy; if you get caught, there may be no deal at all, or the other side will come back with an unreasonable offer.

Herb Cohen (author of *You Can Negotiate Anything*) was visiting my class. That provided an opportunity to ask how he would handle this situation. Herb proposed revealing you made a mistake and asking for their help. That doesn't mean opening your wallet. Even at a low price Moffett Studio is coming out ahead. Explain the situation and ask permission to use the photograph. You should still point out that using the photograph will be in Moffett's interest. The pie is large as both sides will benefit. And you can owe Moffett a big favor down the road. Moffett has photographed presidents since Lincoln, and should Roosevelt win, Moffett will be continuing that tradition.

You are unlikely to get Moffett to pay you once you reveal the true situation. But I expect you can still get the rights to use the photograph at a reasonable price.

It is easy to get carried away and think that Perkins turned a $3 million liability into a $250 win. That is far too extreme. The campaign could likely have bought the license at a price below $500. In today's dollars, that's around $13,000. (To put this in perspective, Getty Images licenses most of its photographs for commercial use at prices below $1,000.) Thus, we are more likely talking about a $750 swing, the difference between the campaign paying $500 and having the studio pay the campaign $250. Sure, it is better to get paid $250 than to pay $500, but not at the cost of risking everything.

One might reasonably ask how this differs from a teacup buyer not saying anything to the flea market seller about how this particular cup is especially valuable to him or her. Why is it okay to omit this information but it is not okay to leave out that the booklets have already been printed?

This issue kept me up for several nights.

For starters, I have the feeling Moffett was being misled and manipulated. To bring this close to home, imagine your eleven-year-old daughter calls you at work and asks if it is okay to have a friend sleep over. You say yes. When you get back home you discover that the friend with her pajamas had been dropped off long before the call asking for permission. At that point, you ask just what would have happened had you said no. Your daughter, absent any contriteness, explains that one of the friend's parents would have come by to pick her friend up. But that doesn't matter, she says. Since you were willing to permit the sleepover, what difference does it make that the sleepover had already started? Perhaps all eleven-year-olds are consequentialists.

I'd feel quite differently about the matter. I'd have felt misled. I might well have approved the sleepover before it had been arranged or even if I had been told that it was already in progress. But I would not be happy giving approval to an action that was nearly a fait accompli and not knowing it at the time.

I admit this is strange in that I would be *more* willing to say yes if I had known that the friend was already there and the parent would have to make an extra trip to pick her up. So why would I care if I'd have made the same decision? Besides feeling duped, I might have negotiated a more even split of the pie. Had the daughter revealed the truth, she would have revealed her high valuation. She would have agreed to do some extra chores or math problems in return for a yes. She got more of the pie through her lie of omission.

I think Moffett Studio would've felt the very same way had Perkins got caught. Moffett was willing to pay $250 to have its name on the photo whether or not the booklets were already printed and whether or not Perkins had any alternatives. The publicity was worth it. But just because something is worth it to you doesn't mean you'd agree to the deal.

If Alice offers Bob 3 slices, he might well accept if all he knew was he was getting 3 slices rather than his BATNA of 2. But if he became aware that his getting 3 went along with Alice getting 9, his answer changes. Now he holds out for an even split of the pie.

We know that Moffett was willing to sell the license at a reasonable price—even a negative price—before the booklets were printed. Though the price might not be negative, I'm betting the price would be reasonable even if they had been told the booklets were already printed by mistake. But Moffett would not want to give their permission to use the photograph without knowing the true situation. The campaign didn't trust Moffett with the truth. People care about being treated with respect separate from the money they may make in a negotiation.

When the campaign asked to get paid, this compounded the misperceptions. Why would Moffett Studio be willing to pay the campaign? They would do so under the assumption there was another photo option the campaign could use and thus a rival studio would get the publicity. The telegraph contributed to Moffett Studio's misperception. That was an act of commission, even if indirect. Had the campaign simply asked the studio to state its regular price and provide a discount given the positive public relations, they would have taken advantage of the studio's misperception, but would not have compounded it.

If you aren't going to disclose that the booklets have already been printed, the following offer seems less likely to backfire:

> *Planning to distribute three million copies of convention speech with pictures of Roosevelt and Johnson on front page. This will be great advertisement for photographer. Do not want to spend time negotiating on price. Willing to offer small fee in addition to the publicity. Is $100 okay?*

This lacks Perkins's killer instinct. Were Moffett to come back with a price of $200, I'd call that a win. Were Moffett to discover the booklets were already printed, I think they'd feel less taken advantage of.

When the buyer of a teacup asks the flea market seller for a price and agrees to the $20 price, there is no sense in which the dealer feels lied to. Even if the buyer has a very high idiosyncratic valuation for the teacup, the buyer is not contributing to any misperception the seller may have. And the seller is getting a normal or even above-average level of profit in the transaction. But if the teacup is really worth $300 to the buyer, that's still nowhere near an even split.

To summarize: First, prepare by being allocentric. Start by understanding the other side's position. They don't know what you know, so when you put yourself in their shoes you have to erase some part of your knowledge. Second, when you are in a tough spot, don't leave false impressions. Perkins looks like a hero, but I fear he was too clever by half. He risked a huge loss for a small win (and a great story).

I don't claim you should never lie. If Nazis are asking if there are any Jews hiding in the attic, you can lie. If Perkins thinks the fate of the election hangs on distributing these booklets and is worried Moffett is a Wilson supporter, it is justifiable to hide the desperate situation. But leaving out the desperation is different than pushing Moffett to pay you.

Improving Your BATNA

Another aspect of preparation is working to understand your true BATNA. While most people have a sense of their "Alternative" if the negotiation breaks down, they tend not to focus enough on the "Best" part of BATNA. Imagine you are fortunate enough to have a job offer from both Apple and Microsoft. The Apple offer is $120,000. Microsoft is your first choice and Apple is your fallback. Is your BATNA a $120,000 salary?

The answer is no, for two reasons. The first is that your BATNA takes into account more than just salary. You have to include the value of the lifestyle, location, colleagues, mentorship, and all that comes with the job. Most people get that point. The alternative is better described as "Working for Apple in Cupertino at a $120,000 salary."

What they miss is that the $120,000 may not be the *best* offer you could get from Apple. If you were to say to the recruiter that you are keen to join them and would do so if they were to bump their salary offer to $130,000, do you think they would say yes?* If so, the salary that goes with the BATNA is not $120,000 but $130,000. If you think the chance is 50 percent, you might put a $125,000 salary with the BATNA. My point is that your best alternative is likely better than what the alternative is currently offering you.

---

* Getting you to say yes may be reason enough for them to raise the salary. If you have other reasons—such as the lower state tax rate in Redmond compared to Cupertino or the salary at competing offers—I'd use those, too.

That doesn't mean you should negotiate with the #2 option at the start. It's time consuming and it is hard to get the most out of them if you are not prepared to commit to taking the job. What you should do is estimate what your #2 option might do to improve their offer were you prepared to say yes and then incorporate that estimate into your BATNA.

Chapter 21

WHAT TO
REVEAL (AND WHAT
TO KEEP HIDDEN)

To create a pie, people need to share information. Sharing means both asking questions and answering them. All too often, negotiators keep things hidden or imagine the other side can read their mind. Here is an exchange between my married friends Adam and Barbara.

> **Adam:** I really want you to know what it is that I want *without* my having to tell you. It would mean much more that way.

> **Barbara:** Communication is hard. Even if you say what you want there's a good chance you'll be misunderstood. You might get what you want. But if you don't say anything, the chance is near zero.

People are often afraid to reveal what it is that they want. They fear that the other side will use this information against them in the negotiation. Is that really right?

Imagine that you are selling a car and will use the money to pay off your loan to the mob. The mob enforcer is coming to collect at 5:00 p.m. this evening. He will break your knees if you don't come up with the $10,000 you owe.

A potential car buyer comes along at noon and asks why you are selling. Do you explain your predicament? You might at first think that revealing your level of desperation would put you in a weak position. If you tell them about your need to come up with $10,000, the buyer knows they don't have to pay you much, if anything, more than $10,000. On the other hand, they also know they shouldn't waste time. If they want a great deal, they have to come up with the money right now. If you keep the information hidden, you might get more for the car . . . and you can use that extra money to pay for the leg casts.

In this obviously extreme, even cartoonish, example, the seller cares about both the price and the speed of the transaction. Ideally, the seller would get a high price quickly. But if speed really is the number one priority, revealing this will help ensure the transaction is done quickly.

That said, one doesn't have to reveal information that isn't relevant to the transaction. For example, if you are selling a house you purchased thirty years ago for $100,000 and thus have a low tax basis, that is not relevant to today's valuation. The fact that you stand to make a lot of money doesn't change what the house is worth today. And it isn't relevant to the buyer's valuation. If asked, you could reveal the original purchase price or you could politely decline to share, explaining that it doesn't seem relevant. Even here, I don't see any real harm in sharing, though I don't see any potential benefit, either.

In general, I come down on the side of revelation. The reason is that it is hard, if not impossible, for the other side to give you what you want if you hide it or lead them astray. Returning to the gas station negotiation (from Chapter 16), the buyer will typically ask the seller why he or she is selling. The seller will often answer with a white lie, as in "I'm planning to retire." The problem with this answer is that it doesn't lead the buyer to follow up with a job offer. Why would you offer a job to someone who has just announced plans to retire?

Is there any reason not to reveal the true reason they are selling? Think about it. The buyer knows there is some reason for the sale. From the buyer's perspective, there are good reasons and bad reasons for a sale. A bad reason would be there's a leak in the underground storage tank and the station is about to become a superfund site or the highway exit ramp that leads customers to the station is about to be closed.[35] A good reason is the owner has a lifelong dream to take a sailing trip around the world. It's a good reason because it means there's nothing wrong with the station. People have a knee-jerk reaction to hiding information—they don't even disclose information that would redound to their benefit.

When you are deciding upon what to reveal, focus on two factors. How will the other party react to your information? And how will it change the pie?

Deadlines

The case of a hidden deadline offers a good way to test your thinking. Alikiah and Brenise are involved in a negotiation that has a deadline of Friday at 5:00 p.m. If they don't have a signed deal by that time, the opportunity will vanish, and both will be left with nothing. Both sides are fully aware of this deadline.

As things turn out, Alikiah has an earlier deadline, Wednesday at 5:00 p.m. Brenise is entirely unaware of this fact. Should Alikiah tell Brenise?

My students are equally divided on this question. Those who choose not to reveal are worried that Brenise will use Alikiah's time pressure to get a better deal. Is that really right?

What is Brenise's deadline? It is also Wednesday at 5:00 p.m.—except she doesn't know it. Alikiah and Brenise have the exact same deadline. This goes back to our early discussion of the pie. Alikiah can't create a pie without Brenise, and Brenise can't create a pie without Alikiah. The two of them are equally needed to create pie. For the very same reason they should split the pie, they should share information about deadlines.

If Alikiah doesn't share his early deadline with Brenise, he will feel time pressure and she won't. In contrast, if he shares the news, the two sides will both feel the time pressure. I advise Alikiah to say something like: "Brenise, I have some bad news to share. I need to have this negotiation wrapped up by Wednesday at 5:00, not Friday at 5:00. That means if we can't reach a deal by then, we will both lose this opportunity. So, that's your new deadline, too. Let's get cracking."

My advice is backed up by experimental evidence. Professors Francesca Gino and Don Moore find that hiding the shorter deadline increased the chance of impasse by more than half, from 23 percent up to 37 percent.[36] Among those who reached a deal, the party with the shorter deadline got half the pie on average when the deadline was revealed, but only a 43 percent share when it was kept hidden. Unless you frame things using symmetry, this isn't intuitive. Indeed, when participants with the shorter deadline were asked beforehand if revelation would help, almost 60 percent thought it would put them in a weaker position. They were wrong.

BATNAs

If there is one thing negotiation experts agree on it's that you should keep a weak BATNA hidden. According to the Harvard Program on Negotiation, this is Negotiation 101:

Don't reveal a weak BATNA.[37]

Since I'm not one to go with the crowd, allow me to offer an alternative perspective.

To set the scene, you're selling your business and the best offer you have on the table is $400,000. That feels like a weak BATNA because you think the business is worth at least $500,000. A new potential buyer seems interested and asks what other offers you have. There are several potential replies:

None of your business
Something that begins with a 4
$400,000.

While "None of your business" is a rude way of saying it, one can employ symmetry to communicate the same message: "I don't imagine you will be willing to tell me the most you are willing to pay. For the same reason, I am leery of telling you the least I am willing to accept." This is the standard approach.

But would you have said "None of your business" or the more polite version if your other offer were $500,000? There's a reason to reveal your BATNA even when it's weak. If you don't, the other side may infer that your BATNA is even weaker.

If you had a high offer, say $500,000, you'd want to share this information. Thus, if you don't share, the buyer will infer that your other offer is at best in the $450,000 range. The logic snowballs. If you had a $450,000 offer, you'd now want to reveal that information. If you don't, the seller will believe that your other offer, if you even have one, is at best $400,000. It then becomes advantageous to reveal a $400,000 offer to distinguish yourself from a seller with no other offer. You can try to keep a weak BATNA hidden, but an unwillingness to share your BATNA speaks volumes about its weakness.

Another reason to reveal your BATNA is to avoid wasting time. Edward jumped down from his $2,500 initial ask to $1,100 right after I revealed to him that my BATNA was going to ICANN at a cost of $1,300. When selling your business, if the new potential buyer offers $275,000, you can quickly determine if the person is serious by revealing there's a competing bid that starts with a 4. It's true that the potential buyer will recognize that if the offer were anything like $450,000 or more, you would have said "and it is close to $500,000." Thus, they will be able to infer that the offer is in the low $400,000 range. If they can't beat $400,000, there's no point in continuing the conversation.

> When you share information, do it in steps and look for reciprocity. Say it begins with a 4 rather than presenting the exact number. Ask to see their spreadsheet or model so that their numbers can be verified. You can be more open when you are committed to splitting the pie and when there's less room for the other side to hide the true size of the pie.

The full-information reply isn't nearly as bad as it sounds. Even if you reveal your current high bid is only $400,000, that doesn't mean you will accept $401,000:

I had a bid of $400,000 and I turned it down. It was too low. If you want to buy this business, you are going to have to make a much better offer.

While you revealed the other offer of $400,000, you didn't reveal your BATNA. Your BATNA could be continuing with the status quo and not selling. I admit this keeps your BATNA partially hidden, so I haven't fully proven my case.

What if a sale at $400,000 really is your BATNA? If you believe the buyer is willing to pay $480,000, then even if your BATNA is revealed, you can hold out for $440,000 or half the pie. There's no reason to accept $401,000 any more than the buyer will pay $479,000. Go back to Edward and the domain name. I told him my BATNA was $1,300, but I wasn't going to pay him anything more than $650.

Revealing a weak BATNA doesn't stop you from getting half the pie, and not revealing it may lead the other side to infer that your BATNA is even weaker than it is.

I think there's confusion over what it means to have a weak BATNA. Was my BATNA weak in the negotiation with Edward? His BATNA was $0 and mine was paying $1,300. My BATNA was worse than his, but that isn't a relevant comparison.

Here's what I suspect is really going on. The other party will have some belief about your BATNA (after taking into account the fact you haven't revealed it to them). If they think your BATNA is better than it really is, you don't want to correct them by revealing your BATNA. If they think your BATNA is worse than it really is, you do want to correct them.

Of course, they may not tell you what they think your BATNA is. In that situation, your decisions are based on what you think they think your BATNA is (again, after taking into account the fact you haven't revealed it to them). If you think they think your BATNA is better than it really is, you don't want to correct them by revealing your BATNA. If you think they think your BATNA is worse than it really is, you do want to correct them.

The meaning of a weak BATNA is that you think the other side has overestimated your BATNA. The weakness is not from some absolute low value of your BATNA but the fact that your true BATNA is worse than what you think they think it is. If that's the case, mum's the word.*

---

* Why do we say "mum's the word" for keeping silent? It's the "mmm" sound from humming when one's lips are sealed. The expression goes back to Middle English. As Shakespeare wrote in *Henry VI, Part 2,* "Seal up your lips and give no words but mum."

_____

Chapter 22

OPENING MOVES

There is a well-known Chinese adage: A journey of a thousand miles begins with a single step. True. It is also easy to begin with a misstep. Let's see if I can help you avoid getting the negotiation off on the wrong foot.

In this chapter we examine excerpts from a series of negotiations. Over the past fifteen years, I've filmed hundreds of negotiations and the excerpts are from transcripts of those recordings. Because the negotiations involve real people, I can't show you the actual video. To solve this issue, I hired actors to re-create the scenes. The actors watched the originals and then used the transcripts as their script. There are links to these videos on the book's companion website, SplitThePieBook.com. The actors were students at the Yale School of Drama. When they win their Academy Awards, you can say you saw them here first.

The excerpts focus on opening moves, whether they be first offers, lies, good cop/bad cop routines, or ultimatums. There are several train wrecks. One takeaway is that the traditional approach to negotiation is deeply flawed. If you can agree at the start to different ground rules—to split the pie—you won't have to worry about playing these games. I recognize you won't always have this opportunity. Here's what to do or mostly what not to do in those cases, and how to respond when others don't follow my advice.

Anchoring (and How Not to Get Dragged Down by Your Own Anchor)

In trying to get more of the pie, some think it's a smart move to start the negotiation with an extreme offer. If the other side is asking for $100 and you are prepared to pay $70, offer $20.

The idea is to anchor the other side with your number. When they hear $20, that will drag down their expectation of what you are willing to pay. Instead of countering with $80, they will meet you halfway at $60.

There are two potential problems with this approach.

1. Offering $20 or some other very low number may lead the other side to walk away or decide they don't want to negotiate with you.
2. If the market price is somewhere in the $80 to $100 range, you will have to make large concessions in order to get to the right price range. Having moved, for example, from $20 to $50, the seller will interpret this as you still have significant flexibility in your offer. They will expect to see additional large concessions.

An example of an extreme anchor sinking the negotiations took place on January 26, 2017. President Donald Trump was scheduled to meet President Enrique Peña Nieto of Mexico at the White House. A contentious part of their agenda was a discussion of the border wall. President Trump preempted the negotiations with an 8:55 a.m. tweet, reiterating his insistence that Mexico pay for the wall construction.

It seemed that President Trump was trying to anchor the negotiations with his lowball offer. That anchor backfired as it was seen as an insult—and, even worse, as a public insult. By 11:30, the Mexican foreign minister was instructed to cancel his meeting with then homeland security secretary John Kelly. Soon thereafter, President Peña Nieto publicly canceled his meeting with President Trump.[38] Ultimately, the United States ended up paying all $15 billion of the construction costs.

The academic literature on anchoring is based on experiments unconnected to negotiation. In 1974, Amos Tversky and Daniel Kahneman introduced the world to behavioral decision making—how the quirks of the human mind lead to predictable deviations from rationality. This work ultimately led to a 2002 Nobel Memorial Prize in economics for Kahneman. (Tversky would surely have shared the prize with him but had died prematurely at age fifty-nine from cancer.) They demonstrated the effect of anchoring by priming subjects with two different questions. Half were asked if the number of African countries in the United Nations was above or below 10. The other half were asked if the number was above or below 65. After their first answer, everyone was then asked to estimate the actual number. Those primed with the above or below 10 estimated 25 as the number. Those who began with above or below 65 settled on 45 countries. While both estimates were below the truth (54), it was a remarkable demonstration of how simply considering the numbers 10 or 65 can have a large effect on people's estimates. Hearing 65 first rather than 10 almost doubled the estimate.

The reason why anchoring is different in negotiation is that the other side is aware of what you are doing and will be insulted. No one is insulted when asked if the number of African countries in the United Nations is above or below 10. But they will be insulted if you offer them 10 percent of what their car or house or business is worth. Either you have no idea of what you are doing or, more likely, you are trying to take advantage of them.

That doesn't mean you can't use this tactic at all. You have to use it with more moderation.

Whatever offer you make, you should always be able to defend it. If you offer $20 and the buyer says "How did you come up with that number?" it isn't a satisfactory answer to reply: "I was trying to anchor you with a low bid." Pick a defensible number. In the case of real estate, for example, if there is a Zillow range of estimates, you can justify picking the low end of the range.

Let's turn to the second problem with anchoring: it forces you to make big moves in order to reach a potential deal. Having done so, the other side will think there are more concessions to follow. But sometimes there aren't any more concessions to be made. The end result is no deal, as we see in the following transcript.

> **Buyer:** Let's say how we can begin.
>
> **Seller:** It would be around $660,000 to reproduce my petrol station.
>
> **Buyer:** Well, I have to admit that you are very, very, very far from what we were thinking . . . Around this amount we simply build a new station. I am not willing to pay more than $300,000. Maybe we can negotiate a bit on the fact that it is maybe worth more a bit more than $300,000. But, of course, the price you are hoping to get is absolutely out of the question.
>
> *[some more back-and-forth]*
>
> **Buyer:** If we can reach an agreement at $375,000—
>
> **Seller:** See, I don't have to sell.
>
> **Buyer:** I personally was thinking really not to go over $375,000, but I might go a bit higher because . . . because we would like to keep this between us and shake hands. Today, now, now, I can give you a check for $470k if you agree, but above that I can't do it.
>
> **Seller:** No. I'd agree but my other options are better.
>
> **Buyer:** I will translate your message to my board.

The buyer started with a lowball bid of $300,000. The market price is closer to $470,000. He does get there, but the process of quickly moving up to $375,000 and then $470,000 leaves the impression that if the seller holds out there will be even more attractive offers to come. There are no higher offers forthcoming, as $470,000 is the buyer's limit. The big price jumps—which were necessitated by the lowball starting point—created a false sense of buyer flexibility that, in turn, made the seller unwilling to accept the buyer's true best offer.

You might ask if the buyer should just move more slowly, but that, too, creates a different set of problems. If the buyer doesn't come up to a reasonable range, the seller will think the buyer isn't serious.

The underlying source of the problem is the unreasonably low initial offer. That low starting point requires making some big steps and that creates a different anchor—that you are a negotiator willing to make big moves.

Not to pile on, but there's one more problem with this strategy. The lowball offer leads to a lack of trust. If someone starts out offering you $300,000 and ends up at $470,000, that suggests, actually screams, they were trying to take advantage of you. That puts you on alert. You have to keep your guard up. You don't say anything that can be used against you. As we see in the transcript, the two parties don't do a good job or any job at all in finding ways to expand the pie.

I don't want you to conclude that there's no place for anchoring. Instead, I want you to appreciate that a heavy-handed anchor can be worse than no anchor at all. Use a light touch. It's possible to make even a light anchor very sticky, as we now discuss.

Make Precise Bids

I love this sign: speed limit 24 gets my attention much more than 25 would. For the same reason, if you want to make a bid stick, make it precise. It is better to ask for $485 than to ask for $500. If you ask for such a round number, the other side will think you are just making something up and haven't done the research to figure out what the item is worth. They will come back with a much lower number. In contrast, if you ask

for $485, the other side will infer that there is some reasoning behind your ask.

This result was documented in an ingenious paper by business school professors Matt Backus and Steven Tadelis and eBay researcher Tom Blake.[39] They looked at millions of negotiations that took place on eBay. As seen in the chart, they compared the final sale price with the initial asking price. For example, if the initial asking price was $200, the seller ended up with around 57 percent of the asking price when the item sold. This is the filled-in circle above $200. You will notice a pattern to the filled-in circles. When the asking price is a round number, especially a multiple of $100, the sale price tends to be a much lower ratio of the ask compared to the case when the asking price is more precise.

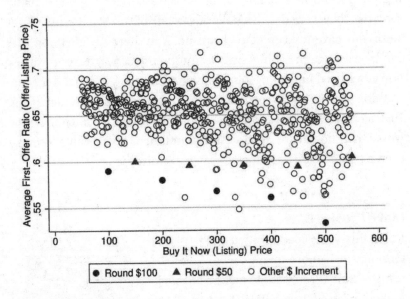

It isn't surprising that someone who asks for $515 will end up with more than someone who asks for $500. But it is surprising that someone who asks for $485 also ends up with more. The precise number sticks.

Of course, don't get carried away and ask for $485.12. If the other side asks where you came up with that number, it isn't helpful to reply that you read in a book that precise numbers are stickier. You have to be able to justify that precise number you have come up with.

Often people shoot themselves in their bid by rounding the bid or ask. If you are looking to make an offer on an apartment and the apartment is 1,145 square feet and the Zillow range on price/square foot is $900 to $1,000, go ahead and offer $900 × 1,145 = $1,030,500. If you round down and offer $1m, the other side won't believe this is a firm bid. If the seller asks how you came up with the $1,030,500 price, you can explain that it came from the low end of the Zillow estimate multiplied by the square feet.

Don't Lie about Your BATNA

In trying to get more of the pie, some people exaggerate their BATNA. And by exaggerate, I mean lie. The easiest way to get the other side to move up is to make them believe they are in competition with someone else.

In the following exchange, the seller claims to have a competing offer for $500k.

> **Seller:** We have a couple of other offers on the table.
>
> **Buyer:** What's the offer?
>
> **Seller:** Best offer is $500k. So that's the number to beat.
>
> **Buyer:** Wow, [*laugh*] that's a really good offer. I'd take that if I were you.

The buyer isn't prepared to offer anything more than $470k. If the seller already has an offer for $500k, there is little point in continuing the negotiation.

At that point, the seller might add a second lie and claim that for some reason she prefers selling to this buyer than the one offering $500k. That will likely raise further suspicions about her honesty.

Don't lie and get yourself in this mess to start with.

Good Cop/Bad Cop

The buyer opens the next negotiation all nice and friendly.

Buyer: I just wanted to start out by saying, I think this deal is going to go more smoothly than it could have. Luckily for you, my coworker who would usually be here to do this deal is working another deal. She couldn't be here today and she's a hard hitter. [*laugh*] I'm easygoing. I'm not trying to lowball you.

She's saying, you're lucky to be working with me. I'm easygoing. Everything is all smiley, but it isn't really smiley below the surface.

This is the classic good cop/bad cop routine. She is really saying if you don't do this deal with me, you're going to face somebody else who's mean and tough. You'd better do this deal with me or else!

Now the question: If you were the seller, how would you respond to this implicit threat?

You could ignore it. This is dangerous because if you do so, you are implicitly saying you accept the good cop/bad cop threat. That means you are scared of facing the other person or that the buyer thinks you will be scared.

You could call the person on it and say I can't believe you're playing a good cop/bad cop game with me. That is better than saying nothing, though it runs the risk of starting the negotiations off on a bad footing.

If you don't want to call the person explicitly and you don't want to let it pass, how do you reply? Here we continue with the transcript. The seller has the perfect retort to the buyer's ploy.

Buyer: . . . I am easygoing. I'm not trying to lowball you.

Seller: I guess we're both lucky. My wife's not here either. She's a hard hitter, too. [*laugh*]

Buyer: Okay. Fair enough. Should we just get started?

Call the person out on the tactics, but do so in a humorous way. The seller is saying I see what you are doing, and I could play the same game. Let's cut the BS and get to work.

I am a big fan of employing symmetry. But there's a catch. You sometimes want to employ hypothetical symmetry rather than actual symmetry. That's what the seller's humor accomplished. It was saying I could hypothetically play the same game, not that I'm going to play the same game. If someone is being a jerk to you, I don't want you to apply symmetry and be a jerk back to them. Instead, I want you to employ symmetry to help them see how their actions are being perceived.

How to Put Out a Fire: Fight Fire with Water

When the other side lights a fire, the natural reaction is to respond in kind, to fight fire with fire. But as any firefighter will tell you, the better answer is to fight fire with water (FFWW). You want to put out the flame.

In the negotiation that follows, we have three parties involved. There is the seller, the seller's lawyer, and the buyer. The seller has an ingenious idea for making an ultimatum.

> **Seller:** I love you. You're family. But this is business. We've spoken. It's either going to be A or B or the deal is off. I am going to let you guys discuss. I know we're going to reach a solid conclusion. I've left my phone here so you can . . . Well, you can't call me. A or B? That's how it is for us. Thank you.
> *[Seller exits the room and leaves cell phone on the table.]*
>
> **Seller's lawyer:** *[laugh]* I think she said it all. My client has told me that all we can accept on our end is A or B. That's it.

The buyer could respond in kind: it's D or E or there's no deal. That's fighting fire with fire and is unlikely to lead to a deal. The buyer could acquiesce and accept their preferred option. I don't like that answer as it rewards bad behavior by the other party. I want the buyer to get the seller's lawyer to show some flexibility, essentially to override the instructions provided by the client.

Here's how the buyer extinguished the ultimatum.

Buyer: It's A or B?

Seller's lawyer: Yes, that's it.

Buyer: That's it. Nothing else?

Seller's lawyer: That's exactly what we're dealing with here.

Buyer: Well, let's see, A is $25 million.

Seller's lawyer: That's right.

Buyer: You wouldn't take $26 million?

Seller's lawyer: Are you offering $26 million?

Buyer: I'm not offering $26 million. I'm just saying, would you take $26 million?

Seller's lawyer: Yes.

What we've seen here was truly remarkable. We had a seller who seemed stuck on only A or B. The buyer figured out a clever way to create new options. The buyer comes in and says, well, you're happy with $25 million. How about $26 million? Who could say no to that?

It wasn't a real offer. It was a hypothetical offer. And yet, it established the fact that the seller would consider things beyond A or B.

You make a simple superior proposal to get the person's attention and to demonstrate that their ultimatum or intransigence isn't really true. And then, once you've established that they're open to other ideas, it's time to start exploring.

There's something else I want to point out about how the buyer put out the fire. The buyer didn't say: Would you consider an offer of $20m today with 10 percent profit sharing and a 5 percent preferred dividend over the next 5 years? The likely answer would be no, even if it's an offer far superior to A. The offer fails to put out the fire because it's too complicated. No one has to think or take out a spreadsheet to figure out $26m beats $25m. To get someone off their ultimatum you want to employ a simple offer that hits them in the head with its obvious superiority.

If the lawyer says no to $26m then you really are stuck on A or B. If, as above, the lawyer says yes, you've established that the seller is willing to consider things other than A or B. Having established that, now it's time to explore creative and more complicated options. In the Zinc-It case, there are deals worth well more than $26 million for the seller and yet don't cost nearly as much for the buyer. For example, consider a $50 million payment in the event of FDA approval and nothing otherwise. That's worth $30m to the seller, but only costs the buyer $5m.

Negotiating with Jerks

As former Treasury secretary and Harvard president Larry Summers famously wrote in an unpublished paper: "There are idiots. Look around." He could equally well have written: "There are jerks. Look around."

Not everyone will have read this book or will choose to negotiate in a principled manner. To help the reader navigate the challenge of negotiating with jerks, I offer some simple advice: don't you be a jerk.

Don't be the person someone else has to seek advice about. I love my students. They are smart, empathetic, and principled—until they start negotiating. Then some strange disorder takes over and many of them become a caricature of the tough-guy negotiator. They give up the skills that allow them to succeed and grow the pie and instead become the very person they would not want to negotiate with.

Yes, there are jerks out there. When you find yourself on the other side, explain the pie and hold firm in terms of getting half. Use symmetry to turn their arguments around. But, more important, don't copy them. Don't add one to the number of jerks.

What to Say

How can you discover what the other party is truly looking to accomplish? The easiest thing is just ask. Do so before you start talking about money. Early on, you might ask them: What is it that excites you about this deal? What gives you pause?

Another way of trying to get at this is to preempt the money talk:

> *I know you want more money; everybody wants more money. What else can I do besides giving you money that would make your life better? Later we'll talk about money and that will be an issue of contention, but right now what are things I can do to help make this deal work better for you that don't involve money?*

That conversation is how you discover the interests that allow you to trade broccoli for beets and create a bigger pie.

Some people, perhaps you, will think "I don't really want to reveal that at the opening, because if I do they're likely to pay less." And there is some truth here; they probably *will* pay a little less if you reveal there is something else you care about and they give it to you. On the other hand, the two of you have made the pie bigger and you will have gotten something you really care about. Both sides end up better off and the deal is more likely to happen.

Of course, if you've first agreed to split the pie, the conversation will go even smoother. You still want to ask the same questions (What excites them? What gives them pause?), because that's how you expand the pie. And you want to answer their questions when they ask you.

45 TAKEAWAYS

Here are my forty-five main lessons from the book. I hope you'll put them to good use and feel free to share them.

The Basics
These are the table stakes in any negotiation.

1. **Start by asking.** If you don't ask, you're unlikely to receive. You can have the greatest understanding of negotiation, but if you don't negotiate, it doesn't matter.

2. **Don't just ask; make principled arguments.** There's a famous experiment done in the 1970s by Ellen Langer, Arthur Blank, and Benzion Chanowitz in which a person asks to cut in line to make copies.[40] Most people only know their first result, namely that asking "May I use the Xerox machine, because I have to make copies?" led to 90 percent success compared to just saying "May I use the Xerox machine?" which was only 60 percent effective. The wrong conclusion people draw is that any reason works, no matter how inane. But the inane reason ("I have to make copies") only worked when the person wanted to make five copies. Once the person wanted to make twenty copies, both approaches had an identical

24 percent success rate. If you wanted to cut in line, you had to provide a legitimate reason, as in "I'm in a rush." In a negotiation, I don't advise asking for more just because "I'd like more money." The pie framework provides logical and principled arguments that persuade others.

3. **Know your BATNA.** Your BATNA (Best Alternative To a Negotiated Agreement) is what you will do if you can't agree on a deal. If you don't know your BATNA, you won't know how well you are doing in the negotiation or even if you should walk away. When your BATNA is uncertain, you should still make an estimate. And remember that your *best* alternative may be better than your current second-place option, as there may be the potential to improve the offer should you go down that route.

4. **Never accept something worth less than your BATNA.** Ending up with no deal is better than accepting a bad deal.

5. **Work to understand the BATNA of the other party.** You may be doing well in absolute terms, but if you don't consider how much the other side is getting relative to its BATNA, you don't know how well the other side is doing.

The Pie

These are the main contributions of this book.

6. **Calculate the pie.** In any negotiation, employ the pie perspective. What is really at stake? With two parties, the pie is how much more the two can achieve by working together compared to what they can get if they don't reach an agreement. To calculate the pie requires three numbers: what the two can achieve together, your BATNA, and the other party's BATNA.

7. **Recognize the equal power in any two-party negotiation.** Since each party is essential to the deal, each has equal power. For this reason, you should split the pie evenly.

8. **Recognize the symmetry in any two-party negotiation.** Parties that otherwise look different become symmetric under the pie lens.

People in symmetric positions should be treated equally. For this reason, you should split the pie evenly.

9. **Employ symmetry.** Once you are in the pie framework, everything is symmetric. Any argument the other side makes can be flipped. If they propose a 90/10 division in their favor, you can counter with 90/10 in yours. But you may want to do this as a hypothetical rather than actual flip.

10. **A poor BATNA does not mean low power.** If there is no deal, neither party beats their BATNA. Just as you want to beat your BATNA, the other side is looking to do the same. A low BATNA means there is more at stake in the negotiation as the pie is bigger; it doesn't mean you should accept less than half the pie.

11. **Splitting the pie is the fair outcome.** All our notions of fairness come down to a form of equal treatment. But equality of what? Proportional division treats all dollars equally. I want to treat people equally. The pie framework will help you figure out how to treat parties equally.

12. **Beware the lure of proportional division.** It is easy to fall into the trap of proportional division, especially as larger parties will present this as the default.

13. **Just because you care more doesn't mean you should get less.** The side that cares less should find it easier to make a sacrifice. Each side should get the same share of the maximum potential gain *as they perceive it*. When valuations are linear, that means each side gets half their ideal pie. When valuations are nonlinear, it may be possible for each side to get more than half their ideal pie.

14. **Present this new way of negotiating up front.** People jump too quickly to numbers and offers. Start with principles and ground rules. Don't expect the other side will be familiar with this approach. If you meet resistance, at least you know up front what type of person is on the other side.

15. **Even if the other side doesn't care about fairness or the pie, you can still get half the pie.** Use the pie perspective to explain what the negotiation is really about. You can do so without having to use the pie terminology. ("The reason we are negotiating is to save the $1,300 ICANN fee.") Explain why both parties are equally essential

to create the pie. Symmetric power implies an equal split. Use this logic to explain why you are holding firm on requiring half the pie. The other side won't have a principled counter. Principles and logic beat arbitrary positions.

16. **Agree to split the pie to grow the pie.** If you can resolve the issue of pie division, you will find it easier to work in a cooperative fashion to grow the pie.

17. **Use the pie as a measuring stick.** It is all too easy to fall into the trap of comparing an offer to your BATNA. The offer handily beats your BATNA and so you accept. But you have no idea how good the offer is (or how much better it could be) until you look at what share of the pie you are getting. If you are going to accept less than half the pie, you should know it at the time. And if you are asking for or already getting more than half the pie, you should know that, too.

18. **Use the pie as a beacon.** You don't just want to get half of a small pie. Your objective is to create a massive pie (of which you get half). Think about what type of deal structures create the biggest pie.

Growing the Pie

19. **Give the other side what they want.** If they get what they want, you can get what you want. To do so, begin by learning what it is that they want (and what they don't want). Let me share some advice here I learned from Daylian Cain: time spent trying to change minds is better spent figuring them out.

20. **Be empathetic (or at least curious).** Ask questions. Ask about their goals for the deal. Figure out what is important to them. What are their concerns? Besides giving more money, how can you help?

21. **Answer along with asking.** If you don't answer their questions, they'll stop answering yours. Moreover, if you don't share information, the other side won't be able to figure out what you want and give it to you. People are too afraid that anything they say can and will be used against them. But if you don't answer their questions, what you don't say may lead to inferences that can and will be used against you.

22. **Make smart trades.** Figure out what is and is not important to you. Give up items that are valuable to the other party and less valuable to you. Get the items valuable to you and less valuable to them. This is how you expand the pie.

23. **Remember beets versus broccoli.** A good deal gives each party more of what they value. Don't be afraid to go to extremes. If A likes beets more than broccoli and B likes broccoli more than beets, A should get all the beets and B should get all the broccoli.

24. **Use creativity as a first resort, not a last resort.** If you wait too long, both sides will be frustrated, and you may run out of time or patience. Try to expand the pie at the start of the negotiation, when people are in a more cooperative mood and there is less time pressure.

25. **Demonstrate you understand the other side's perspective.** This is best done by making their argument for them. Check that you've got it right.

26. **Create new options.** Don't limit yourself to the options on the table. People spend too much time debating different poor alternatives. One reason you may be having trouble reaching an agreement is that none of the options are fair (in that they lead to an equal split) and none lead to the largest pie. Focus on devising new options that maximize the pie and provide an even split.

27. **Employ contingent deals (I).** One reason to propose a contingent deal is that you are unsure as to the size of the pie but fear that the other side has better information. To ensure you aren't taken advantage of, set payments based on how big the pie turns out to be. This also applies when both sides are equally unsure about the size of the pie and would prefer not to take a risk.

Selling Your Solution

28. **A negotiation solution should be consistently applied across any range of parameters.** Part of selling your solution is demonstrating flaws with other approaches. A negotiation solution shouldn't be ad hoc.

It should be based on a single procedure that applies across a broad range of situations. One can't make an argument in favor of proportional division in one context and then make an argument against proportional division in another when proportional division is no longer favorable. The consistency test leads to splitting the pie. With any other rule, there are always inconsistencies. In the pizza example, we saw how an equal division of the twelve slices fails the consistency test as it breaks down when one side has a BATNA of seven or more slices; a division in proportion to the BATNA fails when one of the BATNAs is close to zero. In the negotiation between Anju and Bharat, Anju showed that dividing up the interest in proportion to the amount invested was no longer fair (to Bharat) when the interest rate on a $20,000 and $25,000 CD were the same.

29. **Anticipate potential objections to your proposal.** You won't need a plan if the other side says: "Great, I never thought of that. Let's split the pie." Since that is unlikely, have a plan for what to do when the other side says no. What are the objections you'd make if representing the other side and how can you counter them? Anticipate their proposal by considering what heuristic approach works best for them. Plan to show how their approach might hurt them if the numbers were different or how their heuristic breaks down as the numbers become extreme.

30. **When presenting a new idea, frame it in a way that the other side wants to hear.** Be allocentric. Think about what they will like in the new idea, not what you like. If you plan to offer a big bonus and a low up-front payment, lead with the large bonus, not the low up-front payment. It seems obvious once you say it, but people tend to lead with the part of the deal they like the most. At that point, the other side may stop listening.

31. **Employ contingent deals (II).** If you aren't sure that you have the authority to try something new, propose two deals: one that is conventional and one that you both prefer if permitted.

32. **Say "Yes if" rather than "No unless."** People are more willing to give you what you want if they know that doing so will lead to a deal. Figure out what it would take for you to say "Yes if."

Cautions

33. **Don't overask.** I started by advising you to ask. Don't get carried away. If you are already getting half (or more) of the pie, accept what you've been offered. There's an old saying: pigs get fat and hogs get slaughtered.

34. **Beware opportunities to get more than half the pie.** Even if the other side doesn't understand the pie, you will have to rely on their misunderstanding. It's not the best way to build trust.

35. **Don't fight fire with fire. Fight fire with water.** If the other party says something inflammatory, instead of escalating, try to diffuse the situation. Use humor.

36. **If someone gives you an ultimatum, don't give one in return.** That's fighting fire with fire. Instead, look to find an option that would make them clearly better off. Even if hypothethical, it demonstrates they are open to options other than the ultimatum.

37. **Let them say no to you.** Rather than saying no to an unfavorable deal, consider what it would take to get you to say yes. Ask for it. You have nothing to lose.

38. **Choose a reasonable anchor.** The first offer can affect the outcome of the negotiation, but being too aggressive may lead to no deal. Exact numbers are stickier than round numbers, e.g., $1,217 vs. $1,200. But be prepared to defend where your exact number came from.

39. **Many procedures that sound fair aren't.** While it's important to reciprocate in sharing information, there is nothing inherently fair about meeting in the middle of two arbitrary points or reciprocally taking options off the table.

40. **When there are more than two parties, things get complicated fast.** The same idea of the pie applies, but the challenge is that the BATNAs are no longer exogenous. Consider who is likely to partner with whom if things go south.

41. **Even if you have no power in a negotiation, you may have power in terms of changing what others get.** Don't settle for Diet Squirt. Get paid for changing the game.

42. **Don't tell white lies.** White lies may seem harmless, but they can lead to misdirection. You don't know what problems the other party can help you solve, and they don't know what problems you have.

43. **Don't tell bald-faced lies.** It is unethical. As a strategic matter, if you get caught in the lie, you may lose any chance to reach an agreement. Even if you don't get caught, you may lose the agreement if the other side thinks your BATNA is better than what they can offer: "That's a good offer, I would take it if I were you."

44. **Care, but not too much.** It's easier to negotiate on behalf of others, instead of for yourself, because you're not as emotionally invested. When you are negotiating for yourself, it may help to think of yourself as negotiating for this other person who happens to be a lot like you.

45. **Be aware of cultural differences.** Listen to the other parties and be aware that what is important to them may not be important to you and vice versa. Herb Cohen says that *every* negotiation is cross-cultural. He explains: We don't see things as they are, but as we are. Indeed, negotiating with someone who looks like you may be even harder as you assume you are being understood.

Start with ground rules.
Split the pie.
Solve problems.
Make a giant pie.
Enjoy half.

AUTHOR'S NOTE

There are four types of negotiations described in this book. There's the obviously made-up examples such as with Alice and Bob dividing up a pizza or Sisyphus rolling up a rock. There's the historical examples (Moffett Studio, Ionity). Here I tracked down original source material or interviewed some of the executives involved. There's the negotiations I've been involved in, ranging from buying a domain name to selling Honest Tea. These are told as they happened, perhaps with a biased recollection. The fourth category is the examples from my students. Along with changing the names, I've taken a bit of artistic license. We have transcripts from their actual negotiations, but the negotiations were from case studies, not real negotiations. In the other group (such as negotiating the CD), I've created composites based on what I've learned from my students' experiences and seen in class.

When it comes to choosing names, I've tried to move beyond the traditional Alice and Bob. I was pleasantly surprised how many of my friends and star students had names beginning with A and B. This was a small way to honor them.

ACKNOWLEDGMENTS

Recipe to make one very large pie.

Ingredients: Mix together academics and practitioners.

2 co-teachers who shared their trade secrets (Cade Massey and Daylian Cain)

7 tough but fair critics (Bharat Anand, Max Bazerman, Jack Fanning, Brian Hanessian, Igor Kirman, Bradley Kuszmaul, and Ann Olivarius)

7 thoughtful colleagues who cut the fat and fixed the facts (Ian Ayres, Florian Ederer, Dan Esty, Kyle Jensen, Sharon Oster, Frances Rosenbluth, Kelly Shue)

1 second-cousin eye surgeon who thinks like an economist (Howie Weiss)

1 old college roommate who supplied (re)generative kibitz (Jeffrey Macklis)

1 sprinkling of former all-star students (Corey Baron, Greg Camp, Ezra Goldschlager), a dash of supersmart readers (Seth Masters, Dan Rube, Robert Schonberger, Andrew Weiss), and a few generous individuals who let me look under their kitchen hood (Richard Brooks, Don Moore, Michael Salinger, Shayne)

Bake in head for ten years at 98.6 degrees. Be patient. At this point, it's only half-baked.

Add mixing agent and rearrange ingredients in the right order (James Levine).

Edit recipe to cut numbers in half and keep serving size small (Hollis Heimbouch).

Knead at kitchen table for one year during pandemic. Spread out paper and let cool. Divide into 12 slices. Stores well.

———————

I had plenty of help in the kitchen. There were sous chefs (Courtney Paganelli and Wendy Wong) and thousands of food tasters (my MBA students, Schwarzman scholars, Coursera students) who helped refine the recipe. Katie Pichotta's voice in my head helped ensure ~~that~~ no superfluous "that"s appear—only 1,188 remain. The talented editors Elizabeth Brown, Tom Pitoniak, and Nikki Baldauf put back the ones I shouldn't have cut along with making my writing seem like I majored in English, not math.

Thank you all. I've said from the beginning you can't make a pie by yourself. Let me go further: each and every ingredient was essential.

One colleague deserves special mention. Adam Brandenburger is a coauthor (Co-opetition) and lifelong friend. We've written several articles together on negotiation that lay out the theory of the pie and multi-party negotiations. His pioneering work on cooperative game theory helped set me on this path. His influence is on every page.

Writers often end by thanking their life partner for letting them spend time locked away in their office working on the book. But in this case, it was my office that was locked up. I decamped to the kitchen table, where I wasn't alone, quite the opposite—Helen and I were both working from home. I think the distraction may have saved us from splitting up things other than pie. Here's to another forty-two years of making pies together.

Illustrations by Dan Ashwood. Dan is a graphic designer, animator, and illustrator. In an earlier life, he was a cartoonist at the *Harvard Lampoon.* You can see his animations in Barry's online negotiation course at coursera.org/learn/negotiation and more of his illustrations at danashwood.myportfolio.com.

NOTES

1. See Nejat Anbarci and Nick Feltovich, "How sensitive are bargaining outcomes to changes in disagreement payoffs?" *Experimental Economics* 16, no. 4 (2013): 560–96.

2. See Robin Pinkley, Margaret Neale, and Rebecca Bennett, "The Impact of Alternatives to Settlement in Dyadic Negotiation," *Organizational Behavior and Human Decision Processes* 57, no. 1 (1994): 97–116.

3. See Francesca Gino and Don Moore, "Why Negotiators Should Reveal Their Deadlines: Disclosing Weaknesses Can Make You Stronger," *Negotiation and Conflict Management Research* 1, no. 1 (2008): 77–96.

4. We were helped by George Lloyd and Jeremy Halpern, two brilliant lawyers who are counselors in the truest sense of the word.

5. How do we know that Alice's true valuation was $11,500 and not something higher or lower? This is not a number that can be verified. We might have to take Alice's word that the car was worth $11,500 to her. Or we could provide some deference to her in terms of how much evidence she would need to bring to bolster her claim that the car was worth $11,500 to her.

6. Under the default, the seller saved $2,400. If they split the pie, each side would have saved $7,000, so the exact difference was $4,600.

7. David Messick discusses the myriad of heuristics people use for equality in "Equality as a decision heuristic," which appears in B. A. Mellers and J. Baron (eds.), *Psychological Perspectives on Justice: Theory and Applications* (Cambridge: Cambridge University Press, 1993). In an earlier study, Richard Harris and Mark Joyce demonstrate the importance of framing. They ran a series of experiments in which several partners worked equally long but different shifts (at a flea market in one case or a carpentry shop in a second).

The way the partners proposed to split the total profits strongly depended on the way the question was phrased. When asked to allocate profits in a fair manner, the most common answer was equal profits. But when asked to allocate joint expenses in a fair manner, the most common response was to divide costs equally and not in a way that equalized profits. The experiments are described in their article "What's fair? It depends on how you phrase the question," *Journal of Personality and Social Psychology* 38, no. 1 (1980): 165–79.

8.   The modern connection between negotiation and the Talmud was first made in Barry O'Neill's paper "A Problem of Rights Arbitration from the Talmud," *Mathematical Social Sciences* 2 (1982): 345–71. The results were extended in Robert Aumann and Michael Maschler, "Game Theoretic Analysis of a Bankruptcy Problem from the Talmud," *Journal of Economic Theory* 36 (1985): 195–213. The Talmudic text can be found at sefaria.org/Bava_Metzia.2a.1–12.

9.   For those sticklers who worry about the clippers breaking down or depreciating, don't worry about that. There's no issue with the two of them using the same clippers.

10. In this case, the cloth is only $50 and both parties have a claim to more than $50. The entire cloth is disputed, and so it is divided up $25/$25.

11. The folks on the ground floor may have friends up on the top floor they would like to visit. That said, I don't think they should be charged more for visiting the top floor than those who live outside the apartment. Those who live on the top floor are the ones responsible for covering the charge of the elevator used to transport people up to them.

12. Sources: wikipedia.org/wiki/List_of_development_aid_country_donors and reliefweb.int/sites/reliefweb.int/files/resources/GHA%20report%202019_0 .pdf.

13. Source: worldpopulationreview.com/countries/countries-by-gdp.

14. See Rudy Nydegger and Guillermo Owen, "Two-person bargaining: An experimental test of the Nash axioms," *International Journal of Game Theory* 3 (1974): 239–49.

15. The research was part of her PhD thesis. It is available at ninaroussille.github .io/files/Roussille_askgap.pdf.

16. The caveat is that the result is mainly through a reduction in the growth rate of male wages; see Morten Bennedsen, Elena Simintzi, Margarita Tsoutsoura, and Daniel Wolfenzon, "Do Firms Respond to Gender Pay Gap Transparency?" available at nber.org/papers/w25435.

17. Sources: iwpr.org/wp-content/uploads/2020/09/Q068-Pay-Secrecy.pdf and nytimes.com/2019/01/20/smarter-living/pay-wage-gap-salary-secrecy -transparency.html.

18. Zoë Cullen and Bobak Pakzad-Hurson are professors at Harvard Business School and Brown University, respectively. Their paper, "Equilibrium Effects of Pay Transparency," is available at https://www.nber.org/papers/w28903.

19. Most people think an increase in the minimum wage will lead to a reduction in employment (because it becomes more expensive to hire people). But an increase in the minimum wage defeats the spillover logic, and therefore can lead to an *increase* in employment. Consider a firm with ten employees each earning $10/hour. At that wage, the firm finds it hard to hire new employees. Were it to pay $15/hour, the firm could double the staff and expand hours and service. The problem is that doing so would cost the firm $20/hour, the $15/hour it pays the ten new hires plus the $5/hour raise it would have to provide to its ten existing employees. That's not worthwhile. Because the minimum wage forces the firm to raise the wage to $15/hour for existing employees, the cost of hiring new employees is only $15/hour, not $20/hour, as the $5/hour raise has already been implemented. The firm has lower profits due to the higher minimum wage, but it's also less costly to expand as the firm has already borne the cost of raising the wage for its existing workers.

20. For legal buffs, the case is known as *American-Hawaiian*, 38 Cal.App.3d 73, 112 Cal. Rptr. 897.

21. See nytimes.com/1989/11/19/business/nutrasweet-s-bitter-fight.html.

22. He is also the Massey behind the Massey-Peabody football rankings.

23. See Cade Massey and Richard Thaler, "The Loser's Curse: Decision Making and Market Efficiency in the National Football League Draft," *Management Science* 59, no. 7 (2013): 1479–95.

24. I've had a few readers who say I should attribute the orange story to Mary Parker Follett, a brilliant thinker and pioneer in dispute resolution. While there are dozens of citations to her to this effect, and the solution is a perfect example of her integrative approach to conflict resolution, I can't find any reference to this story in her work. But there is an interesting backstory. The first editions of *Getting to Yes* shared a story about a conflict over an open window. That story was taken without attribution from Mary Parker Follett's 1925 article, "Constructive Conflict." Later editions of *Getting to Yes* provided proper attribution. Perhaps people infer the orange story was also borrowed. The proper history is due to Deborah Kolb in a 1995 *Negotiation Journal* article about Mary Parker Follett's contributions. Professor Kolb originally thought the orange story "was but another example of a good idea from a woman co-opted by a man." As she dug deeper, she traced the story back to a case written by Robert House and published in 1975 in *Experiences in Management and Organizational Behavior*. Perhaps Robert House was thinking about Jack Sprat translated into fruit.

25. The full agreement is 360 pages long, as there are literally hundreds of details that need to be specified. You can download the agreement on the National Basketball Players Association website: nbpa.com/cba.

26. See espn.com/nba/story/_/id/7127448/nba-lockout-talks-break-early-thursday-planned and northwesternbusinessreview.org/how-the-nba-lockout-came-to-be-169cfa0bcf0d.

27. See Daylian Cain, George Loewenstein, and Don Moore, "The Dirt on Coming Clean: Perverse Effects of Disclosing Conflicts of Interest," *Journal of Legal Studies* 34 (2005): 1–25.

28. See www.williamury.com/getting-to-yes-in-colombia/.

29. An earlier version of the Tyson quote is attributed to Joe Louis: Everyone's got a plan until they get hit. In Tyson's case, he was responding to a reporter's question if he was worried about Evander Holyfield's preparation for the fight. At first, it seemed Tyson's quote was prescient as he sent Holyfield reeling with a devastating right cross in the first round. And yet, ten rounds later, Holyfield's planning and skill were enough to beat Tyson.

30. Conn. Gen. Stat. § 22–357: If any dog does any damage to either the body or property of any person, the owner or keeper . . . shall be liable for such damage . . .

31. See cdc.gov/rabies/exposure/index.html.

32. The historical details and quotes come from John Garraty's biography *The Right Hand Man: The Life of George Perkins* (Westport, CT: Greenwood Press, 1960).

33. The mere printing of the booklets is a statutory violation of copyright. According to the 1909 Copyright Act, the $1 penalty is applied "for every infringing copy made or sold by or found in the possession of the infringer or his agents or employees"; see copyright.gov/history/1909act.pdf. Were they distributed, it would become a willful violation. It is possible that were the campaign to destroy the pamphlets without distributing them, this would end up being what is today called an innocent violation and could lead the court to reduce the statutory damages.

34. In this case, there is no duty to disclose, so it may not pass the legal test of a lie of omission. But it passes the smell test.

35. Generally speaking, when there are such bad reasons, the seller has a legal duty to disclose them.

36. See Francesca Gino and Don Moore, "Why Negotiators Should Reveal Their Deadlines: Disclosing Weaknesses Can Make You Stronger," *Negotiation and Conflict Management Research* 1, no. 1 (2008): 77–96.

37. See pon.harvard.edu/daily/batna/negotiation-research-you-can-use-should-you-brandish-your-batna-nb/.

38. See nytimes.com/2017/01/26/world/mexicos-president-cancels-meeting-with-trump-over-wall.html.

39. See Matthew Backus, Thomas Blake, and Steven Tadelis, "On the Empirical Content of Cheap-Talk Signaling: An Application to Bargaining," *Journal of Political Economy* 127, no. 4 (2019): 1599–1628.

40. See Ellen Langer, Arthur Blank, and Benzion Chanowitz, "The Mindlessness of Ostensibly Thoughtful Action: The Role of 'Placebic' Information in Interpersonal Interaction," *Journal of Personality and Social Psychology* 36, no. 6 (1978): 635–42.

INDEX

ABOUT THE AUTHOR

BARRY NALEBUFF is the Milton Steinbach Professor at the Yale School of Management. An expert on game theory, he has written widely on its application to business strategy. Alongside *Split the Pie,* he is the coauthor of six books: *Thinking Strategically* and *The Art of Strategy* are two popular books on game theory. *Co-opetition* looks beyond zero-sum games to emphasize the potential for cooperating as well as competing. *Why Not?* provides a framework for problem solving and ingenuity. *Lifecycle Investing* introduces a new strategy for retirement investing. *Mission in a Bottle* provides lessons for entrepreneurs and tells the story of Honest Tea in graphic format.

In addition to his academic work, Barry has extensive experience consulting with multi-national firms. He served on the board of Nationwide Insurance and Q Mixers, and currently serves on the boards of Calicraft and AGP.

In the field of negotiation, he advised the NBA in their prior negotiations with the Players Association. He has also advised firms in major M&A transactions and his daughters in negotiations with their roommates over how to fairly split the rent. Barry has been teaching this method at Yale for the last decade in the MBA core and then turned it into an online course on Coursera. The course has over 350,000 enrolled students and a 4.9/5.0 rating.

He is also an entrepreneur. He cofounded Honest Tea with his former student Seth Goldman. The company was sold to Coca-Cola in 2011. His next company, Kombrewcha, makes a slightly alcoholic kombucha and was sold to AB InBev in 2016. His third venture, Real Made Foods, makes overnight oats. This allowed him to be a cereal entrepreneur and bad pun artist.

A graduate of MIT, a Rhodes scholar, and a Junior Fellow at the Harvard Society of Fellows, Barry earned his doctorate at Oxford University.